Saving Data on Android

By Jennifer Bailey, Dean Djermanović, Aldo Olivares Dominguez,

Fuad Kamal,Subhrajyoti Sen & Harun Wangereka

Saving Data on Android

By Jennifer Bailey, Dean Djermanović, Aldo Olivares Dominguez, Fuad Kamal, Subhrajyoti Sen & Harun Wangereka

Notice of Rights

Notice of Liability

Trademarks

ISBN: 978-1-950325-43-6

Table of Contents

Book License

Before You Begin

This section tells you a few things you need to know before you get started, such as what you'll need for hardware and software, where to find the project files for this book, and more.

What You Need

To follow along with this book, you need:

- **Android Studio 4.1+:** Available at https://developer.android.com/studio/. This is the environment in which you'll develop most of the sample code in this book. If you didn't install it already, now is the right time to do that!
- **Java SE Development Kit 8+**: Most of the code in this book will be run on the Java Virtual Machine or JVM, for which you need a Java Development Kit or JDK. The JDK can be downloaded from Oracle at http://www.oracle.com/technetwork/java/javase/downloads/index.html.
- **Kotlin Playground**: You can also use the Kotlin Playground available at the Kotlin home page at https://play.kotlinlang.org.
- **Android 6.0+:** The `minimumSdkVersion` for the projects targets API 23. Therefore, you need an emulator or device running API 23 or higher.

Book Source Code & Forums

Where to download the materials for this book

The materials for this book can be cloned or downloaded from the GitHub book materials repository:

- https://github.com/raywenderlich/sda-materials/tree/editions/2.0

Forums

We've also set up an official forum for the book at https://forums.raywenderlich.com/c/books/saving-data-on-android. This is a great place to ask questions about the book or to submit any errors you may find.

About the Cover

Saving Data on Android Cover

Dragons are an extremely common and ancient piece of folklore in nearly all cultures around the world. Most dragons are thought to breathe fire, or even ice, but legend has it that green dragons breathe acid. Any warrior brave enough to charge a green dragon would have the story of her battle permanently etched on her armor and shield from the dragon's acid.

Saving data on Android etches the story of data in a persistent manner on the user's device. There's hardly an app out there that doesn't persist data in some way. After reading Saving Data on Android, you'll be armed and ready to charge fearlessly into battle with the dragons of development, to save your users' data!

Dedications

"In loving memory of my wife, Huma. Not every warrior carries a sword."

— Fuad Kamal

"To my parents, friends and colleagues, who have always supported me and pushed me to achieve more. This book wouldn't have been possible without them."

— Subhrajyoti Sen

"To my Mum for always supporting me. To my wife for the encouragement and amazing support in everything that I work on. To my extended family, friends and colleagues who always push me to be a better version of myself. And to Apps:Lab for nurturing and providing me the opportunity to better myself, as well as all the Android Bits members for the guidance throughout my journey as a developer."

— Harun Wangereka

About the Authors

Fuad Kamal is one of the authors of this book. Fuad provides mobile strategy, architecture and development for the Health, Fitness and Telematics markets. If you've ever been to an airport, you've likely seen his work — the flight arrival and departure screens are a Flash 7 interface he wrote near the beginning of the millennium. He's also into photography. He's https://twitter.com/FlexRonin on Twitter and Instagram or you can contact him through anaara.com.

Subhrajyoti Sen is one of the authors of this book. Subhrajyoti is a Google Developer Expert for Android and an Android Engineer at KeepTruckin, where he develops apps to improve the trucking industry. Before this, he also worked on apps to improve the experience of Indian investors. He believes in the power of Open Source and communities and actively tries to give back. When not writing code, you can find him binge-watching anime, reading up on public policy or playing Rocket League.

Harun Wangereka is one of the authors of this book. Harun is an Android Developer who is passionate about creating quality Android apps. He never tires of learning, building the tech community and helping other developers upscale their skills. He loves contributing to open-source projects and writing technical articles on the topics of Android and Kotlin. He's very passionate about giving back to the community and sharing his knowledge and experiences.

About the Editors

Gabriela Angebrandt is the technical and final pass editor of this book. Gabriela is a tech enthusiast with a master's degree in Computer Science who specializes in Java, Kotlin and Swift. She is an Android and iOS developer at Code Consulting Ltd. She got into programming during college and has been developing apps for several years. Her passion for sharing knowledge drives her to contribute to the developer community through books and articles. In her spare time, Gabriela attends tech talks and invests time to learn new things from the programming world. When she's not crushing it in the tech world, she enjoys spending time with her horse and cat, rock climbing and playing the piano.

Sandra Grauschopf is the language editor of this book. She is a freelance writer, editor, and content strategist as well as the Editing Team Lead at raywenderlich.com. She loves to untangle tortured sentences and to travel the world with a trusty book in her hand. You can follow her on Twitter at https://twitter.com/sgrauschopf or learn more about her at http://www.grauschopf.com/.

About the Artist

Vicki Wenderlich is the designer and artist of the cover of this book. She is Ray's wife and business partner. She is a digital artist who creates illustrations, game art and a lot of other art or design work for the tutorials and books on raywenderlich.com. When she's not making art, she loves hiking, a good glass of wine and attempting to create the perfect cheese plate.

Acknowledgements

Content Development

We would like to thank **Jennifer Bailey**, **Dean Djermanović** and **Aldo Olivares Dominguez** for their work as authors on the previous edition of this book.

Introduction

Welcome to the Second Edition of Saving Data on Android, completely updated for Kotlin 1.5 and Android Studio 4.2!

Kotlin has been improved a lot for the past few years. It also has been announced as Google's preferred programming language for Android developers. Since then, Kotlin becomes more popular with each new day and one of the main reasons is its simplicity.

Saving Data on Android explains how to use Kotlin to manage data persistence in your app. Once you read this book, you won't ever doubt how to store your app's data.

The most important part is to learn how to avoid cluttering app storage. If you're dealing with sensitive and unique content, you'll find out how to store data in a safe environment as well. Since the last book version, there are some new tools launched to our Android world, and this book covers them as well. Lucky you!

In this book, you'll learn everything about saving data possibilities. You'll start with simple data persistence mechanisms — managing data using files, storing a small amount of data in form of key—value pairs, creating SQLite type of database and manipulating data in it using queries. You'll find out how to share stored data across more clients and what is the new and improved version of storing key—value pairs delivered by Google.

Once you learn the basics, you'll find out how to create a Room database that can contain more complex data and in which way you can store, retrieve, update and delete data from it.

Finally, you'll meet some options of storing data remotely.

These chapters include several plain code blocks what makes simultaneous reading and coding pretty easy. This also means you'll have a bunch of room for experimenting. With a lot of practice, this book will make you an expert on data persistence!

How to read this book

In this book, every chapter contains theory about the specific topic and a simple practical task to learn implementation faster.

Each section is based on a certain type of data persistence. Also, there are three awesome applications you'll develop — each one per section.

To learn and notice every little detail, read chapters in order. However, this book is for advanced users and there is a possibility you want to skip some chapters. In that case, be sure to continue from the starter project of the chapter you are moving to. The starter projects contain all steps implemented in the previous chapters of a certain section.

Assuming you have some experience in Android, all code used in this book is written in Kotlin and applications are built-in Android Studio.

While going through the chapter, you can type the code in Android Studio immediately. Feel free to play with the code and investigate the references provided in the chapter. Also, in the first section we prepared one fun **challenge** for you to test how much you learned. :]

This book is split into 3 main sections:

Section I: Saving Data Using Android SDK and Jetpack DataStore

Managing persistence is one of the main features that every mobile environment should provide, and Android is no different. In this chapter, you'll learn, through practical examples, how to use the API that Android SDK provides to persist data. You'll learn when and how to manage persistence depending on the type and quantity of data. The main focus will be on storing data to **Files**, **SharedPreferences** and **SQLite Database**. You'll also learn how to share data across multiple applications with **ContentProvider**. At the end of the section, you'll get familiar with Google's latest tool for handling data persistence —**Jetpack DataStore** — and how to migrate from SharedPreferences to it.

Section II: Using Room

At Google I/O 2018, Google presented a set of new components for Android development with the name of **Architecture Components**. The goal was to provide a set of solutions for the most common problem in the development of Android applications. The solution for persistence is **Room** which is the topic of this section. You'll learn how to use this library in the most common scenarios. Also, this section includes steps on how to safely **migrate data** once database schema changes.

Section III: Using Firebase

Firebase is a mature suite of products that allow you to implement Android applications that persist information in a safe, secure and reliable way. In this section, you'll learn the fundamentals and more advanced concepts of **Firebase**, including how to read and write to **Realtime Database**, how to use it in offline mode, as well as its usage and performance. You'll learn a few things about managing and securing data in **Cloud Firestore**. The last part of the section contains basic about **Cloud Storage**.

It's always the right time to explore data persistence possibilities. Are you ready to dive into it? :]

Section 1: Saving Data Using Android SDK & Jetpack DataStore

Ready to learn all about how to persist data in your app? In this chapter, you'll use practical examples to see how to use the API that Android SDK provides to persist data. You'll learn when and how to manage persistence depending on the type and quantity of data.

Your main focus will be on storing data to **Files**, **SharedPreferences** and **SQLite Database**. You'll also learn how to share data across multiple apps with **ContentProvider**.

Finally, you'll learn how to use **Jetpack DataStore**, Google's latest tool for handling data persistence. Along the way, you'll see how to migrate from SharedPreferences to Jetpack DataStore.

Chapter 1: Using Files

By Fuad Kamal

There are many ways to store data in an Android app. One of the most basic ways is to use **files**. Similar to other platforms, Android uses a disk-based file system that you can leverage programmatically using the **File API**. In this chapter, you'll learn how to use files to persist and retrieve information.

Reading and writing files in Android

Android separates the available storage into two parts, **internal** and **external**. These names reflect an earlier time when most devices offered built-in, non-volatile memory (internal storage) and/or a removable storage option like a Micro SD card (external storage). Nowadays, many devices split the built-in, permanent storage into separate partitions, one for internal and one for external. It should be noted that external storage does not indicate or guarantee that the storage is removable.

There are a few functional differences between internal and external storage:

- **Availability**: Internal storage is always available. On the other hand, external storage is not. Some devices will let you mount external storage using a USB connection or other options; this generally makes it removable.
- **Accessibility**: By default, files stored using the internal storage are only accessible by the app that stored them. Files stored on the external storage system are usually accessible by everything. However, you *can* make files private.
- **Uninstall Behavior**: After uninstalling the app, files saved to the internal storage are removed and the ones in the external storage are not. The exception to this rule is if the files are saved in the directory obtained by `getExternalFilesDir`.

Here's a usage hint: Use internal storage when you don't want the user or any other apps to access the files, like important user documents and preferences. Use external storage when you want to allow users or other apps access to the files. This might include images you capture within the app.

Getting started

To get started, you'll build an app that uses internal storage. Locate **using-files/projects** and open **starter** using Android Studio. Sync the project and run the app on a device or emulator. For now, you can ignore the warnings in the code.

The Simple Note app has a simple user interface with two `EditTexts`, one for the filename and one for a note. There are also three buttons along the bottom: **READ**, **WRITE** and **DELETE**. The user interface looks like this:

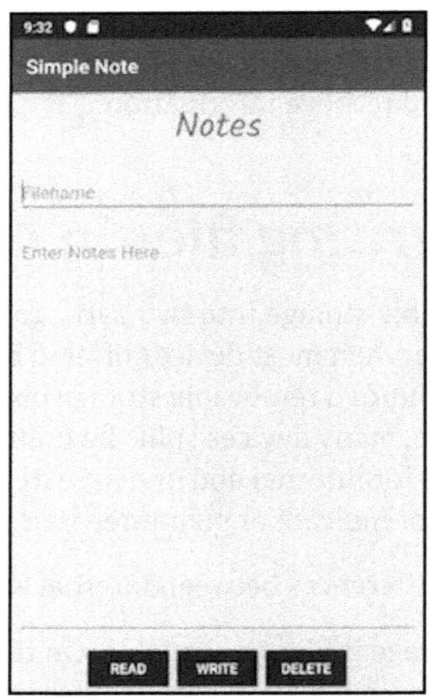

The SimpleNote App User Interface.

The sample for this project includes three sub-packages:

- **model**: Includes a simple data class to represent a single note in **Note.kt**. **NoteRepository.kt** contains the interface declaration with methods to add, get and delete a `Note`. `ExternalFileRepository`, `InternalFileRepository` and `EncryptedFileRepository` are implementation classes of `NoteRepository`.
- **ui**: This package includes **MainActivity.kt**. `MainActivity` implements the `OnClick` methods for each button. Because the code to read, write, encrypt and delete is abstracted behind `NoteRepository` and placed into separate classes, the code to handle the button click events remains the same regardless of the type of storage being utilized. This code is dependent on a single repository, and only the concrete type of the repository needs to change.
- **app**: This package includes **Utility.kt**, which contains a utility function to produce `Toast` messages.

Using internal storage

The internal storage, by default, is private to your app. The system creates an internal storage directory for each app and names it with the app's **package name**. When you uninstall the app, files saved in the internal storage directory are deleted. If you need files to persist — even after the app is uninstalled — use external storage.

Are you ready to see internal storage in action?

Writing to internal storage

Open **MainActivity.kt**. Notice the code immediately below the class definition:

```
private val repo: NoteRepository by lazy
{ InternalFileRepository(this) }
```

This is a lazy value. It represents an object of a class that implements `NoteRepository`. There's a separate implementation for each storage type demonstrated in this chapter.

The `repo` is initialized the first time it's used and will be utilized throughout `MainActivity`. This includes the button click events that call the add, get and delete methods required by `NoteRepository`.

In `onCreate()`, locate `binding.btnWrite.setOnClickListener()` add the following code for the **WRITE** button's click event:

```
// 1
if (binding.edtFileName.text.isNotEmpty()) {
  // 2
  try {
    // 3
    repo.addNote(Note(binding.edtFileName.text.toString(),
        binding.edtNoteText.text.toString()))
  } catch (e: Exception) { // 4
    showToast("File Write Failed")
  }
  // 5
  binding.edtFileName.text.clear()
  binding.edtNoteText.text.clear()
} else { // 6
  showToast("Please provide a Filename")
}
```

Here's how it works:

1. Use an `if/else` statement to ensure the user entered the required information.
2. Put `repo.addNote()` into a `try/catch` block. Writing a file can fail for different reasons like permissions or trying to use a disk with not enough space available. Using a try/catch block will ensure the app doesn't crash.
3. Call `addNote()`, passing in a `Note` that contains the filename and text provided in the `EditText` fields.
4. If writing the file fails, display a `Toast` message and write the stack trace of the error to Logcat.
5. To prepare the interface for the next operation, clear the text from `edtFileName` and `edtNoteText`.
6. If the user didn't enter a filename, display a toast message within the `else` block. `showToast()` is a utility function that exists in **Utility.kt**.

The code for **READ** and **DELETE** click events are similar to what you added for **WRITE**; these already exist in the sample project.

Now, open **InternalFileRepository.kt** and locate addNote(). Then, add the following to the body of the method:

```
context.openFileOutput(note.fileName, Context.MODE_PRIVATE).use
{ output ->
  output.write(note.noteText.toByteArray())
}
```

This code opens the file in fileOutputStream using the Context.MODE_PRIVATE flag; using this flag makes this file private to this app. The FileOutputStream is a Closeable resource so we can manage it using use(). The note's text is converted to a ByteArray and written to the file.

Build and run. Enter **Test.txt** for the file name and some text for the note. Then, tap **WRITE**. If the write is successful, the EditText controls will clear. Otherwise, the stack trace is printed to **Logcat**.

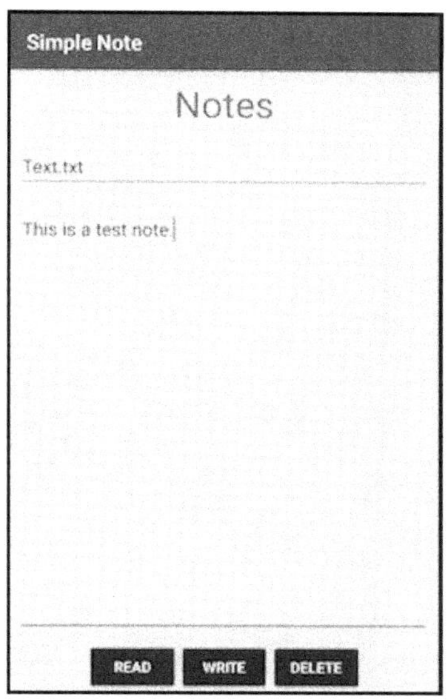

Creating a file named Text.txt.

Now that you've learned how to read, write and delete files from internal storage, wouldn't it be nice to see a visual representation of the files in the file system?

Viewing the files in Device File Explorer

In Android Studio, there's a handy tool named **Device File Explorer**. This tool allows you to view, copy and delete files that are created by your app. You can also use it to transfer files to and from a device.

> **Note**: A lot of the data on a device isn't visible unless the device is rooted. For example, in **data/data/**, entries corresponding to apps on the device that aren't debuggable aren't expandable in the Device File Explorer. Much of the data on an emulator isn't visible unless it's an emulator with a standard Android (AOSP) system image. Be sure to enable USB debugging on a connected device.

Open the **Device File Explorer** by clicking **View ▸ Tool Windows ▸ Device File Explorer** or by clicking the **Device File Explorer** tab in the window toolbar.

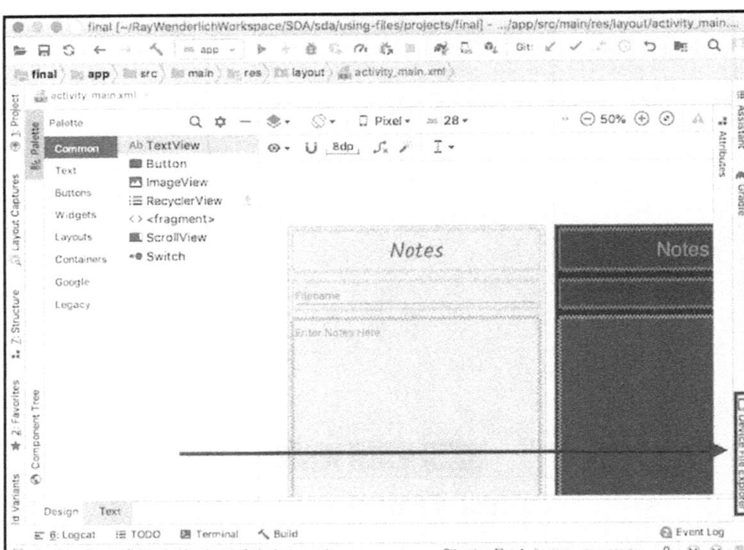

The Button to Open the Device File Explorer.

The Device File Explorer displays the files on your device. Open **data > data > com.raywenderlich.android.simplenote > files**; you'll see **Test.txt** and any other files you've saved. Files are saved in a directory with the same name as the app's package name.

> **Note**: The file location depends on the device; some manufacturers tweak the file system, so your app directory might not be where you expect it. If that's the case, you can locate the folder using the app's package name as this never changes.

The files stored on the external storage are located in **sdcard/Android/data/app_name/**.

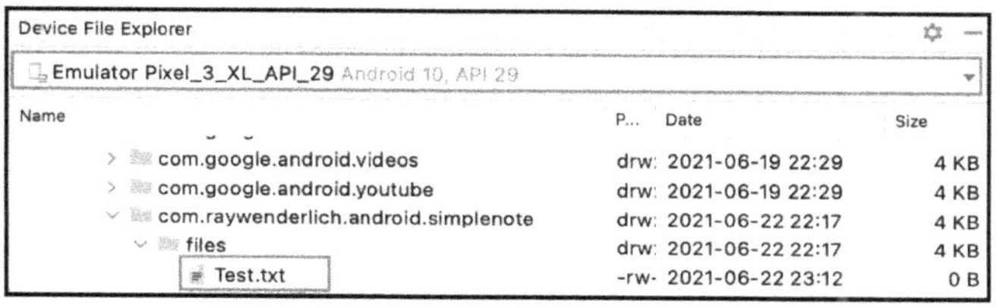

Seeing the File in Device File Explorer.

At the top of the Device File Explorer, there's a drop-down you can use to select the device or emulator. After making your selection, the files appear in the main window. You can expand the directories by clicking the triangle to the left of the directory name.

Right-click the filename, and a menu pops up that allows you to perform different operations on the file.

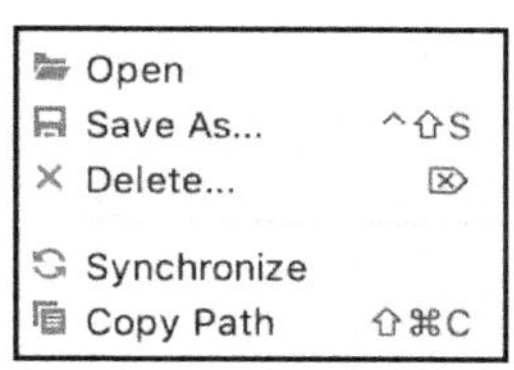

Seeing the File in Device File Explorer.

1. **Open** lets you open the file in Android Studio.
2. **Save As...** lets you save the file to your file system.
3. **Delete** allows you to delete the file.
4. **Synchronize** synchronizes the file system if it's changed since the last run of the app.
5. **Copy Path** copies the path of the file to the clipboard.

Now, it's time to learn how to make your app read files.

Reading from internal storage

In **InternalFileRepository.kt** , replace `return` in `getNote()`with the current code:

```
// 1
val note = Note(fileName, "")
// 2
context.openFileInput(fileName).use { stream ->
  // 3
  val text = stream.bufferedReader().use {
    it.readText()
  }
  // 4
  note.noteText = text
}
// 5
return note
```

Here's how it works:

1. Declare a `Note`, passing in a `fileName` and an empty string so that a valid object gets returned from this function even if the read operation fails.
2. Open and consume the `FileInputStream` with `use()`.
3. Open a `BufferedReader` with `use()` so that you can efficiently read the file.
4. Assign the text that was read to the file to `note.noteText`.
5. Return `note`.

Build and run. Next, enter the name of a file you previously saved and then tap **READ**. The note's text displays in the app.

And that's it! Your app can now write and read notes. Up next, you'll write the code to delete a file.

Deleting a file from internal storage

In **InternalFileRepository.kt**, replace `return` of `deleteNote()` with the following line of code:

```
return noteFile(fileName).delete()
```

This function returns a value of successful file deletion.

Build and run. Delete a file by tapping **DELETE**; you'll see the appropriate message. To confirm the file was deleted, use the Device File Explorer.

A Toast message is displayed after deleting a file.

Internal storage is great for storing private data in an app. But what if you want to store data temporarily? To do this, you can use **Internal Cache Files**.

Internal cache files

Each app has a special and private cache directory to store temporary files. Android may delete these files when the device is low on internal storage space, so it's not safe to store anything other than temporary files in this space. There's also no guarantee that Android will delete these files for you, so you must maintain this directory yourself.

To write to the internal cache directory, use `createTempFile()` as shown in the following example:

```
File.createTempFile(filename, null, context.cacheDir)
```

A good use case for temporary files is when you're uploading images to a server. You may not need the image persisted on the device, but you still need to upload some files. You'd store the image in this temp file, upload it, and then delete the file upon completion.

Next, it's time to look at how to store files on **External Storage**.

Using external storage

External storage is appropriate for data you want to make accessible to the user or other apps. Files saved on the external storage system aren't deleted after uninstalling the app. The external storage is made up of standard public directories. Files saved to the external storage are world-readable and can be modified by enabling mass storage and transferring the files to the computer via USB.

External storage isn't guaranteed to be accessible at all times; sometimes it exists on a physically removable SD card. Before attempting to access a file, you must check for the availability of the external storage directories, as well as the files. You can also store files in a location on the external storage system, where they **will be deleted** by the system when the user uninstalls the app.

Now that you know the theory, it's time to replace usage of internal storage with external. You'll start by adding the necessary permissions to the manifest.

Adding permissions in the manifest

To use external storage, you must first add the correct permission to the manifest. If you wish to only **read** external files, use the **READ_EXTERNAL_FILE** permission.

```
<uses-permission
  android:name="android.permission.READ_EXTERNAL_STORAGE" />
```

If you want to both **read and write**, use the **WRITE_EXTERNAL_STORAGE** permission.

```
<uses-permission
  android:name="android.permission.WRITE_EXTERNAL_STORAGE" />
```

Beginning with API level 19, reading or writing files in your app's **private** external storage directory doesn't require the above permissions. If your app supports Android API level 18 or lower, and you're saving data to the private external directory only, you should declare that the permission is requested only on the lower versions of Android by adding the `maxSdkVersion` attribute:

```
<uses-permission
  android:name="android.permission.WRITE_EXTERNAL_STORAGE"
  android:maxSdkVersion="18" />
```

In this app, you'll be reading and writing to the external storage, so add the **WRITE_EXTERNAL_STORAGE** permission inside the `<manifest>` element in **AndroidManifest.xml**.

Writing the notes to external storage

Now that the correct permissions are in place, it's time to write the file to the external storage. Open **ExternalFileRepository.kt** and add the following code to `addNote()`:

```
// 1
if (isExternalStorageWritable()) {
  // 2
  FileOutputStream(noteFile(note.fileName)).use { output ->
    // 3
    output.write(note.noteText.toByteArray())
  }
}
```

Here's how it works:

1. Check to see if the external storage is available.
2. Open a `FileOutputStream` with `use()`.
3. Write `note.noteText` to the file.

Next, in **MainActivity.kt**, change the instance of the `NoteRepository` you're initializing to the following:

```
private val repo: NoteRepository by lazy
{ ExternalFileRepository(this) }
```

Finally, build and run to write a file to the external storage. Name the file as **ExternalStorageTest.txt** and add a random note. Then, press **WRITE**.

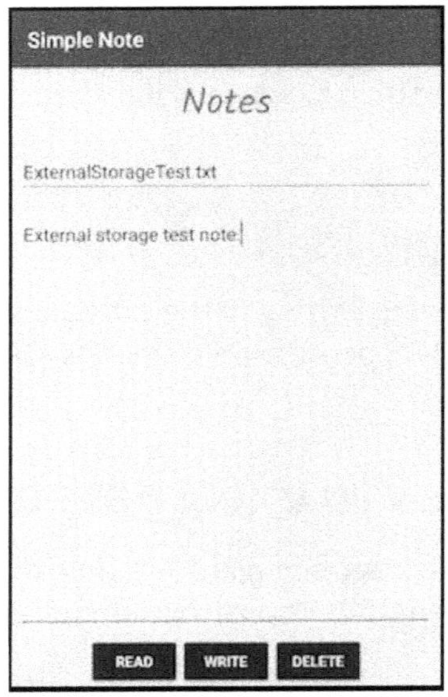

Writing a file to external storage.

To view the file using the Device File Explorer, look in **sdcard/Android/data**, within the app's package name folder.

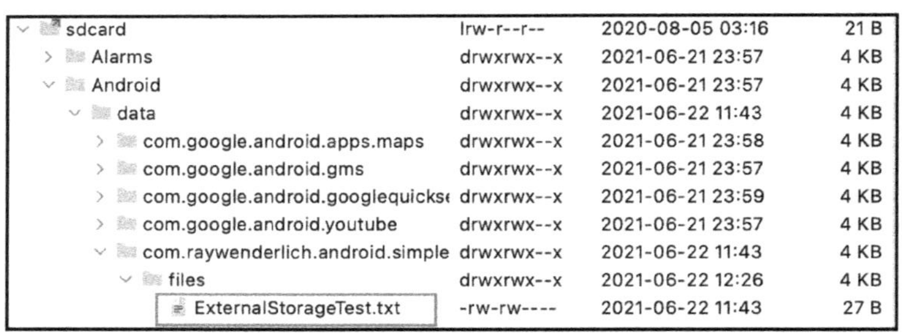

Name	Permissions	Date	Size
sdcard	lrw-r--r--	2020-08-05 03:16	21 B
Alarms	drwxrwx--x	2021-06-21 23:57	4 KB
Android	drwxrwx--x	2021-06-21 23:57	4 KB
data	drwxrwx--x	2021-06-22 11:43	4 KB
com.google.android.apps.maps	drwxrwx--x	2021-06-21 23:58	4 KB
com.google.android.gms	drwxrwx--x	2021-06-21 23:57	4 KB
com.google.android.googlequicks	drwxrwx--x	2021-06-21 23:59	4 KB
com.google.android.youtube	drwxrwx--x	2021-06-21 23:57	4 KB
com.raywenderlich.android.simple	drwxrwx--x	2021-06-22 11:43	4 KB
files	drwxrwx--x	2021-06-22 12:26	4 KB
ExternalStorageTest.txt	-rw-rw----	2021-06-22 11:43	27 B

Reading from external storage

To read from the storage, open **ExternalFileRepository.kt**, and replace `return` of `getNote()` with the following code:

```
val note = Note(fileName, "")
// 1
if (isExternalStorageReadable()) {
  // 2
  FileInputStream(noteFile(fileName)).use { stream ->
```

```
        // 3
        val text = stream.bufferedReader().use {
          it.readText()
        }
        // 4
        note.noteText = text
      }
    }
    // 5
    return note
```

For the most part, the procedure here is the same as reading from the internal storage but with a small difference. Here's how it works:

1. Ensure the external storage is readable.
2. Open and consume the `FileInputStream`, with `use()`, as you did before.
3. Open a `BufferedReader` with `use` so that you can efficiently read the file.
4. Assign the text that was read to the file to `note.noteText` .
5. Return the `note`.

The above code blocks rely on the following two functions: `isExternalStorageWritable()` and `isExternalStorageReadable()`. The first one determines if the external storage is mounted and ready for read/write operations, whereas the other determines only if the storage is ready for reading.

You're ready to add the capability to delete a file from external storage.

Deleting a file from external storage

In **ExternalFileRepository.kt**, replace `return` with the following code into `deleteNote()`:

```
return isExternalStorageWritable() &&
noteFile(fileName).delete()
```

The first part of the condition checks if the external storage can be written to or altered; the second part, if the first condition is true, returns the result of deleting the file. This way, you can be sure that the file will be deleted only if you can manipulate external storage.

Securing user data with a password

Security is important for the credibility of your app, especially when it comes to securing users' private data. Storing data on external storage allows the data to be visible to other apps. That's why it's advised to avoid using external storage. Or at least doing so, without a strong security system and encryption. To prevent users from installing the app on external storage you can add `android:installLocation="internalOnly"` to the manifest file.

Another best practice you can use to enhance your app's security is to prevent the contents of the app's private data directory from being downloaded with `adb backup`. You do this by setting the `android:allowBackup="false"` in the manifest file.

One way to secure your data beyond the best practices listed above is to encrypt the files before writing them to the external file system with a user-provided password.

Using AES and Password-Based Key Derivation

The recommended standard to encrypt data with a given key is the **AES (Advanced Encryption Standard)**. In this example, you'll use the same key to encrypt and decrypt data - known as **symmetric encryption**. The preferred length of the key is **256 bits** for sensitive data.

It's not realistic to rely on the user to select a strong or unique password. That's why it's never recommended to use passwords directly to encrypt the data. Instead, produce a **key** based on the user's password using **Password-Based Key Derivation Function** or **PBKDF2**.

PBKDF2 produces a key from a password by hashing it over many times with **salt**. This creates a key of a sufficient length and complexity, and the derived key will be unique even if two or more users in the system used the same password.

In this example, `passwordString` that represents the user's password has been hardcoded at the top of **EncryptedFileRepository.kt**.

Find `encrypt()` and add the code inside the empty `try` block:

```
// 1
val random = SecureRandom()
// 2
val salt = ByteArray(256)
// 3
random.nextBytes(salt)
```

Here's how it works:

1. Generate a random value using the `SecureRandom` class. This guarantees the output is difficult to predict as `SecureRandom` is a cryptographically strong random number generator.
2. Create a `ByteArray` of 256 bytes to store the salt.
3. Pass the salt to `nextBytes()` which will fill the array with 256 random bytes.

Next, add the following code below the previous code block to *salt* the password.

```
// 4
val passwordChar = passwordString.toCharArray()
// 5
val pbKeySpec = PBEKeySpec(passwordChar, salt, 1324, 256) //
1324 iterations
// 6
val secretKeyFactory =
SecretKeyFactory.getInstance("PBKDF2WithHmacSHA1")
// 7
val keyBytes =
secretKeyFactory.generateSecret(pbKeySpec).encoded
// 8
val keySpec = SecretKeySpec(keyBytes, "AES")
```

Here's how it works:

4. Convert the password into a character array.
5. Pass the password in `char[]` form, along with the salt, to `PBEKeySpec`, as well as the number of iterations, `1324`, and the size of the key, `256`.
6. Generate an instance of a `SecretKeyFactory` using **PBKDF2WtihHmacSHA1**.
7. Pass the `pbKeySpec` to the `secretKeyFactor.generateSecret()` method and assign the `encoded` property which returns the key in bytes.
8. Finally, `keySpec` is produced to use when you initialize the **Cipher**.

All of these steps seem a bit complex, but it's the kind of thing that's always the same to use; only the data changes. You're almost done!

Using an initialization vector

The recommended mode of encryption when using AES is the **cipher block chaining**, or **CBC**. This mode takes each next unencrypted block of data and uses the **XOR** operation with the previous encrypted block. One problem with this procedure is that the first block is less unique as subsequent blocks. If one encrypted message started the same as another message, the beginning blocks of the two messages would be the same. This would help an attacker to find out what the message(s) are. To solve this problem, you'll create an **initialization vector** or an **IV**.

An IV is a block of random bytes that are XOR'd with the leading block of the data. All subsequent blocks are dependent on the previous block, so using an IV uniquely encrypts the entire message.

Inside `encrypt()`, below the last code block, add the following code to create an IV:

```
// 9
val ivRandom = SecureRandom()
// 10
val iv = ByteArray(16)
// 11
ivRandom.nextBytes(iv)
// 12
val ivSpec = IvParameterSpec(iv)
```

Here's what's happening:

9. Create a new `SecureRandom` object so that you're not using a cached, seeded instance.

10. Create a byte array with a size of `16` to store the IV.

11. Populate `iv` with random bytes.

12. Create the `IvParameterSpec` with the random `iv` so that you can use it when performing the encryption.

Now, it's time to use `keySpec` and `ivSpec` to encrypt a note. Below previously added block, add:

```
// 13
val cipher = Cipher.getInstance("AES/CBC/PKCS7Padding")
cipher.init(Cipher.ENCRYPT_MODE, keySpec, ivSpec)
// 14
val encrypted = cipher.doFinal(plainTextBytes)
// 15
map["salt"] = salt
map["iv"] = iv
map["encrypted"] = encrypted
```

Here's the explanation:

13. Create and initialize the **Cipher** using **AES/CBC/PKCS7Padding**. This specifies AES encryption with cypher block chaining. PKCS7 refers to an established standard for padding data that doesn't fit into the specified block size.

14. Encrypt the bytes of the data with the `cipher`.

15. Place the `salt`, `iv`, and `encrypted` bytes into a **HashMap**.

Now `encrypt()` can be used to encrypt the note text before writing to a file. To finish off the file encryption, insert the following code into `addNote()`:

```
if (isExternalStorageWritable()) {
  ObjectOutputStream(noteFileOutputStream(note.fileName)).use
{ output ->
    output.writeObject(encrypt(note.noteText.toByteArray()))
  }
}
```

The code above creates an `ObjectOutputStream` with `use()` and utilizes it to write the encrypted message out to the file.

Lastly, you have to change the instance of the `NoteRepository` in **MainActivity.kt** to this:

```
private val repo: NoteRepository by lazy
{ EncryptedFileRepository(this) }
```

Build and run. Name a file as **EncryptedTest.txt**, add a random note and press **WRITE** to create an encrypted file. Open the file with Device File Explorer a notice that it's filled with unreadable data because the file is encrypted.

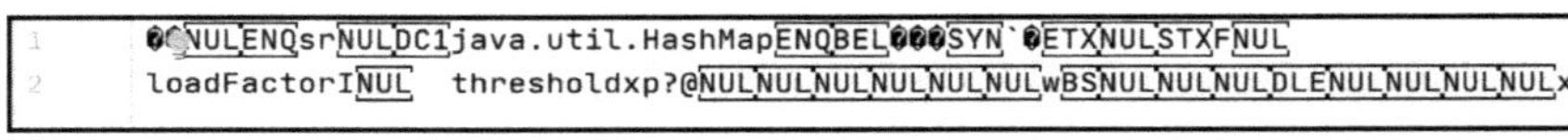

Encrypted data.

Now you must add a mechanism to decrypt the file.

Decrypting the file

Locate `decrypt()` and add the following code in it:

```
var decrypted: ByteArray? = null
  try {
    // 1
    val salt = map["salt"]
    val iv = map["iv"]
    val encrypted = map["encrypted"]
    // 2
    val passwordChar = passwordString.toCharArray()
    val pbKeySpec = PBEKeySpec(passwordChar, salt, 1324, 256)
    val secretKeyFactory =
SecretKeyFactory.getInstance("PBKDF2WithHmacSHA1")
    val keyBytes =
secretKeyFactory.generateSecret(pbKeySpec).encoded
    val keySpec = SecretKeySpec(keyBytes, "AES")
    // 3
    val cipher = Cipher.getInstance("AES/CBC/PKCS7Padding")
    val ivSpec = IvParameterSpec(iv)
    cipher.init(Cipher.DECRYPT_MODE, keySpec, ivSpec)
    decrypted = cipher.doFinal(encrypted)
  } catch (e: Exception) {
    Log.e("SIMPLENOTE", "decryption exception", e)
  }
  // 4
  return decrypted
```

Here's what's happening:

1. Retrieve the `salt`, `iv` and `encrypted` fields from the **HashMap**.
2. Regenerate the key from the password.
3. Decrypt the encrypted data.
4. Return the decrypted data.

Call `decrypt()` after reading the file in `getNote()`.

```
val note = Note(fileName, "")
if (isExternalStorageReadable()) {
  // 1
  ObjectInputStream(noteFileInputStream(note.fileName)).use
{ stream ->
    // 2
    val mapFromFile = stream.readObject() as HashMap<String,
ByteArray>
    // 3
    val decrypted = decrypt(mapFromFile)
    if (decrypted != null) {
      note.noteText = String(decrypted)
    }
  }
}
return note
```

Here's how it works:

1. Open an `ObjectInputStream` with `use()` for reading data.
2. Read the data and store it into the `HashMap`.
3. Decrypt the file with `decrypt()`; if it was successful, assign the decrypted text to `note.noteText`.

Build and run. Notice the weird, encrypted data is now decrypted and understandable again! :]

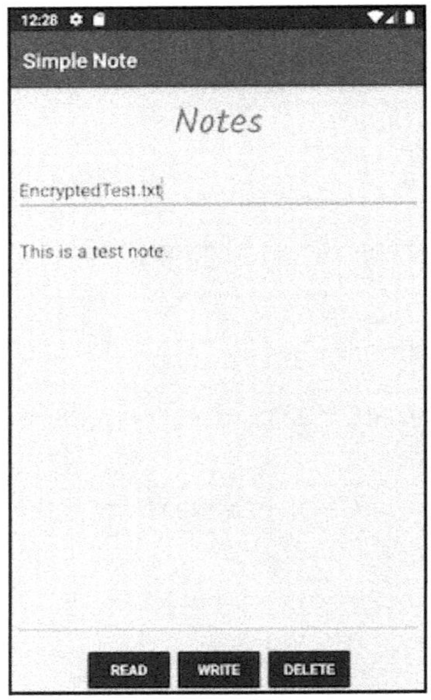

Decrypted data.

Understanding Parcelization and Serialization

In computer science, **marshaling** is the process of transforming an object into a format that is suitable for transmission or storage. Android apps often transfer data from one activity to another, where **Parcelization** and **Serialization** are the means of marshaling objects.

By default — and because your app utilized `ObjectOutputStream` to write the file — the encrypted data, iv and salt values were all **serialized** when written to the file.

Serializable

Serializable is a standard Java tagging interface. This interface has no operation but it can be used to define the corresponding type as serializable. An object is serializable when it can be converted into an array of bytes and vice versa. If an object is **Serializable** it can also be written into a file or read from a file. However, when you restore an object you still need a compatible version of the class used during serialization. Implementing the **Serializable** interface isn't enough - some properties are implicitly not serializable like **Thread** or **InputStream**. The Serialization process implies the use of **reflection**.

Reflection is the ability for an object to know things about itself. Therefore, using serializable can result in a lot of garbage collection which then translates to poor performance and battery drain. Fortunately, there's another way to marshal objects in Android.

Parcelable

Parcelable is also an interface. However, unlike Serializable, Parcelable is part of the Android SDK. Because it's designed not to use reflection, it requires the developer to be explicit about the marshaling process, making it more tedious to use. Despite this complication, using Parcelable can result in better app performance — although the gain in performance is usually imperceptible to the user.

Parcelable is often used when passing data between activities in a **Bundle**.

> **Note**: The Parcelable API isn't for general purposes. It's designed to be a high-performance IPC transport. It's not appropriate to place Parcel data into persistent storage.

Key points

- The **internal storage** is a great place to store files that are specific and private to your app.
- Use the **internal cache** to store temporary files.
- Use **external storage** to store files that you want users or other apps to have access to.
- External files are **persistent**, even after the app is uninstalled. However, internal files are deleted after uninstalling the app.
- To write files to the external storage, the correct **permissions** must be set in the manifest.
- Because the external storage isn't secure, it's a good idea to use **AES encryption** with a password-based generated key.
- Serializable and Parcelable are ways of **marshaling** data for transport or storage.

Where to go from here?

File encryption — and encryption in general — is a broad topic. To learn more about it, read the tutorial located at https://www.raywenderlich.com/778533-encryption-tutorial-for-android-getting-started. There is also a course on Jetpack Security https://www.raywenderlich.com/10135609-jetpack-security, which covers using Jetpack Security for the keychain and file encryption. To dig deeper into file management on Android, also read the official documentation available at https://developer.android.com/guide/topics/data/data-storage.

Chapter 2: Using SharedPreferences

By Fuad Kamal

Files are a quick and convenient way to store unstructured data in Android. But there are other convenient, more organized ways to store small bits of data. One of them is by using **SharedPreferences**.

Understanding SharedPreferences

The **SharedPreferences**, or **prefs** for short, API provides the means to read and write to a file that is formatted as **XML**. The API is especially useful when you need to store things like application-wide flags to style your app, user progress, data filters and so on.

The prefs file you create, edit and can delete is stored in the **data/data/{application package name}** directory. The location of this file can be obtained programmatically by calling `Environment.getDataDirectory()`. Like files, the data is app—specific and will be lost if the application data is cleared through settings or if the app is uninstalled.

You already learned that `SharedPreferences` should not be used to store large amounts of data, but rather small features of your app. As such, the data is structured into **key—value** pairs, where each value has an identifier key, which marks its location in the file. Then, by passing in the key, you can retrieve the last value you stored. If there is no value for the key, you can specify a default that will be returned instead. Furthermore, since the point of `SharedPreferences` is to store simple data, the only supported types to store are `Boolean`, `Int`, `Float`, `Long`, `String` and `Set<String>`.

> **Note**: `SharedPreferences` are also stored at the location where app **Preferences** are. However, the two should not be confused with one another.

The first step to using `SharedPreferences` is obtaining a reference to the app—specific file, let's see how to do that!

Getting a reference to the SharedPreferences file

Depending on how you want to use `SharedPreferences`, there are different ways to access or create the `SharedPreferences` file:

- `getSharedPreferences()` can be called from any `Context` in your app and allows you to specify a name for the file. It's handy if you need multiple `SharedPreferences` files with different names.
- `getPreferences()` is called from `Activity` and doesn't allow you to specify a file name because it uses the default class name of that `Activity`. It's handy if you need to create different preference files for different activities.
- `getDefaultSharedPreferences()` is used for app settings and preferences at the **app level**, and returns the default prefs file for the entire app. You can use this to store data that is useful for your entire app, or features you set up every time a user starts your app.

But getting preferences is only half of the work. You still need to read and write data to the prefs.

Reading from preferences

Reading from prefs is pretty straightforward. Once you get ahold of a preference file, you can use aptly named functions to read the variables of the data types mentioned earlier in this chapter. You can use functions such as `getInt()`, `getString()` and `getLong()`, passing in a key and an optional default value to get the stored value. An example call, to get a `String`, by the key `username`, with a default value of an empty `String` is as follows:

```
prefs.getString("username", "")
```

You will learn more about reading data through the chapter's project, but for now, let's see how to write some data to `SharedPreferences`.

Writing to preferences

Writing to the `SharedPreferences` file is slightly more complicated. To write to the file you must open it for editing, by creating an **Editor**. You can do that using `edit()` on your `SharedPreferences`. The **SharedPreferences.Editor** is essentially a pointer to the `SharedPreferences` file, in the app's data directory. Then you pass key—value pairs to methods such as `putInt()`, `putString()` and `putLong()`. Once the key—value pairs have been added to the **Editor**, call either `apply()` or `commit()` to finalize the changes, and save to the file.

Generally, it's a good practice to choose `apply()` to write the `SharedPreferences`. `apply()` will write the changes to the object out immediately, but then saves those changes to the disk asynchronously. If two `Editors` try to use `apply()` at the same time, the last one to call the function will be the one that has its changes saved. `apply()` will complete before the app switches state so you don't have to worry about it interfering with the lifecycle of your app. `commit()` writes the changes synchronously which can *block* the main thread and result in the app locking up, until everything is properly stored.

Now, it's time to look at an example of `SharedPreferences` in action.

Getting started

To get started with prefs, locate this chapter's folder in the provided materials named **using-sharedpreferences**, and open up the **projects** folder. Next, open the **organizedsimplenotes** app under the **starter** folder. Allow the project to sync, download dependencies and set up the workplace environment. Run the app on a device or in a simulator. For now, ignore any warnings in the code.

The OrganizedSimpleNote App Interface.

The app allows you to create, edit and delete notes that are saved in the internal file system. In the **options menu** items, there is an option to change the background color. You can also filter the notes by priority, or sort them by specific sort order.

The Option Menu Items.

Select a new background color, sort order and one or more priority filters. Now, quit the app and rerun it.

When the app reloads, the background color you selected persists. That is because the background color you selected was saved to prefs and applied when the app was rerun. The sort order and priority filters reset to defaults. They were not stored in prefs.

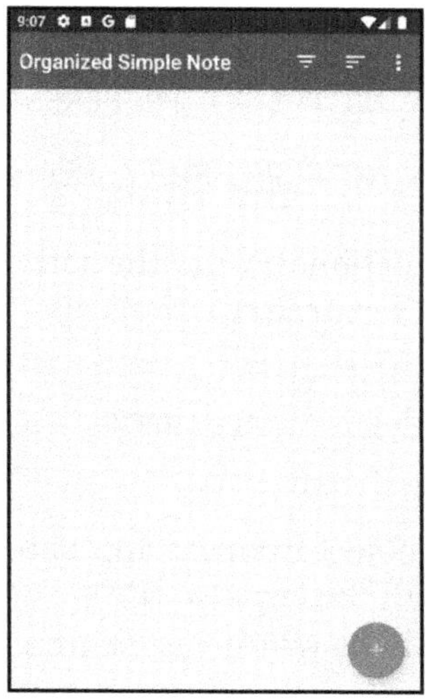

Changed Background Color persist.

To see the saved value for the background color, open the **Device File Explorer** in Android Studio, as you did in the previous chapter and navigate to the **data/data/com.raywenderlich.organizedsimplenote/shared_prefs** directory. You'll see a file named **com.raywenderlich.organizedsimplenote_preferences.xml**.

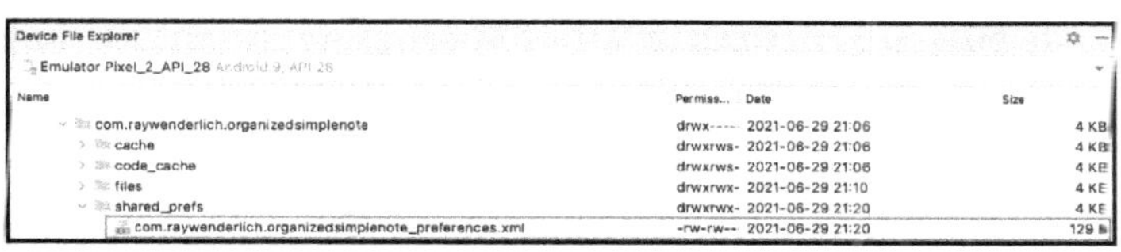

The SimpleNote App Interface

If you open the file, you'll see something similar to the following, depending on the color you chose:

```
<?xml version='1.0' encoding='utf-8' standalone='yes' ?>
<map>
  <string name="key_app_background_color">Orange</string>
</map>
```

In the next steps, you'll add the code to save and retrieve the sort order and priority filters to and from the prefs so that these settings can persist between runs of the app along with the background color.

Saving the user preferences

First, you have to create some constants which will represent the keys for the key—value pairs of data you need to save. Open **NotePrefs.kt** and insert the following declarations right below the declaration of DEFAULT_PRIORITY_FILTER:

```
    private const val KEY_NOTE_SORT_PREFERENCE =
  "note_sort_preference"
    private const val KEY_NOTE_PRIORITY_SET = "note_priority_set"
```

Next, you have to create the function to write the sort order to the prefs file. Insert the code below into saveNoteSortOrder(), replacing TODO:

```
sharedPrefs.edit()
    .putString(KEY_NOTE_SORT_PREFERENCE, noteSortOrder.name)
    .apply()
```

This code retrieves the **Editor** object from the app's prefs and puts the sort order in the preferences as a String with the key KEY_NOTE_SORT_PREFERENCE. It then uses apply() so that the changes will be written asynchronously to the disk.

Now, provide the code to write the selected priority filters. Insert the code below into saveNotePriorityFilters(), once again replacing TODO:

```
sharedPrefs.edit()
    .putStringSet(KEY_NOTE_PRIORITY_SET, priorities)
    .apply()
```

The previous code puts priorities, a Set of Strings, representing the selected priority filters, into the prefs using putStringSet() with the key KEY_NOTE_PRIORITY_SET.

Awesome! The functions to write to the prefs are done. Next, you'll add the code to read the values.

Reading the user preferences

Currently, getNoteSortOrder() returns the default value of NoteSortOrder.FILENAME_ASC. Replace the returned value with the following:

```
NoteSortOrder.valueOf(
  sharedPrefs.getString(KEY_NOTE_SORT_PREFERENCE,
DEFAULT_SORT_ORDER)
      ?: DEFAULT_SORT_ORDER
)
```

The above code uses getString() to retrieve the sort order the user stored, or DEFAULT_SORT_ORDER as the default value if the key KEY_NOTE_SORT_PREFERENCE doesn't exist.

Next, write the function to read the priority filters. Right now getNotePriorityFilters() returns an empty Set. Replace setOf() with the following:

```
sharedPrefs.getStringSet(KEY_NOTE_PRIORITY_SET,
setOf(DEFAULT_PRIORITY_FILTER))
      ?: setOf(DEFAULT_PRIORITY_FILTER)
```

The code above reads a Set of Strings from the prefs with the key KEY_NOTE_PRIORITY_SET, and if nothing is found with that key, it will use DEFAULT_PRIORITY_FILTER as the default - a set with the priority of "1" inside.

Now that the functions to read and write the sort order and priority filters are written, you can use these functions in MainActivity.

Reading and writing the prefs from MainActivity

Right now, in **MainActivity.kt**, you're using hardcoded values for the sort order and the priority filters, which you pass on to NoteAdapter, to display notes in a different order and filter which notes should be in the list. The right way to do this, which involves SharedPreferences, is to read a user's preferred ways of sorting and filtering, from prefs, and then passing those values to NoteAdapter.

To do this, open **MainActivity.kt** if you didn't already, and change the way you create the `priorities` `Set` by changing the statement to the following:

```
private val priorities by lazy
{ notePrefs.getNotePriorityFilters().toMutableSet() }
```

Instead of creating an empty mutable set and then adding values to it, you're now reading from the preferences, in a lazy way. Once you create `NoteAdapter`, the value will be assigned and you can use `priorities`.

Then, change the creation of the `NoteAdapter`:

```
private val noteAdapter: NoteAdapter by lazy {
  NoteAdapter(this,
      priorities,
      notePrefs.getNoteSortOrder(), // Read from preferences
      ::showEditNoteDialog
  )
}
```

Instead of passing in a hardcoded value for `FILENAME_ASC` as the `NoteSortOrder`, you're reading from the preferences to get the ordering the user previously selected.

> **Note**: Do not attempt to modify a string set read from the prefs. The results can be unpredictable. Always make a **copy** of the set instead, if it is going to be modified, like in the case of this app. You can do that by calling `toMutableSet()`, because Kotlin internally creates a new object, instead of just copying the `Set` value.

The app can now load the saved preferences when the app launches, but it also needs to store the values anytime the menu options change. To do that, find `updateNoteSortOrder()` and insert the following, replacing `TODO`:

```
notePrefs.saveNoteSortOrder(sortOrder)
```

The line of code above will save the `sortOrder` to the prefs. Finally, find `updateNotePrioritiesFilter()` at the bottom of `MainActivity` and insert this line of code, once again replacing `TODO`:

```
notePrefs.saveNotePriorityFilters(priorities)
```

The above statement will save the list of priority filters to the prefs. If you look in `onOptionsItemSelected()`, the above two functions you just wrote the code for are called anytime the appropriate menu options are changed.

Finally, build and run. You can now filter and sort notes to your heart's content and the app will save your personalized preferences. Once you come back, everything will be ready and waiting for you!

SharedPreferences Saving Successful.

Key points

- **SharedPreferences** are a great way to store **small bits of data** for an app.
- User—specific app configuration data is often stored in `SharedPreferences`.
- **Preferences** are also stored in an app's default `SharedPreferences`, but they are not to be confused with each other.
- `SharedPreferences` are not a good choice to store structured data, like various entities, use a database for that.
- `SharedPreferences` are organized in **key—value pairs** that are ultimately written out to a file in .xml format.
- Each app has its own `SharedPreferences`. When the app is uninstalled or the data is deleted, these stored values are wiped away.
- You can create custom-named `SharedPreferences` files and store user's choices in them.
- To edit `SharedPreferences`, you first have to fetch its **Editor**, by calling `edit()`.
- When writing `SharedPreferences`, use `apply()` instead of `commit()` to perform an asynchronous, thread—safe write.

Where to go from here?

- Check the tutorial on location https://www.raywenderlich.com/2705552-introduction-to-android-activities-with-kotlin about the utilization of SharedPreferences.
- To view the documentation on SharedPreferences, visit the developer guide here: https://developer.android.com/training/data-storage/shared-preferences.
- To read more about SharedPreferences, see the documentation found here: https://developer.android.com/reference/android/content/SharedPreferences.
- As with encrypted files, you can also encrypt SharedPreferences, using the JetPack Security library. You can learn more about this in the "Security Best Practices" chapter of *Android App Distribution* as well as the RayWenderlich.com course on JetPack Security: https://www.raywenderlich.com/10135609-jetpack-security

Chapter 3: SQLite Database

By Fuad Kamal

Using **Files** and **Shared Preferences** are two excellent ways for an app to store small bits of data. However, sometimes an app needs to store larger amounts of data in a more structured manner, which usually requires a database. The default database management system (DBMS) that Android uses is called **SQLite**. SQLite is a library that provides a DBMS, based on SQL. Some distinctive features of SQLite include:

- It uses dynamic types for tables. This means you can store a value in any column, regardless of the data type.
- It allows a single database connection to access multiple database files simultaneously.
- It's capable of creating in-memory databases, which are very fast to work with.

Android provides the APIs necessary to create and interact with SQLite databases in the `android.database.sqlite` package.

Although these APIs are powerful and familiar to many developers, they are low-level and do require some time and effort to use. Currently, it's recommended to use the **Room Persistence Library** instead, which will provide an abstraction layer for accessing the data in your app's SQLite databases. One disadvantage to using the SQLite APIs is that there is no compile-time verification of the raw SQL queries, and if the database structure changes, the affected queries have to be updated manually. Another is that you need to write a lot of boilerplate code to connect and transform SQL queries and data objects.

If you have written an app in the past that utilizes the SQLite APIs in Java, this chapter will show you how to use them with Kotlin, instead. However, if you have never seen an app that utilizes the SQLite APIs, this section will show you an example of how to use them in your apps. Overall, this section will give you a greater understanding and appreciation for the new and improved **Room Persistence Libraries**.

Understanding database schemas

The first step to creating an app that reads from a SQLite database is to decide on a database **schema**. The schema is the formal declaration of how the data in a database is **structured**. It's good practice to define constants that describe the database schema in a self-documenting way in their own class or file. These can be organized into subclasses for databases with multiple tables and should be visible throughout the scope of the project.

The schema you'll define is going to create a database called **todoitems.db**, with one table inside. Inside this table will be three columns:

1. The **primary key** column will be an auto incrementing `Integer` named **todoitemid**.
2. The **todoname** column will contain the actual text of the TODO item.
3. The **todoiscompleted** column will contain a `Long` value that will represent whether a TODO item is completed or not.

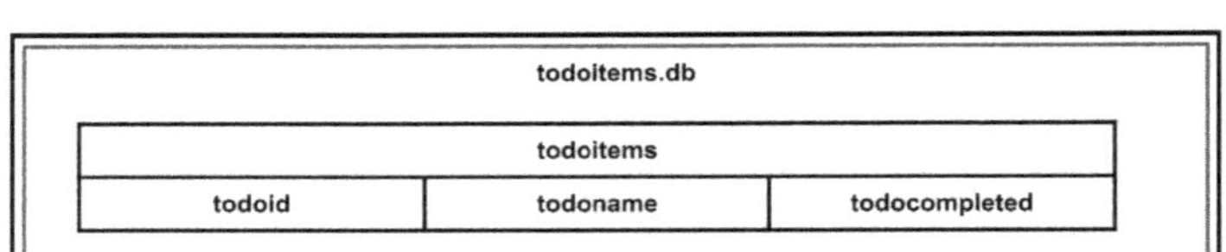

The Database Schema.

Understanding CRUD operations

CRUD stands for **Create**, **Read**, **Update** and **Delete**. These are the basic operations that can be done with a database, to store, maintain and utilize data. Each in turn:

- **Create**: This operation adds a new record to the database. In **SQL** or **Structured Query Language**, this is accomplished using an **INSERT INTO** statement.
- **Read**: The read operation **queries** the database or searches and returns zero to many records meeting a specific criteria. In SQL, this is done by using a **SELECT FROM** statement.
- **Update**: The update operation performs a change to an existing record or set of records that meet a specific criteria. In SQL, the **UPDATE** statement is used.
- **Delete**: The delete operation is used to delete records meeting specific criteria. In SQL, the **DELETE FROM** statement is used to delete a record.
- To specify criteria, the **WHERE** clause is used in SQL, along with the commands listed above.

Fortunately, the SQLite APIs in Android provide a useful class called **SQLiteOpenHelper**, which will simplify the integration with the database. This will reduce the amount of knowledge you must have of raw SQL. However, if you'd like more information about SQL and how to syntactically use it with SQLite, refer to the documentation found in the **Where to go from here?** section at the end of this chapter.

Getting started

Open the starter project for this chapter and ignore the errors you get initially. Notice there are three sections in the **com.raywenderlich.android.sqlitetodo** package: **model**, **view** and **controller**.

- **model** contains the class **ToDo**, which represents a singular item on the TODO list.
- **view** contains **SplashActivity.kt** and **MainActivity.kt**. The first file contains a class which interface you see once you start the app. The second one contains the class used to allow the user interacting with TODO tasks.
- **controller** contains two files that serve as a bridge between the data and the interface. **ToDoAdapter** retrieves the data from the database and places it into the **RecyclerView** list, whereas **ToDoDatabaseHandler** contains the code that interacts with the database.

Now, it's time to create the database schema utlilizing a **contract class**.

Creating the database constants using a contract class

In the **model** package, create a new file and name it **TodoDbSchema.kt**. Place the following code into the file:

```
object ToDoDbSchema {
  // 1
  const val DATABASE_VERSION = 1
  // 2
  const val DATABASE_NAME = "todoitems.db"
  object ToDoTable {
    // 3
    const val TABLE_NAME = "todoitems"
    object Columns {
      // 4
      const val KEY_TODO_ID = "todoid"
      // 5
      const val KEY_TODO_NAME = "todoname"
      // 6
      const val KEY_TODO_IS_COMPLETED = "iscompleted"
    }
  }
}
```

Here's what each part is:

1. The version of the database. Manually increment this number each time the database version is new, and you need to use the version to add **update** or **migration logic**.
2. The name of the database as it will be stored in the app-specific database folder on the device.
3. The name of the table will use to store the TODO items.
4. The column that contains the **unique primary key** for each TODO item.
5. The column that contains the text of the TODO item.
6. The column that will store an indicator whether or not you completed a TODO item.

Now, it's time to create your own database!

Using SQLiteOpenHelper

SQLiteOpenHelper is a helper class designed to help manage database creation and version management. To use it, you need to create a subclass of it and implement `onCreate()`, `onUpgrade()` and optionally the `onOpen` methods. This class will then open the database if it exists, create it, if it does not exist, and upgrade it when necessary. It does all these things automatically, using the above-mentioned methods.

Now that the constants are in place and you've learned a bit about **SQLiteOpenHelper**, it's time to create the database and add the CRUD operations.

Open **ToDoDatabaseHandler.kt** and add replace the class declaration with:

```
class ToDoDatabaseHandler(context: Context):
SQLiteOpenHelper(context, DATABASE_NAME, null, DATABASE_VERSION)
```

The above code makes the database handler class a subclass of `SQLiteOpenHelper`. This will allow the class to utilize the Android SQLite APIs in a simpler way.

Next up, you have to give the helper the schema data required to build the database.

Creating the database

First, the database must be created if it doesn't already exist. This is automatically done by `onCreate()`, which will run only when it needs to. If the database already exists, this method will not run.

> **Note**: When testing an app that utilizes SQLite, you must uninstall the app to delete the old database and reinstall the app to recreate it or completely clear the data of an app.

Add the following method to `ToDoDatabaseHandler`:

```
//This method creates the database
override fun onCreate(db: SQLiteDatabase?) {
    // 1
    val createToDoTable = """
    CREATE TABLE $TABLE_NAME  (
        $KEY_TODO_ID INTEGER PRIMARY KEY,
        $KEY_TODO_NAME  TEXT,
        $KEY_TODO_IS_COMPLETED  LONG );
    """
    // 2
    db?.execSQL(createToDoTable)
}
```

The parts above:

1. Assign an SQL **CREATE** statement which creates the table described in the schema above, to the `createToDoTable` value.
2. Run the command using the database object provided by `SQLiteOpenHelper`.

The above method will be run anytime the app is run and the database isn't found. Otherwise, the database exists, and there's no reason to recreate it.

One of the downsides of SQL, in general, is having to write the statements perfectly. Be very mindful when creating SQL statements using concatenated strings. It's very easy to make an error in doing so. It can be helpful to print the query using a `LOG` statement to check to see if the string is correct. The text of the query string is also displayed at the end of an error message in **Logcat** if the app crashes with an error. Additionally, you could use a local, or a Web SQL database terminal or environment, to try and validate the statement.

Now that the database has been created, you must add a mechanism for upgrading it.

Add the following method to `ToDoDatabaseHandler`:

```
//This method is used to update the database
override fun onUpgrade(db: SQLiteDatabase?, oldVersion: Int,
newVersion: Int) {
    // 1
    db?.execSQL("DROP TABLE IF EXISTS $TABLE_NAME")
    // 2
    onCreate(db)
}
```

The above:

1. Executes the SQL statement to drop the old the table if it exists.
2. Calls `onCreate()` again to recreate the database, this time with an upgrade.

`onUpgrade()` is the one that the framework calls automatically when a different version of the DB is detected. This happens when an instance of the `SQLiteOpenHelper` implementation is created with a different version number in its constructor.

The implementation of this method should provide the code that is necessary to upgrade to the new version of the schema. Since this is a very simple example, you're just dropping the previous table, and recreating it, using the new schema. But in real environments, and big apps, you'd usually do something called a **migration**.

Migration is the process of updating the database, without dropping it. For example, if you decide to add a new field to the TODO model, called `toDoPriority`, you would need to change the database as well, because you need to store that field, and retrieve it, but the old database doesn't have that field defined. You would then update the version number (e.g., from `1` to `2`) and write a SQL statement, to update the table, by adding a new column — `toDoPriority`.

In the next steps, you'll add the CRUD operations to the database handler implementation.

Using ContentValues

Before you add items to the database, it's important to understand a construct known as **ContentValues**. This is a class that allows you to store values that a **ContentResolver** can process. The information that is stored in objects of this class is stored as key-value pairs.

The key consists of the column name for the piece of information being stored, and the value consists of the value to be stored in that column. A key-value pair for each column of the database in a particular row is **put** into the **ContentValues** object before it is then handed to another method, which will resolve the content and perform the database operation.

Simply put, `ContentValues` are similar to a `Map` structures and are used to define the columns and the values to be used in database operations. As such, you'll use them to insert data into the database and update existing models if needed.

Adding a TODO

Add the following code in `createToDo()`, to insert a TODO item into the table:

```
// 1
val db: SQLiteDatabase = writableDatabase
// 2
val values = ContentValues()
// 3
values.put(KEY_TODO_NAME, toDo.toDoName)
values.put(KEY_TODO_IS_COMPLETED, toDo.isCompleted)
// 4
db.insert(TABLE_NAME, null, values)
// 5
db.close()
```

With the above, you:

1. Get a writeable instance of the database and store it in the `db` value.
2. Create an object of the `ContentValues` class called `values`.
3. Take the text of the TODO from the `toDoName` field and put it into `values`. Use `KEY_TODO_NAME` as the key, and `toDoName` as the key's value.
4. Put the key-value pair for the `isCompleted` field into `values`, as well.
5. Close the database, to avoid potential leaks.

Running the program

Build and run. Use the **Floating Action Button** with the plus sign icon to add a TODO item.

Adding an TODO Item.

When you enter the text for the item, tap **ADD**.

Now that you've added the code to create the database and added an item, next step is to take a look at the new database.

> **Note**: The item you added won't be displayed in `RecyclerView` yet, but stay tuned; you'll add that capability after a few more steps.

Viewing the SQLite database

Each app has its own folder to store databases on the device just like files. To look at the database that was just created, open the **Device File Explorer** as you did in Chapter 1, "Using Files". You can found it on the bottom right-hand corner of Android Studio as a collapsed, vertical pane.

Once in the Device File Explorer:

- Expand the **data ▸ data ▸ com.raywenderlich.android.sqlitetodo ▸ databases** folder.
- Right-click on the databases folder and select **Synchronize**.
- Then select **Save As...**.
- Save the entire folder to the location of your choice.

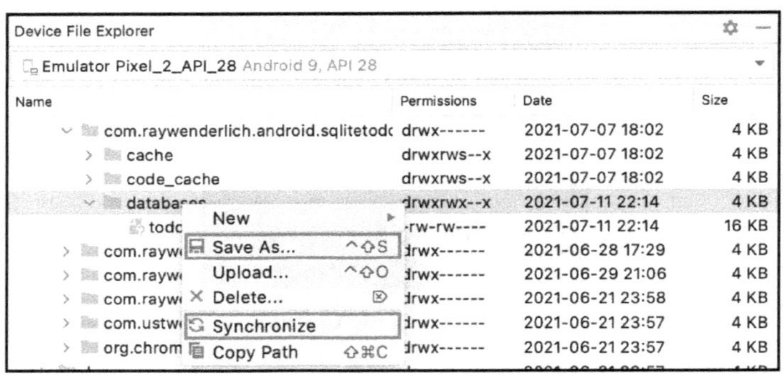

The Database Folder for the App and Context Menu of Device File Explorer

To view the database, you'll need a tool that allows you to open the **.db** file. A tool such as the **SQLite Browser** works nicely; you can find it here: https://sqlitebrowser.org/dl/. Download, install and open the tool.

Select **Open Database** and find and select your .db file. Then, switch to the **Browse Data** tab. Find the drop-down **Table:** and select the **todoitems** item. Now the records in the table will be listed in the main area of the window and you can see the record that you added, along with its unique id and completed status.

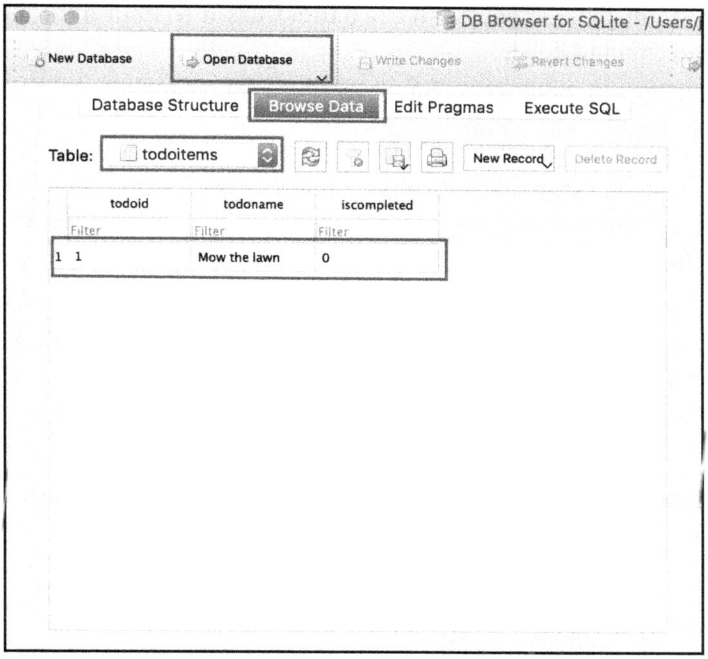

The Database Folder for the App in DB Browser.

Note: Another tool you can use to view the database on the command line is **sqlite3**, which you can find, here: https://developer.android.com/studio/command-line/sqlite3.

Now that you've successfully added a record to your database and viewed it in the file system, it's time to write the rest of the CRUD operations!

Reading from a database

Before the record added in the previous step can be displayed, the app must have the capability to read the records from the database. First, the database must be queried for the records to display. Then, you'll use a tool **Cursor** to iterate through the records and add them to a list.

Understanding the cursor

In Android, `Cursor` is assigned to the result set of a query being run against the database. Then it's used to iterate over the result set in a type-safe manne - **row by row, field by field**.

Internally, the rows of data that are returned by a query are stored in the `Cursor` reads through the data-keeping track of its current position. To start iterating, the current position must be moved to point to a valid row of data, such as the first row. Then, a loop structure is utilized to keep reading while a next record exists, to read in the result set.

In **ToDoDatabaseHandler.kt**, in `readToDos()` replace `return` with the following code:

```
// 1
val db: SQLiteDatabase = readableDatabase
// 2
val list = ArrayList<ToDo>()
// 3
val selectAll = "SELECT * FROM $TABLE_NAME"
// 4
val cursor: Cursor = db.rawQuery(selectAll, null)
// 5
if (cursor.moveToFirst()) {
  do {
    // 6
    val toDo = ToDo().apply {
      toDoId =
cursor.getLong(cursor.getColumnIndex(KEY_TODO_ID))
      toDoName =
cursor.getString(cursor.getColumnIndex(KEY_TODO_NAME))
      isCompleted =
cursor.getInt(cursor.getColumnIndex(KEY_TODO_IS_COMPLETED)) == 1
    }
    // 7
    list.add(toDo)
  } while (cursor.moveToNext())
}
// 8
```

```
cursor.close()
// 9
return list
```

With the above, you:

1. Get a readable instance of the database.
2. Create an `ArrayList<ToDo>` to store the records.
3. Construct the **SELECT** query to get the records.
4. Create a `Cursor` object using **SELECT** on the database.
5. Starting at the **beginning**, and move `Cursor` through all the records one at a time.
6. Assign the fields of each record to the corresponding attribute of a new `ToDo` item.
7. Add the item to the `list`.
8. Close `Cursor`, to avoid memory leaks
9. Return list` as a result.

Build and run. The record added in the previous step is visible now.

The added TODO Item.

So far, you've added a lot of code to the project. The app is now able to create a database, update the database, add records and read the records. Next, you'll add the capability to **update an existing record**, and finally, to **delete records**.

Updating a TODO

To add the capability to update a record, replace `return` in `updateToDo()` with the code below:

```
// 1
val todoId = toDo.toDoId.toString()
// 2
val db: SQLiteDatabase = writableDatabase
// 3
val values = ContentValues()
values.put(KEY_TODO_NAME, toDo.toDoName)
values.put(KEY_TODO_IS_COMPLETED, toDo.isCompleted)
// 4
return db.update(TABLE_NAME, values, "$KEY_TODO_ID=?",
arrayOf(todoId))
```

With this code, you:

1. Prepare the `todoId` argument, for the **UPDATE** clause.
2. Get a writable instance of the database.
3. Create a `ContentValues` object to contain the key-value pairs, and put the TODO item's property values in it.
4. Run the **UPDATE** query on the database and return the result of the operation.

Now build and run. Tap the **edit icon** that looks like a pencil next to the record. Update the record to a new value and tap **Update**.

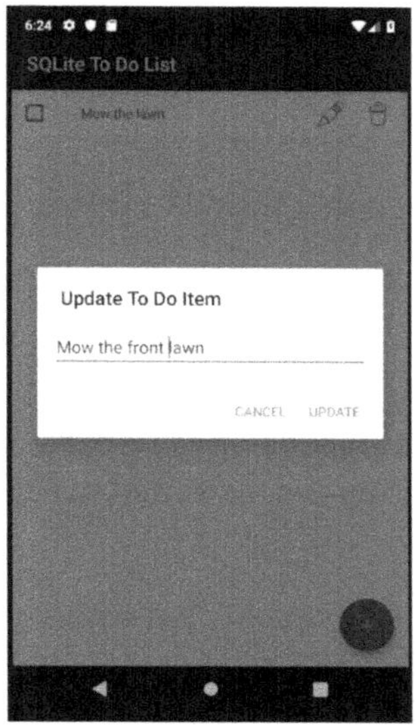

Update a Record.

Now, the record should reflect any changes you made as it is displayed in `RecyclerView`.

Updated Record.

> **Note**: `db.update()` is used in multiple places in the app. First, it was used in the previous example when changes were made to the name of the TODO item. The app also updates TODO items when the completed checkbox is checked.

There is one more bit of functionality to add to this app. The app must also be able to delete TODO items.

Deleting a TODO

In order to delete an item from the database, add the following code to `deleteToDo()`:

```
val db: SQLiteDatabase = writableDatabase
db.delete(TABLE_NAME, "$KEY_TODO_ID=?", arrayOf(id.toString()))
db.close()
```

The above section of code simply gets an instance of the writeable database, deletes the correct TODO item filtered by its id, and closes the database.

Build and run. Tap the **Delete** icon that looks like a wastebasket and the TODO item magically disappears. The list is not empty.

You have successfully written all the CRUD operations! Now, you'll add a unit test to the program with **Robolectric** to see how to unit test the **model** portion of the program.

Unit Testing with Robolectric

You're able to view the contents of the database using the command line or a third-party tool. Wouldn't it also be nice to run a JUnit test on the model portion of the app? This can often be overlooked in the development and testing process.

To create some simple unit tests, you'll use **Robolectric**. Simply put, Robolectric is a framework that allows you to write Android powered unit tests and run them on a desktop JVM while still using the Android API. Robolectric enables you to run your Android tests in your integration environment without any additional setup, which makes it a convenient choice.

Now, you'll create a unit test to test **INSERT** of the database. It will determine if the names of the items are inserting into the database correctly.

To get started, open **build.gradle(Module:app)** and add the following code into the **android** section:

```
testOptions {
  unitTests {
    includeAndroidResources = true
  }
}
```

This will tell gradle to use the `includeAndroidResources` flag, and the name pretty much explains what that means! Next, add the following dependencies in the **dependencies** section:

```
testImplementation "androidx.test:core:1.4.0"
testImplementation "org.robolectric:robolectric:4.4"
```

Sync the gradle file after making these changes. Next, open **ToDoDatabaseHandler.kt** and add the following code inside the class, after `deleteToDo()`:

```
// 1
fun clearDbAndRecreate() {
  clearDb()
  onCreate(writableDatabase)
}

fun clearDb() {
  writableDatabase.execSQL("DROP TABLE IF EXISTS $TABLE_NAME")
}

// 2
fun getAllText(): String {
  var result = ""
  val cols = arrayOf(KEY_TODO_NAME, KEY_TODO_IS_COMPLETED)
  val cursor = writableDatabase.query(TABLE_NAME, cols,
      null, null, null, null, KEY_TODO_ID)
  val indexColumnName =
cursor.getColumnIndexOrThrow(KEY_TODO_NAME)
  while (cursor != null && cursor.moveToNext()) {
    result += cursor.getString(indexColumnName)
  }

  cursor.close()
  return result
}
```

Here's what's happening:

1. You erase and recreate the database once the testing is done. This allows the test to be run multiple times and ensure that residual test data isn't left in the database.

2. `getAllText()` has one job, to create a `String` object that consists of the TODO item names in the database all concatenated together. In the test you'll write soon, you'll see if the database contains the values you expect to see after inserting a few items.

Now, you're ready to create the test. Unit tests are contained in the **test** folder. Open **ToDoDatabaseTest.kt** in **com.raywenderlich.android.sqlitetodo (test)**. Replace the class definition wtih the following code:

```
@RunWith(RobolectricTestRunner::class)
class ToDoDatabaseTest {
  // 1
  lateinit var dbHelper: ToDoDatabaseHandler

  // 2
  @Before
  fun setup() {
    dbHelper =
ToDoDatabaseHandler(ApplicationProvider.getApplicationContext())
    dbHelper.clearDbAndRecreate()
  }

  @Test
  @Throws(Exception::class)
  fun testDbInsertion() {
    // 3
    // Given
    val item1 = ToDo(0, "Test my Program", false)
    val item2 = ToDo(0, "Test my Program Again", false)

    // 4
    // When
    dbHelper.createToDo(item1)
    dbHelper.createToDo(item2)

    // 5
    // Then
    val allText = dbHelper.getAllText()
    val expectedData = "${item1.toDoName}${item2.toDoName}"
    Assert.assertEquals(allText, expectedData)
  }

  // 6
  @After
```

```
    fun tearDown() {
      dbHelper.clearDb()
    }
  }
```

With the above, you:

1. First, declare a database helper property.
2. Perform setup by initializing the database, then clear and recreate the database to start with a fresh copy every time. The function annotated with `@Setup` will be the first function to run before every test.
3. The test is written in **cucumber style** or **Given/When/Then**. You first create two TODO items with two different names. Given those items...
4. ...when they are added to the database...
5. ...then Assert that `getAllText()` matches the expected value.
6. Clear the database after the test, just to be sure.

To run the test, click the **green arrow** next to the class declaration and select **Run 'TestDatabase'**:

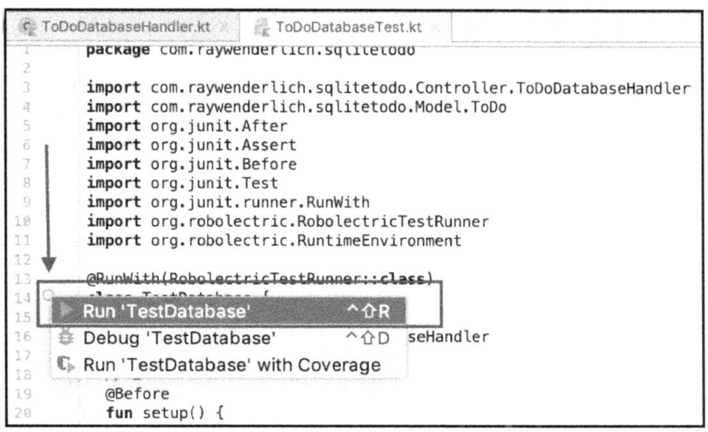

Run the Test.

Then you can see the result of the test at the bottom of the screen:

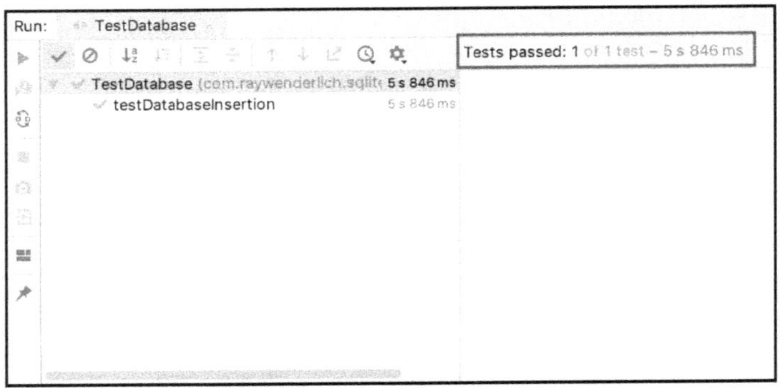

The Test passed.

The positive result indicates that the values returned from the database handler matched the expected string based on the two items that were manually created and inserted.

This proves that the name fields were inserted into the database correctly.

Another neat feature of Robolectric is the .HTML report it can produce. To see this report, make sure you are in project view utilizing the dropdown at the top-left of the editor. Expand the **Gradle** pane with the tab on the right-hand of the screen, and click the **elephant** icon to execute a new task. Then, in the dialog enter **gradle testDebugUnitTest** and press **Enter**.

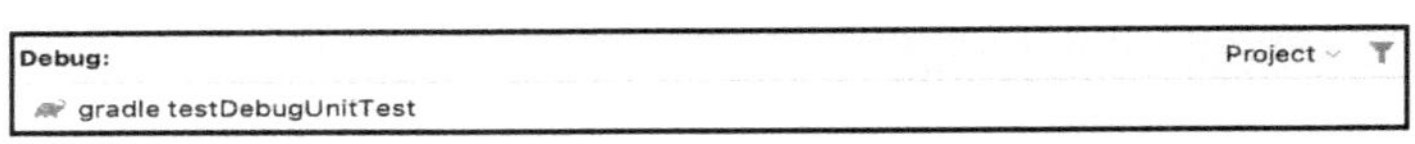

Gradle testDebugUnitTest Action.

This will create the report. Then, in **Project** view browse** to **app/build/reports/tests/debug/index.html**, right-click the file and select **Open in Browser**.

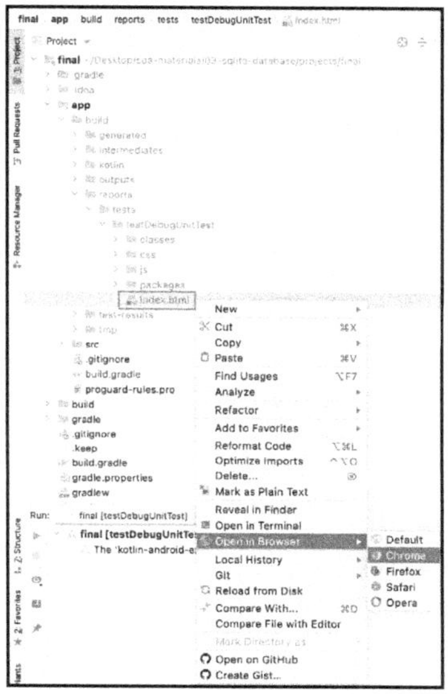

Generate test summary

Now you can see a fantastic report of your testing. Excellent work!

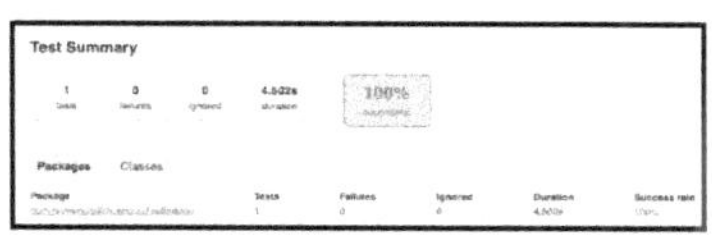

Test report

Key points

- When creating an SQLite database, you should define a **database schema** — a group of `String` constants, used to define your **database structure**.
- A database needs to be **created** and **updated**, according to the context of the app, and the **version of the database**.
- If an app doesn't have a database with the same name as in your schema, it will create one, using the defined schema.
- If the app already has a database with the same name, it will run the **update** process, but only if the database version **changed**.
- You should avoid **dropping the database** if it changes, and try to **migrate** the structure between versions.
- Every database consists of the four standard operations - **Create**, **Read**, **Update**, and **Delete**, or **CRUD** for short.
- To help you avoid so much **SQL** code, and to simplify the operations, Android utilizes the **SQLiteOpenHelper**.
- To store data for operations, the **SQLiteOpenHelper** uses **ContentValues**.
- `ContentValues` are just a key-value pair structure, just like a Map, which is used to insert or update data in the database.
- You can inspect the database by copying it from the **Device File Explorer**, and opening it with a tool, like the **SQLite Browser** or **DB Browser**.
- It's a good practice to write some **Unit tests** for your database, to be sure everything works as expected, **without running the application**.

Where to go from here?

If you would like to know more about SQLite and the syntax that makes up SQLite queries, a more in-depth guide for SQLite can be found in SQLite's Language Guide, which you can access here: https://sqlite.org/lang.html.

This "Unit Testing with Robolectric" article is also an interesting guide about how using Robolectric with Android, which you can read here: https://github.com/codepath/android_guides/wiki/Unit-Testing-with-Robolectric.

Chapter 4: ContentProvider

By Fuad Kamal

Being able to persist structured data in a SQLite database is an excellent feature included in the Android SDK. However, this data is only accessible by the app that created it. What if an app would like to share data with another app? **ContentProvider** is the tool that allows apps to share persisted files and data with one another.

Content providers sit between the app's data source and provide a means to manage this data. This can be a helpful organizational tool in an app, even if the app is not intended to share its data externally with other apps. Content providers provide a standardized interface that can connect data in one process with code running in another process. They encapsulate the data and provide mechanisms for defining data security at a granular level. A content provider can be used to aggregate multiple data sources and abstract away the details.

Although it can be a good idea to use a content provider to better organize and manage the data in an app, this isn't a requirement if the app isn't going to share its data.

One of the simplest use cases of a content provider is to gain access to the Contacts of a device via a content provider. Another common built-in provider in the Android platform is the user dictionary. The user dictionary holds spellings of non-standard words specific to the user.

Understanding content provider basics

In order to get data from a content provider, you use a mechanism called **ContentResolver**. It provides methods to query, update, insert and delete data from a content provider. A request to a content resolver contains an URI to one of the SQL-like methods. These methods return a **Cursor** instance.

> **Note**: Cursor is defined and discussed in more detail in the previous SQLite chapter. It's essentially a pointer to a row in a table of structured data that was returned by the query.

There are two basic steps to interact with a content provider via content resolver:

1. Request permission from the provider by adding a permission in the manifest file.
2. Construct a query with an appropriate content URI and send the query to the provider via content resolver object.

Understanding Content URIs

To find the data within the provider, use a **content URI**. The content URI is essentially the address of where to find the data within the provider. A content URI always starts with `content://` and then includes the **authority** of a provider which is the provider's symbolic name. It can also include the names of tables or other specific information relating the query. An example content URI for the user dictionary looks like:

```
content://user_dictionary/words
```

Oftentimes, providers allow you to append an ID value to the end of the URI to find a specific record, or a string such as **count** to denote that you want to run a query that counts the number of records. You must refer to the provider documentation to figure out what a specific content provider exposes.

Requesting permission to use a content provider

The application will need **read access permission** for the specific provider. Utilize the `<uses-permission>` element and the exact permission that was defined by the provider. The provider's application can specify which permissions requesting applications must have in order to access the data. Users can see the requested permissions when they install the application. For example, the code to request read permission of the user dictionary is:

```
<uses-permission
android:name="android.permission.READ_USER_DICTIONARY" />
```

If you want to use the user dictionary, the above permission should be added inside the **manifest** tag in **AndroidManifest.xml**.

Permission types

The types of permission that can be granted by a content provider include:

- Single read-write provider-level permission – This permission controls both read and write access to the whole provider. It's one permission to rule them all. :]
- Separate read and write provider-level permission – Read and write permissions can be set separately for the whole provider.
- Path-level permission – Read, write or read/write permissions can be applied to each content URI individually.
- Temporary permission – Temporary access can be granted to an application even if it doesn't have the permissions that would otherwise be required. This means that only applications that need permanent permissions for your providers are apps that continually access your data.

Constructing the query

The statement to perform a query on the user dictionary database looks like this:

```
cursor = contentResolver.query(
    // 1
    UserDictionary.Words.CONTENT_URI,
    // 2
    projection,
    // 3
```

```
    selectionClause,
    // 4
    selectionArgs,
    // 5
    sortOrder
)
```

`contentResolver` that is part of a **context** is utilized to call the query function and a list of arguments can be passed if necessary. The only required argument is the **content URI**. Below is an explanation of each of the parameters.

1. The content URI of the provider including the desired table.
2. The columns definitions to return for each row, this is `String` array.
3. The selection clause, similar to the **WHERE** clause only excluding the where. A ? is used in place of arguments.
4. The arguments to be utilized for the selection clause that fill in the `?`.
5. The sort order such as `"ASC"` or `"DESC"`.

> **Note**: Allowing raw SQL statements from external sources can lead to malicious input from SQL injection attempts. Using the selection clause with ? representing a replaceable parameter and an array of selection arguments instead can prevent the user from making these attempts.

A content provider not only allows data to be read by an outside application, the data can also be updated, added to or deleted.

Inserting, updating and deleting data

The insert, update and delete operations look very similar to the query operation. In each case, you call a function on the content resolver object and pass the appropriate parameters in.

Inserting data

Below is a statement to insert a record:

```
newUri = contentResolver.insert(
        UserDictionary.Words.CONTENT_URI,
        newValues
)
```

`newValues` is a **ContentValues** object which is populated with key-value pairs containing the column and value of the data to be inserted into the new row. `newURI` contains the content URI of the new record in the specific form — content://user_dictionary/words/<id_value>.

Updating data

To update data, call `update()` on the content resolver object and pass in content values that include key-values for the columns being updated in the corresponding row. Arguments should also be included for selection criteria and arguments to identify the correct records to update. When populating the content values, you only have to include columns that you're updating, and including column keys with a `null` value will clear out the data for that column. One important consideration when updating data is to sanitize user input. The developer guide to protecting against malicious data has been included in the **Where to go from here?** section below. `update()` returns an `Integer` value that contains the count of how many rows were updated.

Deleting data

Deleting data is very similar to the other operations. Call `delete()` on the content resolver object passing in arguments for the selection clause and selection arguments to identify the group of records to delete. `delete()` returns an `Integer` value which represents the count of how many rows were deleted.

Adding a contract class

A contract class is a place to define **constants** used to assemble the content URIs. This can include constants to contain the authority, table names and column names along with assembled URIs. This class *must* be created and shared by the developer creating the provider. It can make it easier for other developers to understand and utilize the content provider in their application.

MIME types

Content providers can return standard MIME types like those used by media, or custom MIME type strings, or both. MIME types take the format `type/subtype` an example being `text/html`. Custom MIME types or **vendor-specific** MIME types are more complicated and come in the form of `vnd.android.cursor.dir` for multiple rows, and `vnd.android.cursor.item` for single rows.

The **vnd** stands for **vendor** and isn't part of the package name of the app. The subtype of a custom MIME type is provider-specific and is generally defined in the contract class for the provider.

`getType()` of the provider returns a `String` in MIME format. If the provider returns a specific type of data, `getType()` returns the common MIME type for that data. If the content URI points to a row or a table of data, `getType()` returns a vendor specific formatted MIME type including the authority and the table name, e.g. `vnd.android.cursor.dir/vnd.com.raywenderlich.android.contentprovidertodo.provider.todoitems`. This MIME type is for multiple rows in the **todoitems** table with the authority **com.raywenderlich.android.contentprovidertodo.provider**.

A content URI can also perform pattern matches using content URIs that include wildcard characters.

- * – Matches a `String` object of any valid characters of any length.
- # – Matches a `String` object of numeric characters of any length.

Now that you've learned a little bit about content providers, it's time to create one of your own.

Getting started

Locate the **content-provider** folder and open up the **projects** folder inside of it. Next, open the **ContentProviderToDo** app under the **starter** folder. Allow the project to sync, download dependencies, and setup the workplace environment. Build and run to see the main screen.

Add a Content Provider dialog.

You have the shell for a basic todo list app, but if you try to add anything to the todo list now, nothing gets added.

The provider package

It's a good idea to keep the provider classes in their own package. If you look inside the `controller` package, you'll find the `provider` package. It contains the file with a `ToDoContract` class.

The contract class

Now, open **ToDoContract.kt** and examine the contents:

```
// The ToDoContract class
object ToDoContract {
  // 1
  // The URI Code for All items
  const val ALL_ITEMS = -2

  // 2
  //The URI suffix for counting records
  const val COUNT = "count"

  // 3
  //The URI Authority
  const val AUTHORITY =
"com.raywenderlich.android.contentprovidertodo.provider"

  // 4
  // Only one public table.
  const val CONTENT_PATH = "todoitems"

  // 5
  // Content URI for this table. Returns all items.
  val CONTENT_URI = Uri.parse("content://$AUTHORITY/
$CONTENT_PATH")

  // 6
  // URI to get the number of entries.
  val ROW_COUNT_URI = Uri.parse("content://$AUTHORITY/
$CONTENT_PATH/$COUNT")

  // 7
  // Single record mime type
  const val SINGLE_RECORD_MIME_TYPE = "vnd.android.cursor.item/
vnd.com.raywenderlich.android.contentprovidertodo.provider.todoi
tems"

  // 8
  // Multiple Record MIME type
  const val MULTIPLE_RECORDS_MIME_TYPE =
"vnd.android.cursor.item/
vnd.com.raywenderlich.android.contentprovidertodo.provider.todoi
tems"

  // 10
  // Table Constants
  object ToDoTable {
    // The constants for the table columns
    object Columns {
      //The unique ID column
```

```
        const val KEY_TODO_ID: String = "todoid"
        //The ToDo's Name
        const val KEY_TODO_NAME: String = "todoname"
        //The ToDo's category
        const val KEY_TODO_IS_COMPLETED: String = "iscompleted"
      }
   }
}
```

1. The **ALL_ITEMS** constant is used for the URI when `query()` returns all the items in the database.

2. **count** is the suffix used on the URI when the count of items in the table is requested.

3. **AUTHORITY** is the prefix of the URI that serves as the symbolic name for the provider.

4. **CONTENT_PATH** corresponds to the name of the **todoitems** table.

5. **CONTENT_URI** is created by concatenating the authority, or name of the provider with the path, or the name of the table. Then it's parsed into a URI used to get all the records from the provider.

6. **ROW_COUNT_URI** is a second URI that utilizes the same authority but has the count content type. It's used to retrieve the number of records in the table.

7. **SINGLE_RECORD_MIME_TYPE** is the complete, custom MIME type for URIs that return a single record.

8. **MULTIPLE_RECORD_MIME_TYPE** is the custom MIME type for URIs that will return multiple records. Notice the use of **dir** instead of **item** — **item** is used for a single record MIME type.

9. **ToDoTable** is an inner object that contains the name of the main table and definitions for the columns in the database.

`ToDoContract` is the **Contract** class that contains all the constant definitions you need for your content provider. This class can be distributed to client apps that would like to use the provider and will provide insight into what this provider has to provide.

Adding the content provider

Android Studio has a neat feature to automatically add content classes. A content provider class extends **ContentProvider** from the Android SDK and implements all the required methods. By using the automated method of adding the content provider class, many of these method stubs will be provided for you. It will be your job to fill in the functions in the content provider one by one. Ready to get started? :]

Right click the **provider** package and select **New** > **Other** > **Content Provider**. Provide the class name **ToDoContentProvider** and the URI authority **com.raywenderlich.android.contentprovidertodo.provider**. Also check the boxes for **exported** and **enabled**. Ensure that the source language is **Kotlin**, and press **Finish**.

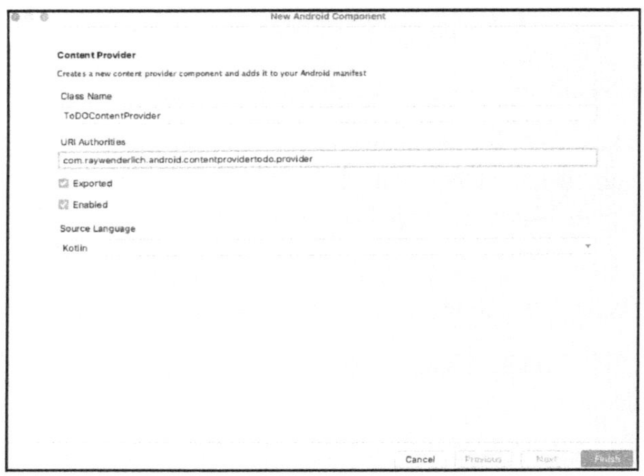

Add a Content Provider dialog.

The class name field provides the name of the new class that will be created in the **provider** package. The URI Authorities field can contain a semicolon-separated list of one to many URI authorities that identify the data under the purview of the content provider. Checking the exported field means that the component can be used by components of other applications. This automatically adds a `<Provider>` element into **AndroidManifest.xml**. Checking the enabled field allows the component to be instantiated by the system.

Now that you have added the template for your content provider, open **AndroidManifest.xml** to see the **provider** tag that has been added.

```
<provider
  android:name=".controller.provider.ToDoContentProvider"
```

```
android:authorities="com.raywenderlich.android.contentproviderto
do"
    android:enabled="true"
    android:exported="true" />
```

Notice how the location, authority and permissions are included in this tag as we specified through the dialog. Next, you need to implement the methods of the content provider.

Implementing the content provider methods

> **Note**: As you add code to the method stubs in the provider, be sure to replace the **TODO** comments with the new code. Also, you may need to press **alt** + **enter** and import libraries as you go along. If given the choice between constants defined in the *ToDoDbSchema* or the new *ToDoContract*, choose **ToDoContract**. The goal is to have the content provider depending on the contract so that it serves as an abstract layer above the database handler. This design allows for the data source to be swapped out as long as it meets the same specifications as the previous data source, and no other code that is dependent on the database will be affected, in this app or other apps that utilize the contract.

Open **ToDoContentProvider.kt**. Notice how the class inherits from `ContentProvider` in the Android SDK. Before implementing the methods, add the following declarations inside the class above all the overridden method stubs:

```
  // 1
  // This is the content provider that will
  // provide access to the database
  private lateinit var db : ToDoDatabaseHandler
  private lateinit var sUriMatcher : UriMatcher

  // 2
  // Add the URI's that can be matched on
  // this content provider
  private fun initializeUriMatching() {
    sUriMatcher = UriMatcher(UriMatcher.NO_MATCH)
    sUriMatcher.addURI(AUTHORITY,CONTENT_PATH,
URI_ALL_ITEMS_CODE)
```

```
        sUriMatcher.addURI(AUTHORITY, "$CONTENT_PATH/#",
URI_ONE_ITEM_CODE)
        sUriMatcher.addURI(AUTHORITY, "$CONTENT_PATH/$COUNT",
URI_COUNT_CODE)
    }

    // 3
    // The URI Codes
    private val URI_ALL_ITEMS_CODE = 10
    private val URI_ONE_ITEM_CODE = 20
    private val URI_COUNT_CODE = 30
```

1. Add an instance of the database handler as the content provider sits between the database and the rest of the program, also create a URI matcher to help construct the URIs.

2. Create `initializeURIMathching()` and add each URI that this content provider can match with. This provider will accommodate a URI to retrieve a single record with an id hence the #, a URI to get all the records, and a URI to get a count of the number of records. Each URI includes the authority, the content path, any arguments represented by special characters, and a unique code.

3. Declare some constants that represent the numeric code for the URI. The contract class gives descriptive names to the corresponding values these codes will match with. These codes are unique and chosen by the developer.

The next step is to start implementing the stub methods one by one. The template doesn't always put them in the most logical order by default. You can reorder them if you like.

Initializing the database and Uris

Insert the code below into `onCreate()` stub replacing `TODO`:

```
context?.let {
    db = ToDoDatabaseHandler(it)
  // intialize the URIs
  initializeUriMatching()
}
return true
```

`onCreate()` prepares the content provider by instantiating the database handler object, calling `initializeUriMatching()` to initialize the URI matcher, and returns `true` to signal that this content provider was created successfully.

Resolving the MIME type

Next, implement `getType()` by replacing the entire stub with the code below:

```
override fun getType(uri: Uri) : String? =
when(sUriMatcher.match(uri)) {
  URI_ALL_ITEMS_CODE -> MULTIPLE_RECORDS_MIME_TYPE
  URI_ONE_ITEM_CODE -> SINGLE_RECORD_MIME_TYPE
  else -> null
}
```

This function accepts `Uri` and matches it with the URI code. Then it returns the correct MIME type. These constants are defined in the contract that has made the code for this function more self-descriptive.

Now that the trivial details are out of the way, you can jump into implementing the CRUD operations.

Querying the database

`query()` queries the database and returns the results. It has been designed so that it can perform *multiple* types of queries, depending on the URI. Insert the code below into the body of the function:

```
var cursor : Cursor? = null
when (sUriMatcher.match(uri)) {
  URI_ALL_ITEMS_CODE -> { cursor = db.query(ALL_ITEMS)}
  URI_ONE_ITEM_CODE -> {
    uri.lastPathSegment?.let {
        cursor = db.query(it.toInt())
    }
  }
  URI_COUNT_CODE -> { cursor = db.count()}
  UriMatcher.NO_MATCH -> { /*error handling goes here*/ }
  else -> { /*unexpected problem*/ }
}
return cursor
```

Here you declare a `Cursor` object and assign it to `null`. Based on the provided `uri`, the URI matcher returns the corresponding code. Then, the **WHEN** statement calls the correct function on the database handler object to retrieve the results, assigns them to the `cursor` and returns `cursor`.

Modifying the adapter

To test the content provider you just created, open **ToDoAdapter.kt** and add the following code inside the class before `onCreateViewHolder()`:

```
private val queryUri = CONTENT_URI.toString() // base uri
private val queryCountUri = ROW_COUNT_URI.toString()
private val projection = arrayOf(CONTENT_PATH) //table
private var selectionClause: String? = null
private var selectionArgs: Array<String>? = null
private val sortOrder = "ASC"
```

These declarations provide the parameters you'll need to pass to the `contentResolver` methods to query, update, insert and delete from the database.

Add the following lines to `bindViews()`:

```
with(binding) {
    // 1
    txtToDoName.text = toDo.toDoName
    chkToDoCompleted.isChecked = toDo.isCompleted
    // 2
    imgDelete.setOnClickListener(this@ViewHolder)
    imgEdit.setOnClickListener(this@ViewHolder)
    // 3
    chkToDoCompleted.setOnCheckedChangeListener
{ compoundButton, _ ->
      toDo.isCompleted = compoundButton.isChecked
      val values = ContentValues().apply {
        put(KEY_TODO_IS_COMPLETED, toDo.isCompleted)
        put(KEY_TODO_ID, toDo.toDoId)
        put(KEY_TODO_NAME, toDo.toDoName)
      }
      selectionArgs = arrayOf(toDo.toDoId.toString())
      context.contentResolver.update(
        Uri.parse(queryUri),
        values,
        selectionClause,
        selectionArgs
      )
    }
 }
```

In this code you:

1. Fill up the `RecyclerView` item with the `toDo` item data — you provide its name and the flag that tells if the item is completed or not.
2. Set `setOnClickListener` for both `imgDelete` and `imgEdit`.
3. Apply `setOnCheckedChangeListener` for `chkToDoCompleted` in which you change the completed state for the `toDo` item and update `contentResolver` with appropriate **ContentValues**, arguments and URI.

Then, add this block to `onClick()`:

```
val cursor = context.contentResolver.query(
  Uri.parse(queryUri),
  projection,
  selectionClause,
  selectionArgs,
  sortOrder
)

if (cursor != null) {
  if (cursor.moveToPosition(bindingAdapterPosition)) {
    val toDoId =
cursor.getLong(cursor.getColumnIndex(KEY_TODO_ID))
    val toDoName =
cursor.getString(cursor.getColumnIndex(KEY_TODO_NAME))
    val toDoCompleted =
cursor.getInt(cursor.getColumnIndex(KEY_TODO_IS_COMPLETED)) > 0
    cursor.close()
    val toDo = ToDo(toDoId, toDoName, toDoCompleted)
    when (imgButton?.id) {
        binding.imgDelete.id -> {
        deleteToDo(toDo.toDoId)
      }
      binding.imgEdit.id -> {
        editToDo(toDo)
       }
    }
    }
}
```

With this code you set an action that will happen once the user click ons the **delete** or **update** button — `deleteToDo()` and `editToDo()`. Both of these methods are currently empty, you'll implement them in a bit. To know which item to update or delete, you use `query()` that returns a `cursor` containing. quieried to-do item's data . You use that data to create a `ToDo` item so you can pass it to `deleteToDo()` and its id to `editToDo()` as parameters.

Next, you'll utilize the content provider by calling the content resolver's functions.

The adapter needs to know how many rows there are to properly configure `RecyclerView`. Locate `getItemCount()` and insert this code above `return`:

```
// Get the number of records from the Content Resolver
val cursor = context.contentResolver.query(
  Uri.parse(queryCountUri),
  projection, selectionClause,
  selectionArgs, sortOrder
)
// Return the count of records
if (cursor != null) {
  if (cursor.moveToFirst()) {
    val itemCount = cursor.getInt(0)
    cursor.close()
    return itemCount
  }
}
```

The query above utilizes the query `String` **queryCountURI**, which is appended with /**count** to query the provider for the count of records instead of returning all the records or a single item. Now wouldn't it be neat if another app could utilize these queries as well?

Now, find `TODO` in `onBindViewHolder()` and replace it wiith this:

```
// 1
val cursor = context.contentResolver.query(
  Uri.parse(queryUri),
  projection,
  selectionClause,
  selectionArgs, sortOrder
)

// 2
if (cursor != null) {
  if (cursor.moveToPosition(position)) {
    val toDoId =
cursor.getLong(cursor.getColumnIndex(KEY_TODO_ID))
    val toDoName =
cursor.getString(cursor.getColumnIndex(KEY_TODO_NAME))
    val toDoCompleted =
cursor.getInt(cursor.getColumnIndex(KEY_TODO_IS_COMPLETED)) > 0
    cursor.close()
    val toDo = ToDo(toDoId, toDoName, toDoCompleted)
    holder.bindViews(toDo)
  }
}
```

In this code you:

1. Call `query()` on the content resolver returns `cursor` that allows the app to iterate through all the records in the table, create a to-do item and bind the fields of the `RecyclerView`'s row to the fields of that to-do item.
2. Create a `ToDo` object from the fields in the query and bind it to the view.

Lastly, add the code to insert a record. Then, you can test the basic functionality of the content provider.

Inserting items

Open **ToDoContentProvider.kt** and locate `insert()`. Replace its `TODO` in with:

```
values?.let {
    val id = db.insert(it.getAsString(KEY_TODO_NAME))
    return Uri.parse("$CONTENT_URI/$id")
  }
return null
```

When inserting a to-do item, the only relevant information that is provided is the name of that item. Completed is false by default and the id field is provided by `insert()` itself. The database handler returns the id, and the content provider uses this id to return a URI where this provider can access the new record.

Next, open **ToDoAdapter.kt** and find `insertToDo()`. Replace `TODO` with:

```
// 1
val values = ContentValues()
values.put(KEY_TODO_NAME, toDoName)
// 2
context.contentResolver.insert(CONTENT_URI, values)
notifyDataSetChanged()
```

Here you:

1. Create and populate a content values object.
2. Run the insert query on the content resolver to insert the record. Then, notify adapter that change happened.

After all your hard work, it's time to run the app and add a couple items! Build and run the app. Click the button in the lower left corner and add some items to your TODO list. They will be displayed in the list as you add them. Nice work! :]

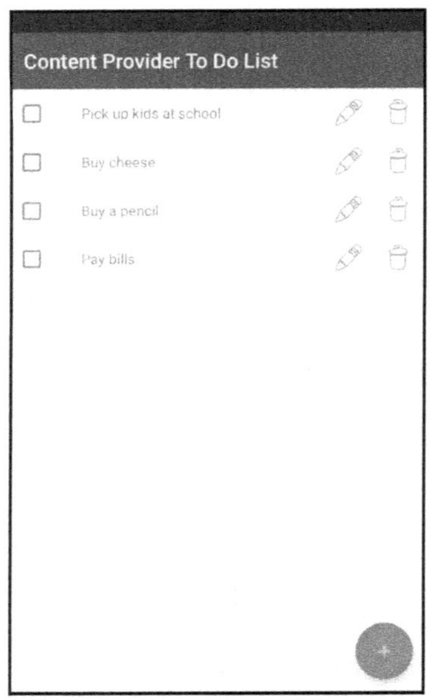

Data appeared in the list.

The **update** and **delete** buttons will not actually do anything, yet. You'll add the functionality to update (edit) an item, next.

Updating items

Open **ToDoContentProvider.kt** and copy the code below into the body of `update()`:

```
values?.let {
  val toDo = ToDo(
    it.getAsLong(KEY_TODO_ID),
    it.getAsString(KEY_TODO_NAME),
    it.getAsBoolean(KEY_TODO_IS_COMPLETED)
  )
  return db.update(toDo)
}
return 0
```

First, you create a `ToDo` item by extracting the values utilizing the key values defined in the contract. Then pass this `toDo` to **db** to update the database.

Now, open **ToDoAdapter.kt** and replace `TODO` in `editToDo()` with the following:

```
 // 1
val values = ContentValues().apply {
  put(KEY_TODO_NAME,
dialogToDoItemBinding.edtToDoName.text.toString())
  put(KEY_TODO_ID, toDo.toDoId)
  put(KEY_TODO_IS_COMPLETED, toDo.isCompleted)
}
// 2
context.contentResolver.update(
  Uri.parse(queryUri),
  values,
  selectionClause,
  selectionArgs
)
// 3
notifyDataSetChanged()
```

In this code block you:

1. Create and populate the `ContentValues` object.
2. Run the update query to update the record.
3. Notify the adapter that the dataset has changed so `RecyclerView` updates.

Run the app and use the pencil icon to update an item that you added previously.

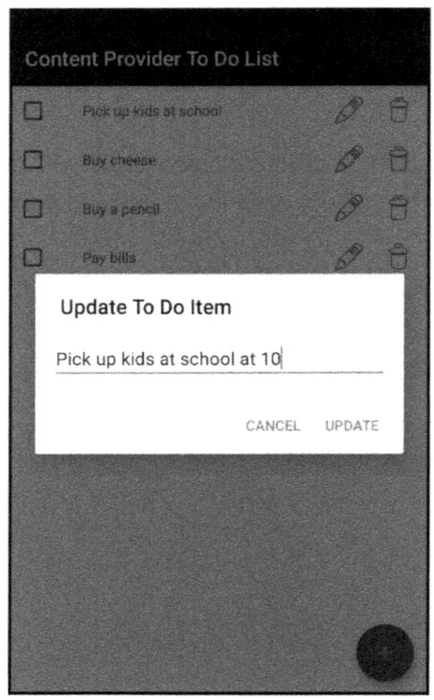

Updating item successful.

The app can now update items. But what about deleting them? You will add the ability to delete items in the next steps.

Deleting items

Deleting a record is simple. Open **ToDoContentProvider.kt** and replace `TODO` of `delete()`:

```
selectionArgs?.get(0)?.let {
    return db.delete(parseLong(it))
}
return 0
```

This gets the id for the record to delete out of the `selectionArgs` and pass that value to the database handler to delete the record from the underlying database. The number of rows that are deleted is returned.

Next, open **ToDoAdapter.kt** and replace `TODO` of `deleteToDo()` with:

```
// 1
selectionArgs = arrayOf(id.toString())
// 2
context.contentResolver.delete(Uri.parse(queryUri),
selectionClause, selectionArgs)
// 3
notifyDataSetChanged()
Toast.makeText(context, "Item deleted.", LENGTH_LONG).show()
```

Here you:

1. Populate **selectionArgs** with the id of the record to delete.
2. Run the query to delete the record.
3. Notify the adapter that the dataset has changed and show a `Toast` message.

Run the app, you are now able to delete items from the list. Great!

Deleting item successful.

Now you have created your very own content provider and content resolver in one. Even though it's not required to utilize a content provider when outside apps aren't accessing the data, sometimes it can provide an organizational layer of abstraction that can improve an app's overall architecture. Now, if you'd like, you can tackle an additional challenge and create a client app that will utilize the content provider.

Challenge: Creating a client

For an additional, interesting challenge, make a copy of the app you just created that creates a content provider and see if you can remove the database and transform it into a client that utilizes the content provider.

Challenge Solution: Creating a client

It's easy to create a client app that utilizes the provider you just created in the previous steps. You can achieve this by making a copy of the provider app and deleting the database and content provider from it. This proves the content provider is shared with an external app. The steps are as follows:

1. Locate your final **contentprovider** app in the file system and make a copy of the project folder with name **final_client**.. Append the word **client** to the name of the folder so you can tell the difference between the two apps.
2. Open the app in Android Studio by going to **File** > **Open...** and select the new folder and click **OK**.
3. Rename the package in the project to **com.raywenderlich.android.contentprovidertodoclient** by right clicking on the package and selecting **Refactor** > **Rename...**. A dialog emerges asking if you'd like to rename the directory or the package. Click **Rename Package**. You are then prompted for the new name so type that in and click **Refactor**. The last step is to click the **Do Refactor** button at the bottom of the editor.

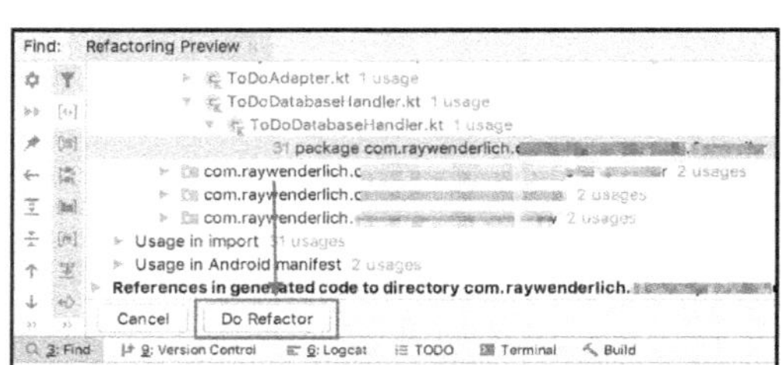

Do Refactor button to rename the package

4. Open the **build.gradle** app module and change the app id to **com.raywenderlich.android.contentprovidertodoclient**.

5. Open **strings.xml** and change the name element value to **Content Provider To Do List Client**.

6. Open **AndroidManifest.xml** and add the following permission just inside the `<manifest>` tag.

```
<uses-permission android:name =
"com.raywenderlich.android.contentprovidertodo.provider.PERMISSI
ON"/>
```

This allows the client to use whatever permissions the provider set.

7. Delete the `<provider>` tag and its contents. This app does not provide data, it simply relies on the data shared by the other app.

8. Remove the files **model/ToDoDbSchema.kt**, **controller/provider/ToDoContentProvider.kt** and **controller/ToDoDatabaseHandler.kt** by right clicking them, selecting **Refactor** > **Safe Delete...**. Uncheck any boxes that would search for usages and hit OK. If the **Usages Detected** dialog pops up simply press **Delete Anyway**. Allow the editor to sync the gradle dependencies if prompted to.

9. Once those files are removed, run the app. Any items you've added in the previous app will show in the new app. But how is this possible? You just deleted the database handler class as well as the schema and the content provider. If you create, update or delete any to-do items and then run the previous app that contains the content provider, those changes will reflect in that app as well. The two apps are sharing data through the same content provider.

Congratulate yourself! You just created two apps that are sharing the same data, think of the possibilities!

Key points

- Content providers sit just above the data source of the app, providing an additional level of abstraction from the data repository.
- A content provider allows for the **sharing** of data between apps.
- A content provider can be a useful way of making a single data provider if the data is housed in multiple repositories for the app.
- It's not necessary to use a content provider if the app is not intended to share data with other apps.
- The content resolver is utilized to run queries on the **content provider**.
- Using a content provider can allow granular permissions to be set on the data.
- Use best practices such as selection clauses and selection arguments to prevent SQL Injection when utilizing a content provider, or any raw query data mechanism.
- Data in a content provider can be accessed via exposed URIs that are matched by the content provider.

Where to go from here?

See Google's documentation on content provider here: https://developer.android.com/guide/topics/providers/content-providers.

Learn more specifics about content provider permissions here: https://developer.android.com/guide/topics/providers/content-provider-basics#Permissions.

Learn more about how to protect against malicious data from this guide found here: https://developer.android.com/guide/topics/providers/content-provider-basics#Injection

Find out more about using content providers with Storage Access Framework here: https://developer.android.com/guide/topics/providers/document-provider.

Chapter 5: Jetpack DataStore

By Subhrajyoti Sen

DataStore is Google's new library to persist data as key-value pairs or typed objects using protocol buffers. Using Kotlin coroutines and Flow as its foundation, it aims to replace SharedPreferences. Since it's part of the Jetpack suite of libraries, it's also known as Jetpack DataStore.

In this chapter, you'll learn about:

- DataStore's advantages over SharedPreferences.
- Types of DataStore implementations.
- Writing to Preferences DataStore.
- Reading from Preferences DataStore.
- Migrating existing SharedPreferences to DataStore.

It's time to jump in!

Getting started

Open the starter project in Android Studio. Build and run to see the main screen of the app.

The Main Screen.

Using `FloatingActionButton`, you can add a note. You can filter and sort the notes using the toolbar menu options. If you restart the app, you'll notice that your sorting and filtering preferences persist.

Right now, you can't change the background color. You'll fix that later.

In the source code, there are two files you should focus on:

1. **NotePrefs.kt**: This file contains a class that takes an instance of `SharedPreferences`. It has methods to read and write the preferences.

2. **MainActivity.kt**: This file includes a class that uses an instance of `NotePrefs` to update the preferences based on user interactions, then updates the UI accordingly.

You'll start updating the app shortly. But first, take a moment to understand more about why to use DataStore and how it works.

Limitations of SharedPreferences

Before you can understand DataStore's advantages, you need to know about the limitations of the `SharedPreferences` API. Even though `SharedPreferences` has been around since API level 1, it has drawbacks that have persisted over time:

1. It's not always safe to call `SharedPreferences` on the UI thread because it can cause jank by blocking the UI thread.
2. There is no way for `SharedPreferences` to signal errors except for parsing errors as runtime exceptions.
3. `SharedPreferences` has no support for data migration. If you want to change the type of a value, you have to write the entire logic manually.
4. `SharedPreferences` doesn't provide type safety. If you try to store both `Booleans` and `Integers` using the same key, the app will compile just fine.

Google introduced DataStore to address the above limitations.

Types of DataStore implementations

DataStore offers two implementations, which you can choose from depending upon your use case:

1. **Preferences DataStore**: Stores data as key-value pairs, similar to `SharedPreferences`. You use this to store and retrieve primitive data types.
2. **Proto DataStore**: Uses **protocol buffers** to store custom data types. When using Proto DataStore, you need to define a **schema** for the custom data type.

In this chapter, you'll focus on Preferences DataStore. However, here's a quick overview of Proto DataStore.

`SharedPreferences` uses **XML** to store data. As the amount of data increases, the file size increases dramatically and it's more expensive for the CPU to read the file.

Protocol buffers are a new way to represent structured data that's faster and than XML and has a smaller size. They're helpful when the read-time of stored data affects the performance of your app.

To use them, you define your data schema using a **.proto** file. A language-dependent plugin then generates a class for you.

Given how vast a topic protocol buffers are, this chapter won't cover them in depth. However, you can refer to the **Where to go from here?** section for resources to learn more about them.

Now, it's time to build your first **DataStore**!

Creating your DataStore

To start working with Preferences DataStore, you need to add its dependency.

Open **build.gradle** and add the following dependency:

```
implementation "androidx.datastore:datastore-preferences:1.0.0"
```

Click **Sync Now** and wait for the dependency to sync.

Similar to other Jetpack libraries, the code to create `DataStore` is very concise. You have to use the property delegate named `preferencesDataStore` to get an instance of `DataStore`.

Open **MainActivity.kt** and add the following code right before the class declaration:

```
private val Context.dataStore by preferencesDataStore(
  name = NotePrefs.PREFS_NAME
)
```

In the code above, you create a property whose receiver type is `Context`. You then delegate its value to `preferencesDataStore()`. `preferencesDataStore()` takes the name of `DataStore` as a parameter. This is similar to how you create a `SharedPreferences` instance using a name.

When you create a `DataStore` instance, the library, in turn, creates a new directory named **datastore** in the **files** directory associated with your app.

Before you can start accessing `DataStore`, you need access to its instance.

Accessing DataStore

Open **NotePrefs.kt** and change the constructor of `NotePrefs` to the following:

```
class NotePrefs(
  private val sharedPrefs: SharedPreferences,
  private val dataStore: DataStore<Preferences>
)
```

> **Note**: Choose `androidx.datastore.preferences.core.Preferences` to add the import for `Preferences`.

The code above adds a constructor parameter of type `DataStore<Preferences>`, which indicates that this is an instance of `DataStore`.

Next, head over to **MainActivity.kt** and change the lazy assignment of `notePrefs` to include the new constructor parameter:

```
private val notePrefs: NotePrefs by lazy {
  NotePrefs(

applicationContext.getSharedPreferences(NotePrefs.PREFS_NAME,
Context.MODE_PRIVATE),
    dataStore
  )
}
```

The code above passes the `DataStore` instance created in `MainActivity` as a parameter to `NotePrefs`.

Now that `NotePrefs` has access to `DataStore`, you'll add the code to write data to it.

Writing to DataStore

To read and write data to `DataStore`, you need an instance of `Preferences.Key<T>`, where `T` is the type of data you want to read and write.

Creating a key

To interact with `String` data, you need an instance of `Preferences.Key<String>`. The DataStore library also contains functions like `stringPreferencesKey()` and `doublePreferencesKey()` that make it easy to create such keys.

Open **NotePrefs.kt** and code the following code inside `companion object`:

```
private val BACKGROUND_COLOR =
stringPreferencesKey("key_app_background_color")
```

The code above creates a key of type `String` and names it **key_app_background_color**.

Writing a key-value pair

Now that you've created a key, you can use it to write a value corresponding to the key. Replace `saveNoteBackgroundColor()` with the following:

```
suspend fun saveNoteBackgroundColor(noteBackgroundColor: String)
{
  dataStore.edit { preferences ->
    preferences[BACKGROUND_COLOR] = noteBackgroundColor
  }
}
```

> **Note**: Here, you create a suspending function. If you need to brush up on suspending functions, or coroutines in general, refer to our book, Kotlin Coroutines by Tutorials https://www.raywenderlich.com/books/kotlin-coroutines-by-tutorials.

In the code above, you use `edit()` to start editing `DataStore`. `edit()` takes in a lambda that provides access to the underlying `preferences`. You then use the key, `BACKGROUND_COLOR`, to store the new color.

Finally, you need to invoke `saveNoteBackgroundColor()` in `MainActivity` inside a coroutine.

Open **MainActivity.kt** and change the invocation of `saveNoteBackgroundColor()` inside `showNoteBackgroundColorDialog()` to the following:

```
lifecycleScope.launchWhenStarted {

notePrefs.saveNoteBackgroundColor(selectedRadioButton.text.toStr
ing())
}
```

A lot is happening in the code above:

- `lifecycleScope` is an extension property that gives you access to `CoroutineScope`, which is tied to the `Activity`'s lifecycle. `CoroutineScope` helps you specify which thread the task will run on and when it can be canceled.
- `launchWhenStarted()` starts a coroutine in `lifecycleScope` when `Activity` is at least in the `STARTED` state.
- `saveNoteBackgroundColor()` is invoked from inside `lifecycleScope`.

The code above makes sure `Datastore` updates asynchronously.

Also, remove the line below from `showNoteBackgroundColorDialog()`.

```
changeNotesBackgroundColor(getCurrentBackgroundColorInt())
```

You don't need this anymore because, using `DataStore`, you'll update your UI reactively whenever the user chances their preferences.

Now, you've set up the method to write the data. Your next goal is to write the mechanism to read this data.

Reading from DataStore

Unlike `SharedPreferences`, `DataStore` doesn't provide APIs to read data synchronously. Instead, it uses **Flow** to give you a way to observe data inside `DataStore` and handle errors correctly. `Flow` is a Kotlin coroutines API that provides an asynchronous data stream that sequentially emits values.

Create a new file called **UserPreferences.kt** in **com/raywenderlich/android/organizedsimplenotes** and add the following lines to it:

```
data class UserPreferences(
  val backgroundColor: AppBackgroundColor
)
```

In the code above, `UserPreferences` acts as a container class that groups different user preferences. For now, it contains only the background color.

Initializing Flow

At this point, you need a way to convert the data you read from `DataStore` into an instance of `UserPreferences`.

Open **NotePrefs.kt** and add the following code at the top of the class, just below the class declaration:

```
// 1
val userPreferencesFlow: Flow<UserPreferences> = dataStore.data
  // 2
  .catch { exception ->
    if (exception is IOException) {
      emit(emptyPreferences())
    } else {
      throw exception
    }
  }.map { preferences ->
    // 3
    val backgroundColor =
AppBackgroundColor.getColorByName(preferences[BACKGROUND_COLOR]
?: DEFAULT_COLOR)

    UserPreferences(backgroundColor)
  }
```

> **Note**: When prompted to add the import for `Flow`, choose `kotlinx.coroutines.flow.Flow`.

The code above does a few important things:

1. Accesses the data inside `DataStore` using the `data` attribute, which returns `Flow` of type `Preferences`.

2. Catches any exceptions thrown into `Flow`. If the exception is an `IOException`, it returns empty preferences using `emit()`. Else, it throws the error to the caller.

3. Reads the preference value using the `BACKGROUND_COLOR` key. If `preferences` don't contain data with the given key, it will return `null`. In that case, you choose `DEFAULT_COLOR`. Finally, it creates an instance of `UserPreferences` and passes it into `Flow`.

Collecting Flow

In the previous step, you accessed the data inside `DataStore`, mapped it to `UserPreferences` and then emitted it into `Flow`.

Now, you need to **collect** `Flow` in `MainActivity` to read its values. Collecting a flow is equivalent to reading the values emitted from `Flow`.

Open **MainActivity.kt** and replace the `changeNotesBackgroundColor()` invocation inside `onCreate()` with the following code:

```
try {
  lifecycleScope.launchWhenStarted {
    notePrefs.userPreferencesFlow.collect { userPreferences ->

changeNotesBackgroundColor(userPreferences.backgroundColor.intCo
lor)
    }
  }
} catch (e: Exception) {
  Log.e("MainActivity", e.localizedMessage)
}
```

Also, add the following imports:

```
import kotlinx.coroutines.flow.collect
import android.util.Log
```

In the code above, you call `collect()` on `Flow` and get access to the `UserPreferences` instance. You then extract the `backgroundColor` value and invoke `changeNotesBackgroundColor()`. Finally, you wrap the entire `collect()` call in a try-catch block since any exception throw by `Flow` will be re-thrown by `collect()` as well.

Next, you need to fetch the background color from `DataStore`.

Making synchronous calls

When you migrate a project from SharedPreferences to DataStore, it isn't always possible to replace all synchronous reads with asynchronous reads.

Open **NotePrefs.kt** and replace getAppBackgroundColor() with the following code:

```
fun getAppBackgroundColor(): AppBackgroundColor =
  runBlocking {
    AppBackgroundColor.getColorByName(dataStore.data.first()
[BACKGROUND_COLOR] ?: DEFAULT_COLOR)
  }
```

In the code above, runBlocking() blocks the current thread while the coroutine runs and effectively lets you make synchronous reads from DataStore.

> **Note**: You should only use runBlocking() to read from DataStore when it's *absolutely necessary* because doing so potentially blocks the UI thread while DataStore reads the values.

You use dataStore.data.first() to access the first item emitted by Flow and then use BACKGROUND_COLOR to access the background color from the preferences.

Build and run. Open the **overflow menu** in the toolbar and change the **background color** to orange. You'll see that the background changes. Close and reopen the app. The background color will still be orange.

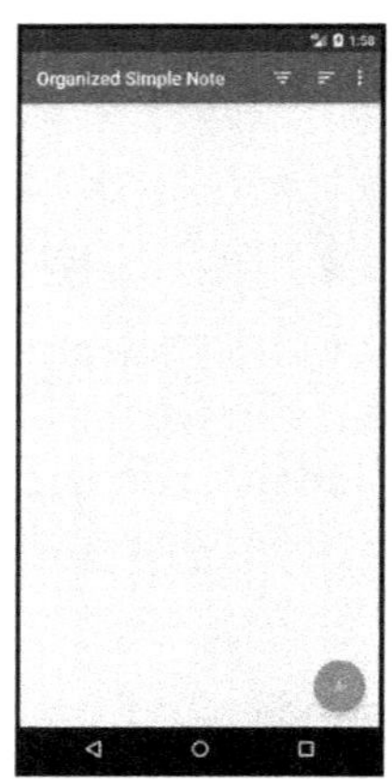

Background Color Changes Based on the User's Preferences.

Congratulations, you've successfully used `DataStore` to store and retrieve user preferences. Next, you'll take a look at how to handle adding `DataStore` to an app that already uses `SharedPreferences`.

Migrating from SharedPreferences

If you're working on a new app, you can use `DataStore` right from the start. But, in most cases, you'll be working on an existing app that uses `SharedPreferences`. The users of this app will already have preferences that you want to persist when you use `DataStore`.

To emulate the second scenario, use the starter project.

Migrating the read/write methods

`NotePrefs` contains methods that persist preferences in `SharedPreferences`. The first step in your migration is to rewrite these methods to use `DataStore`.

Open **NotePrefs.kt** and add the following code to `companion object`:

```
private val NOTE_SORT_ORDER =
stringPreferencesKey("note_sort_preference")
private val NOTE_PRIORITY_SET =
stringSetPreferencesKey("note_priority_set")
```

In the code above, you create keys for the note sort order and priority. This is similar to how you handled the background color.

Next, replace `saveNoteSortOrder()`, `getNoteSortOrder()`, `saveNotePriorityFilters()` and `getNotePriorityFilters()` with the following code:

```
suspend fun saveNoteSortOrder(noteSortOrder: NoteSortOrder) {
  dataStore.edit { preferences ->
    preferences[NOTE_SORT_ORDER] = noteSortOrder.name
  }
}

fun getNoteSortOrder() = runBlocking {
  NoteSortOrder.valueOf(dataStore.data.first()
[NOTE_SORT_ORDER] ?: DEFAULT_SORT_ORDER)
}

suspend fun saveNotePriorityFilters(priorities: Set<String>) {
  dataStore.edit { preferences ->
```

```
      preferences[NOTE_PRIORITY_SET] = priorities
    }
  }

  fun getNotePriorityFilters() = runBlocking {
    dataStore.data.first()[NOTE_PRIORITY_SET] ?:
  setOf(DEFAULT_PRIORITY_FILTER)
  }
```

The code above is similar to what you already wrote for the background color preference. In `saveNoteSortOrder()` and `saveNotePriorityFilters()`, you're assigning provided value to specific key and store it into `DataStore`. Using `getNotePriorityFilters()` and `getNoteSortOrder()`, you're retrieving stored value, or a default value if the real one is `null`.

Open **MainActivity.kt** and replace `updateNoteSortOrder()` and `updateNotePrioritiesFilter()` to make them use `CoroutineScope`, as follows:

```
  private fun updateNoteSortOrder(sortOrder: NoteSortOrder) {
    noteAdapter.updateNotesFilters(order = sortOrder)
    lifecycleScope.launchWhenStarted {
      notePrefs.saveNoteSortOrder(sortOrder)
    }
  }

  private fun updateNotePrioritiesFilter(priorities: Set<String>)
  {
    noteAdapter.updateNotesFilters(priorities = priorities)
    lifecycleScope.launchWhenStarted {
      notePrefs.saveNotePriorityFilters(priorities)
    }
  }
```

`updateNoteSortOrder()` applies provided `sorOrderd` to the note list inside the adapter. Then, it uses `saveNoteSortOrder()` to save the current order filter to `DataStore`. `updateNotePrioritiesFilter()` is doing a similar thing - updates `noteAdapter` about filter priorities, and saves the priorities to `DataStore`.

Now that you have methods to write values to `DataStore` and to read them, you have one final step. You need to copy the user's existing preferences values from `SharedPreferences` to `DataStore`.

Migrating the preferences

To migrate data from `SharedPreferences`, you need to tell `DataStore` the name of the `SharedPreferences` instance that holds the data you want to copy. You use `SharedPreferencesMigration` to achieve this.

To add a migration, change `preferencesDataStore()` to contain the following paramter :

```
  produceMigrations = { context ->
     listOf(SharedPreferencesMigration(context,
NotePrefs.PREFS_NAME))
   }
```

> **Note**: When adding the import for `SharedPreferencesMigration`, choose `androidx.datastore.preferences.SharedPreferencesMigration`.

In the code above, `produceMigrations` is the constructor argument, and takes a lambda of type `(Context) -> List<DataMigration<Preferences>>`.

You create an instance of `SharedPreferencesMigration` that takes a `Context` instance and the name of the existing `SharedPreferences`. You then make a list with the `SharedPreferencesMigration` instance and return it from the lambda.

Similarly, you can migrate multiple `SharedPreferences` to a single `DataStore`.

Without building the app, run it once. Change the priority to **Priority 1** and **Priority 2** and the sort order to **Filename Ascending** from the toolbar. Remember your selections.

Now, build and run for the last time to verify that your sorting and priority choices from the previous session persisted. This proves that you correctly migrated the preferences from `SharedPreferences`.

Note Preferences Persist Across App Launches.

Key points

- `SharedPreferences` has limitations regarding blocking the UI thread, error handling and data migration.
- Google introduced **DataStore** to address the limitations in the SharedPreferences API.
- There are two implementations of DataStore: **Preferences** and **Proto**.
- You use `preferencesDataStore()` to create or get access to a `DataStore` instance.
- `DataStore` instances can have a unique name, just like `SharedPreferences`.
- `DataStore` data is exposed as `Flow` that you can collect when you want to read data.
- You use migrations to migrate data from `SharedPreferences` to `DataStore`.

Where to go from here?

In this chapter, you learned about Preferences DataStore in detail.

To learn about protocol buffers in your favorite programming language, refer to Google's protocol buffers documentation https://developers.google.com/protocol-buffers/docs/tutorials.

To learn about Proto DataStore, refer to the official Android documentation at https://developer.android.com/topic/libraries/architecture/datastore#proto-datastore.

To improve the app, try removing all usages of `runBlocking {}`, then refactor `MainActivity` so it reads the preferences asynchronously.

In the next chapter, you'll start learning about Room and an architecture that integrates with it well.

Section 2: Using Room

Architecture Components made their debut at Google I/O 2018. Google presented them as a set of solutions for the most common problems in the development of Android apps. Data persistence was among those problems, and one solution that Architecture Components offers is **Room**. In this section, you'll learn how to use the Room library to persist data in your apps and how to safely **migrate data** after you change your database schema.

Chapter 6: Room Architecture

By Subhrajyoti Sen

In the previous section, you learned all the basics behind data storage on Android. You learned how to work with permissions, shared preferences, content providers, JetPack DataStore and **SQLite**.

SQLite is a fast, lightweight local database natively supported by Android that allows you to store large amounts of data in a structured way. The only downside of SQLite is that its syntax isn't very intuitive since the way to interact with it can be very different from platform to platform.

Therefore, in this chapter, you'll learn about one of the most popular libraries that helps you simplify your interaction with SQLite: **Room**.

Along the way, you'll also learn:

- How Object Relational Mappers work.
- About Room's integration with Google's architecture components
- The basics behind entities, DAOs and Room databases.
- The advantages and disadvantages of Room.
- The app you are going to build in the rest of this section.

Surely, you're ready to dive in!

Object Relational Mappers

Before using Room properly in your projects, you first need to learn what Room is.

Room is a type of data persistence library commonly known as **O**bject **R**elational **M**apper or **ORM**. ORMs are tools that allow you to retrieve, delete, save and update the contents of a relational database using the programming language of your choice.

ORMs are implemented as libraries or frameworks that provide an additional layer of abstraction called the **data layer**, allowing you to better interact with your database using a syntax similar to the object-oriented world.

To better understand how ORMs work, imagine that you have a `Movie` class with three properties: An `id`, a `name` and a `release_date`.

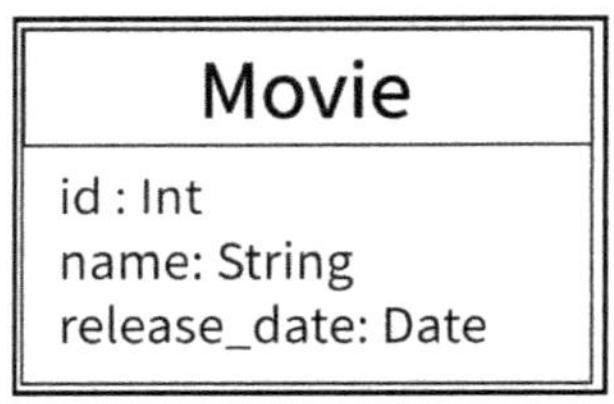

The Movie class with its properties.

The diagram above is a class diagram that represents the `Movie` class. Like most object-oriented languages, each of these properties has a specific data type such as `Int`, `String` or `Date`.

With the help of an ORM, you can easily use the `Movie` class to create a new table in your database. In an ORM, classes represent a table inside your database and each property represents a column. For example, the ORM will translate the `Movie` class into a table like this:

id	name	release_date

Empty table with three columns: id, name and release_date.

Each column would also have the data type that best represents the original data type of the original property. For example, a `String` would be translated as a `varchar` and an `Integer` as an `Int`.

The way to create new records inside the tables differs from each implementation. For instance, some ORMs automatically create new entries each time a new class instance is created. Other ORMs such as Room use **D**ata **A**ccess **O**bjects or **DAO**s to query your tables.

The following is a simple example of how you would use a DAO in Room to create new `Movie` records in the previously mentioned table:

```
movieDao.insert(Movie(1, "Harry Potter", "10-11-05"))
movieDao.insert(Movie(2, "The Simpsons", "03-10-02"))
movieDao.insert(Movie(3, "Avengers", "08-01-10"))
```

And your table would look like this:

id	name	release_date
1	Harry Potter	10-11-05
2	The Simpsons	03-10-02
3	Avengers	08-01-10

The table filled with data and three columns: id, name and release_date.

Easy, right?

> **Note**: Room can autogenerate the primary key, in this case, `ID`. You will learn how to do that in a later chapter.

Now, check out how Room and Google's android architecture components work and interact with each other.

Room and Android Architecture Components

Over the years, Android developers have adopted different practices in developing the architecture of their apps. Some programmers preferred to use an MVVM architecture with SugarORM, while others used MVP with ObjectBox and Firebase. This led to confusion since there was no recommended or official way of doing things.

Therefore, at the 2018 I/O conference, Google introduced the **Android Architecture Components**, a set of libraries focused on creating a robust architecture for your apps.

Room is part of the architecture components and it is Google's ORM meant to replace other libraries such as ObjectBox or SugarORM.

An app built with Room and other architecture components usually relies on a set of components you're going to see in detail in the following sections.

Database

On a device, the data is stored on a local SQLite database. Room provides an additional layer on top of the usual SQLite APIs that avoids creating a lot of boilerplate code using the `SQLiteOpenHelper` class.

For instance, suppose you want to create a simple database that stores a question table for a quiz app, like the one you will be building in the next chapter. A traditional implementation using the standard SQLite APIs would look something like this:

```
private const val SQL_CREATE_ENTRIES =
        "CREATE TABLE question (" +
                "question_id INTEGER PRIMARY KEY," +
                "text TEXT"

private const val SQL_DELETE_ENTRIES = "DROP TABLE IF EXISTS
question"

class QuizDbHelper(context: Context) : SQLiteOpenHelper(context,
DB_NAME, null, DATABASE_VERSION) {
    companion object {
        const val DATABASE_VERSION = 1
        const val DB_NAME = "question_database.db"
    }
    override fun onCreate(db: SQLiteDatabase) {
        db.execSQL(SQL_CREATE_ENTRIES)
    }
    override fun onUpgrade(db: SQLiteDatabase, oldVersion: Int,
newVersion: Int) {
        db.execSQL(SQL_DELETE_ENTRIES)
        onCreate(db)
    }
    override fun onDowngrade(db: SQLiteDatabase, oldVersion:
Int, newVersion: Int) {
        onUpgrade(db, oldVersion, newVersion)
    }
}
```

On the other hand, with Room the code becomes much more concise and easier to understand:

```
@Database(entities = [(Question::class)], version = 1)
abstract class QuestionDatabase : RoomDatabase() {
  abstract fun questionsDao(): QuestionDao
}
```

As you can see, Room drastically reduced the amount of boilerplate code. Room handles most of the database interaction for you under the hood. Instead of you writing the boilerplate code, Room uses code generation to generate the boilerplate code at compile time.

Entities

Entities in Room correspond to tables in your database and are usually defined in Kotlin as data classes. Take a look at the following Entity example:

```
@Entity(tableName = "question") //1
data class Question(
    @PrimaryKey //2
    @ColumnInfo(name = "question_id") //3
    var questionId: Int,
    @ColumnInfo(name = "text")
    val text: String)
```

Room gives you many annotations that allow you to define how you want your data class to be translated into an SQLite table.

Taking each commented section in turn:

1. The `@Entity` annotation tells Room that this data class is an **Entity**. You can use many different parameters to tell Room how this `Entity` will be translated into an **SQLite** table. In this case, you are using the `tableName` parameter to define the name for the table.

2. The `@PrimaryKey` annotation is mandatory and each `Entity` must have at least one field annotated as the primary key. You could also use the `primaryKeys` parameter inside your `@Entity` annotation to define your primary key.

3. The `@ColumnInfo` annotation is optional but very useful since it allows specific customization for your column. For example, you can define a custom name or change the data type.

DAOs

DAO stands for Data Access Object. DAOs are interfaces or abstract classes that Room uses to interact with your database using annotated functions. Your DAOs will typically implement one or more CRUD operations (create, read, update and delete operations) on a particular `Entity`.

The code for a DAO that interacts with the question `Entity` defined above would look like this:

```
@Dao //1
interface QuestionDao {

  @Insert(onConflict = OnConflictStrategy.REPLACE) //2
  fun insert(question: Question)

  @Query("DELETE FROM question") //3
  fun clearQuestions()

  @Query("SELECT * FROM question ORDER BY question_id") //4
  fun getAllQuestions(): LiveData<List<Question>>

}
```

Step-by-Step:

1. The `@Dao` annotation marks this interface as a Data Access Object. DAOs should *always* be abstract classes or interfaces since, at compile time, Room will internally create the necessary implementation for you according to your provided query methods.
2. The `@Insert` annotation declares that this method will perform a **create** operation by performing an **INSERT INTO** query using the object received as a parameter to create a new record.

3. The `@Query` annotation executes the query passed as a parameter. In this case, you are performing a **delete** operation by executing a **DELETE FROM** query.
4. This is another `@Query` annotated method that retrieves all the questions from your database by using **SELECT** query.

Don't worry if something doesn't make sense right now. You'll be learning much more about DAOs in the **The DAO Pattern** chapter.

Repository

This class acts as a bridge between your data sources and your app. The repository class handles the interaction with your Room database and other backend endpoints such as web services and Open APIs. Repositories make it easy to abstract the data and network layers away from the rest of the app. This abstraction makes it easy to add new data sources without affecting the rest of the app.

ViewModel

Just like the **Repository** acts as a bridge between your data sources and your app, the **ViewModels** act as a bridge between your Repository and your user interface. The ViewModel communicates the data coming from your Repository to your Views and has the advantage of surviving configuration changes since it's lifecycle-aware.

ViewModels are implemented independently of the views (Activities or Fragments). The separation makes it easy to change the view layer without affecting the business logic.

LiveData

`LiveData` is a data holder class that implements the **Observer** pattern. This means it can hold information and be observed for changes. Your views such as Fragments or Activities observe `LiveData` objects returned from your `ViewModels` and update the relevant widgets as needed. The unique thing about LiveData is that it emits changes only if the observer is in an **active state**. Hence, if your Activity is in the backstack or the background, LiveData will not emit any changes.

The following diagram illustrates the interaction between the components mentioned above:

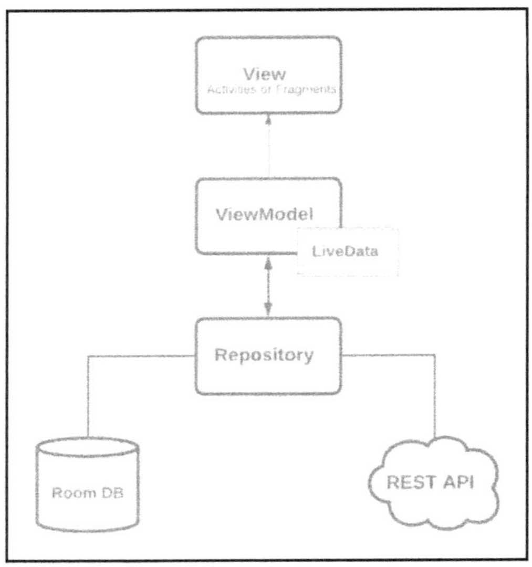

A diagram describing the interaction between Android Architecture components.

You will be learning much more about the above components in the upcoming chapters, but for now, this is all you need to know.

Advantages of using Room

Room uses a local SQLite database to store your data. Therefore, some of the advantages and disadvantages of SQLite apply to Room as well.

Room, however, has some important advantages over the SQLite APIs:

- **Compile-time query verification**: SQLite queries are usually executed at run-time without any verification. If the query has any errors, an exception is thrown, usually crashing your app. Room performs verifications on the SQL queries at compile-time and notifies you of errors early on.
- **Convenience annotations**: As you already noticed in the previous examples, there are some awesome annotations for reducing number of repetitive code parts and boilerplate code.
- **Data migration**: Writing migrations between different versions of your database can be a tedious task. Room provides a set of APIs that streamline this process and also make it very easy to test the migrations.

Frequently asked Room questions

Are ORMs really necessary? Can't I just use plain old SQLite?

Of course, you can use plain old SQLite! In fact, Android standard libraries include many utilities and classes that help you work directly with SQLite. The only downside with this approach is that you often have to deal with a lot of boilerplate code that can slow down your development.

Are there other ORMs for Android besides Room?

Sure! There many ORMs out there like ObjectBox or SugarORM.

What are the advantages of using Room vs. other ORMs?

The main advantage of using Room vs. ORMs is that Room offers the best integration with other architecture components like ViewModel and LiveData. Since Google develops it, you can be sure this library will be maintained and improved for a very long time to come.

Your app

This chapter has been full of theory and concepts. You're probably wondering when you are actually going to start writing some code.

Well, the rest of the following chapters are going to be focusing solely on how to apply the previously mentioned concepts to build a fun quiz app called **DroidQuiz**. This app will allow your users to test their Android knowledge with a set of questions stored in a Room database:

The main screen of DroidQuiz.

DroidQuiz will help you learn about many important concepts behind Room:

- How to add the appropriate dependencies to your `build.gradle` file for Room and most of the architecture components such as `LiveData`.
- How to create a local SQLite database using Room.
- How to use Database Access Objects or DAOs to interact with your database.

- How to use Google's Android architecture components such as `LiveData` and `ViewModel` to interact with your Room database.
- How to create indices and relationships between your tables.
- How to test your database, migrations, and `ViewModels`, and much more!

As you can see, there is a lot to learn. This section will guide you through every, single step needed to build a final version of the app.

Key points

- Room is an ORM developed by Google as a part of Android Architecture Components to simplify the interaction with your SQLite database and reduce boilerplate code.
- Entities in Room correspond to tables in your database.
- DAO stands for Data Access Object.
- The `Repository` class handles the interaction with your Room database and other backend endpoints.
- The `ViewModel` communicates the data coming from your repository to your views and has the advantage of surviving configuration changes.
- `LiveData` is a data holder class that can hold information and be observed for changes.
- ORMs provide an additional layer of abstraction that allows you to interact with your relational database with an Object-Oriented Language syntax.

Chapter 7: Entity Definitions

By Subhrajyoti Sen

In the previous chapter, you learned the architecture best suited for Room. You also learned about ORMs, Android Architecture Components and the advantages and disadvantages of SQLite.

In this chapter, you'll cover all you need to know about Room entities. Along the way, you'll learn:

- The properties of SQLite tables.
- How to add Room's dependencies to your Gradle files.
- How to create SQLite tables using Room annotations.
- How to define primary keys and column names.

Hopefully, you're ready to get started!

> **Note**: This chapter assumes you have a basic knowledge of Kotlin and Android. If you're new to Android, you can find a lot of beginner Android content to get you started on our site at https://www.raywenderlich.com/category/android. If you know Android, but are unfamiliar with Kotlin, take a look at our tutorial, "Kotlin for Android: An Introduction" at https://www.raywenderlich.com/174395/kotlin-for-android-an-introduction-2.

Getting started

Have you ever played trivia games and thought, "There should be a game like this but with questions for Android developers"? Well, the sample app you'll be working on, **DroidQuiz**, is a trivia game that allows you to answer a series of questions to test your knowledge of Android.

In this chapter, you're going to build entities that represent the tables of your database. If you've had some previous experience with SQL, you probably know this can be somewhat annoying or painstaking to accomplish. Additionally, in "Chapter 3, SQLite Database," you saw how, with SQL syntax, it can sometimes be hard to deduce which parts of it caused an error (if by some chance you get one). The Room database, and its **annotation-driven** system of creating entities and queries, make this process *tremendously easier*.

Start by opening the starter project for this chapter in Android Studio 4.2 or greater. Go to **File ▸ Open**, find app folders in the **entity-definitions ▸ projects** folder, and select the **starter** directory.

Once the starter project finishes loading and building, run the app on a device or an emulator.

Starting Screen of the Sample App.

Right now, the app is just an empty canvas, but that is about to change!

Tables and entities

Most databases consist of **tables** and **entities**. If you were to draw a parallel with object-oriented programming, you could think of entities as a **class definition**, which defines what the objects in the table should look like and how their respective properties behave. Once you create those objects — instances of classes, or entities in your case — you can store them somewhere in memory, which is the table. The table as such is a **container** for all the created objects of some entity type.

This is a very brief, high-level description of how databases work, which is why it's also beneficial to see real-life examples.

Tables

If you reached this section of the book you're probably already familiar with relational databases, tables and SQLite. However, it's important to review other key concepts before you proceed to create your entities using Room.

> **Note**: In this chapter, you are only going to learn the basics of database tables; if you want to learn more, check out the SQLite chapters of the previous section of the book.

Simply put, tables are structures similar to spreadsheets or two-dimensional arrays that let you store records as rows with one or more fields defined as columns — or, as mentioned above, a container for entity data.

For example, the following image shows how a table that stores information about movies could look.

ID	Title	Description	ReleaseDate	Rating
1	Harry Potter	Wizard Movie	10-11-2001	4.4
2	Simpsons	Simpsons Movie	01-02-2002	4.5
3	Hunger Games	Apocalyptic Movie	03-04-2008	5
4	MIB	Men in Black	08-01-1998	4.2
5	X-Men	Mutant Movie	05-05-2001	3.2

Example of a Movie Table.

Columns

Columns represent a field or property of your data like the Title, Description, ReleaseDate or Rating. Columns usually have specific data types such as **INTEGER**, **VARCHAR**, **FLOAT** or **DATETIME** that help preserve the integrity of the information stored in your database.

For most of the tables, the first column will be used to store a **primary key** that uniquely identifies the record. Primary keys are values often represented as a series of `Integers` that are incremented one by one (1,2,3,4,5,...). This isn't always the case since you could also use any `String` that represents a unique value for each entry — like a randomly generated hash or a social security number if you have more complex security requirements. As such, the primary key is, at its core, the differentiating agent between records. You can quickly look up records by primary keys or compare two records to see if they are the same.

Primary keys also help you create relationships by defining a **foreign key** that references a primary key of another table. For example, say that you have an **Orders** table that stores the number of Blu-ray sales for each movie like below:

OrderID	MovieID	OrderDate
1	1	08-08-2018
2	2	01-01-2019
3	1	02-03-2018
4	2	20-09-2017
5	5	02-02-2019

Example of an Orders Table.

In this case, the **MovieID** is a foreign key that identifies a unique movie record in your Movies table. Therefore, if you want to retrieve extra details about an available movie, you would only need to retrieve the movie row from your Movies table with that particular ID. As such, you don't have to store all of the data about ordered movies in the **Orders** table, you can just look up movie details using the foreign key. This makes each order object very light while holding enough data to look up more detailed information.

Although not all database management systems will force you to have a primary key, it's strongly recommended that you have one for each of your tables since it makes it much easier to retrieve information using queries. But, usually, when working with databases, you can specify you want a primary key, and it gets auto-generated, so you don't have to worry about it.

Rows

Rows represent a record in your database and can contain as many columns as needed to represent your data. **Row** and **record** are terms that are often used interchangeably just like **column** and **field**. However, when creating a database, you'll need to make sure that your team is on the same page regarding naming conventions.

In the Movie table example, you have five rows each representing a different movie record added to your database. The **ID** column shows the primary key for each movie. **Title** and **Description** are `String` values, **ReleaseDate** is `Date` field and **Rating** is `Float`. This will help you form the appropriate entity within the Android project so that Room can create the database and tables.

Entities

To create a table using Room you need to create an **entity**, just like you did above. Entities in Room are defined by using a series of different **annotations** on classes. The following are the most common annotations that you will use when defining an entity:

- ### @Entity

`@Entity` declares that the annotated class is a Room entity. For each entity, a table is created in the associated SQLite database to save your data. To add the annotation, simply use the following approach:

```
@Entity
data class Movie(
    //...
)
```

This code would create a **Movie** table in your database. By default, Room always uses the name of your class as the table name, but you can use the `tableName` property of `@Entity` to set a different name like shown below:

```
@Entity(tableName = "movies")
data class Movie(
    //...
)
```

Now that the class is declared as an entity, you can use it in Room's setup, which you'll see in a bit.

- ### @PrimaryKey

`@PrimaryKey` allows you to define a primary key for your table. It's very important to remember that each entity in Room **must have** at least one field defined as the primary key:

```
@Entity
data class Movie(
  @PrimaryKey var id: Int,
  var title: String?,
  var description: String?,
  var releaseDate: String?,
  var rating: Float
)
```

You can also let Room generate the primary keys automatically for you, using `autogenerate` of `@PrimaryKey` :

```
@Entity
data class Movie(
  @PrimaryKey(autogenerate = true) var id: Int,
  var title: String?,
  var description: String?,
  var releaseDate: String?,
  var rating: Float
)
```

In the above code, `id` is the primary key for your Movie table, and it's going to be automatically generated by Room incrementing the value each time by one. It's important to remember that if you set `autogenerate` to `true`, the type affinity for the field must be **INTEGER**, or `Int` in Kotlin.

• @ColumnInfo

In the same way that the `tableName` property of `@Entity` allows you to customize the name of your table, `@ColumnInfo` lets you change the name of your columns — class properties in Kotlin:

```
@Entity
data class Movie(
  @PrimaryKey(autogenerate = true) var id: Int,
  var title: String?,
  var description: String?,
  @ColumnInfo(name = "release_date") var releaseDate: String?,
  var rating: Float
)
```

This annotation is particularly useful because you'll often want to follow different naming conventions for your class properties and your database columns, such as `releaseDate` vs `release_date` naming.

• @Ignore

Room translates all of your class properties into database columns by default. If there is a field that you don't want to be converted into a column, you can use `@Ignore` to tell Room to ignore it:

```
@Entity
data class Movie(
  @PrimaryKey(autogenerate = true) var id: Int,
  var title: String?,
  var description: String?,
  @ColumnInfo(name = "release_date") var releaseDate: String?,
  var rating: Float,
  @Ignore var poster: Bitmap?
)
```

In the above code, you use `@Ignore` to tell Room that you don't want `poster` to be converted as a column in your Movie table. You can also use `ignoredColumn` of `@Entity` to declare which fields you want to ignore:

```
@Entity(ignoredColumns = arrayOf("poster"))
data class Movie(
  @PrimaryKey(autogenerate = true) var id: Int,
  var title: String?,
  var description: String?,
  @ColumnInfo(name = "release_date") var releaseDate: String?,
  var rating: Float,
  var poster: Bitmap?
)
```

- **@Embedded**

You use @Embedded on an entity's field to tell Room that the properties on the annotated object should be represented as columns on the same entity.

For example, say that you have a User table that contains address information. Your entity could look like this:

```
@Entity
data class User(
  @PrimaryKey val id: Int,
  val firstName: String?,
  val street: String?,
  val state: String?,
  val city: String?,
  @ColumnInfo(name = "post_code") val postCode: Int
)
```

However, thanks to @Embedded you can represent the address fields as a separate class but Room will still generate a single table:

```
data class Address(
    val street: String?,
    val state: String?,
    val city: String?,
    @ColumnInfo(name = "post_code") val postCode: Int
)

@Entity
data class User(
    @PrimaryKey val id: Int,
    val firstName: String?,
    @Embedded val address: Address?
)
```

Both implementations will generate a single User table with six fields: id, firstName, street, state, city and postCode.

There are more annotations available, but these are by far the most commonly used when creating your entities.

Now that you know the theory, it's time to put it into practice!

Creating your entities

Since you'll be working on with Room, you need to add the appropriate dependencies to your **build.gradle** files to use Room. To ensure forward compatibility with future versions of Android, you'll use **Androidx** artifacts for this project.

Open the app-level **build.gradle** file and add the following lines under the dependencies block:

```
//Room
implementation "androidx.room:room-runtime:$room_version"
kapt "androidx.room:room-compiler:$room_version"
```

The **room-runtime** library contains all the annotations you read about earlier and all other classes you need from Room. The **room-compiler** library is an annotation processor that reads the above annotations and generates the code used to create the SQLite database.

Click **Sync Now** and wait until Android Studio finishes syncing your new dependencies.

Build and run one more time just to make sure that the project is still working properly after the updates to your Gradle files.

Verifying that The App shows The Main Screen.

Create a new package under the root directory of your app by right-clicking on the package **com/raywenderlich/android/droidquiz** and selecting **New ▸ Package** and name it **data**.

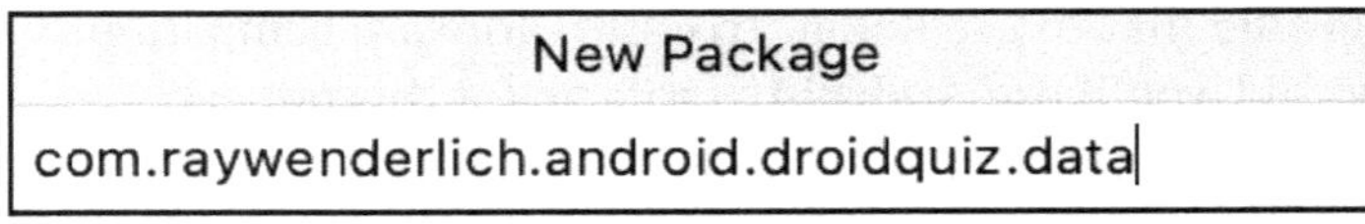

Creating a New Package - Data

Inside the **data** package, you'll store all the code related to your Room database including your entities and data access objects.

Create a new package inside the **data** package and name it **model**. Inside the **model** package, you'll store the data classes that will be converted to entities using annotations.

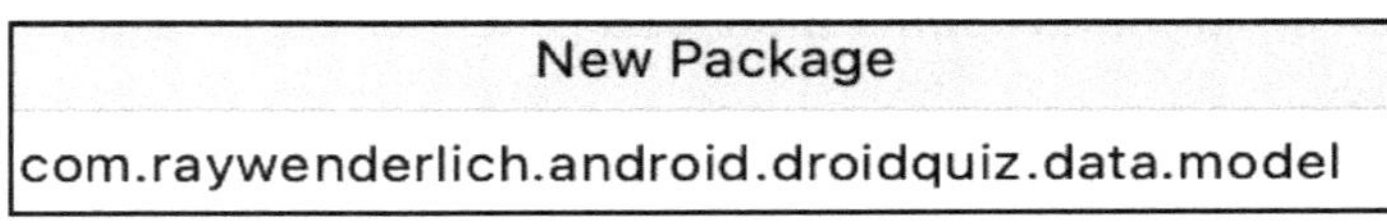

Creating a New Package - Model

The DroidQuiz app will consist of a very simple database with two tables — a **Question** table and an **Answer** table.

The Question table will have two columns:

- **question_id**: A self incrementing `Int` that will act as the primary key.
- **text**: A `String` that represents the text of the question.

The Answer table will have four columns:

- **answer_id**: The primary key for this table.
- **question_id**: A foreign key that references a question in the **Question** table.
- **is_correct**: A `Boolean`, which indicates if this is one of the correct answers or not.
- **text**: A `String` that represents the text of the answer.

Here is how the entity-relationship diagram would look:

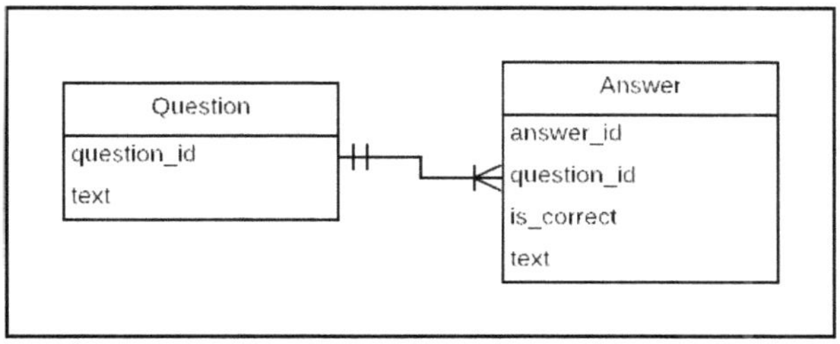

Entity Relationship Diagram

Each question can have one or more answers, but each answer will only have one associated question, thus creating a **one-to-many** relationship. Easy, right?

In this chapter, you'll solely focus on defining entities, without foreign key relationships. You'll learn how to create relations later on in the book.

Create a new class under the **model** package by right-clicking on **model** and selecting **New ▸ Kotlin File/Class**, and name it **Question**.

Replace the class definition with the following code:

```
@Entity(tableName = "questions") // 1
data class Question(
  @PrimaryKey(autoGenerate = true) // 2
  @ColumnInfo(name = "question_id") // 3
  var questionId: Int,
  val text: String
)
```

> **Note**: Remember to use **Alt** + **Enter** on PC or **Option** + **Return/Enter** on a Mac to import any missing dependencies.

This code does the following, step by step:

1. `@Entity` tells Room that this data class should be converted into an entity. The `tableName` property indicates that the table name should be **questions**.
2. `@PrimaryKey` makes the `questionId` field of your `Question` class a primary key of the table. The `autogenerate` property declares that Room will generate the primary key for you as an auto-incremented integer.
3. `@ColumnInfo` allows you to customize your column's properties like the name or the type affinity - `Integer`, `Text`, `Float`, etc.

Now, create another class under the **model** package and name it **Answer**.

Once again, the class definition with the following code:

```
@Entity(tableName = "answers")
data class Answer(
  @PrimaryKey(autoGenerate = true)
  @ColumnInfo(name = "answer_id")
  val answerId: Int,
  @ColumnInfo(name = "question_id")
  val questionId: Int,
  @ColumnInfo(name = "is_correct")
  val isCorrect: Boolean,
  val text: String
)
```

The code is very similar to `Question`, so there isn't much need to explain the steps. With this, your entities are ready, and it's time to create your database!

Creating the database

Create a new package under the **data** directory and name it **db**.

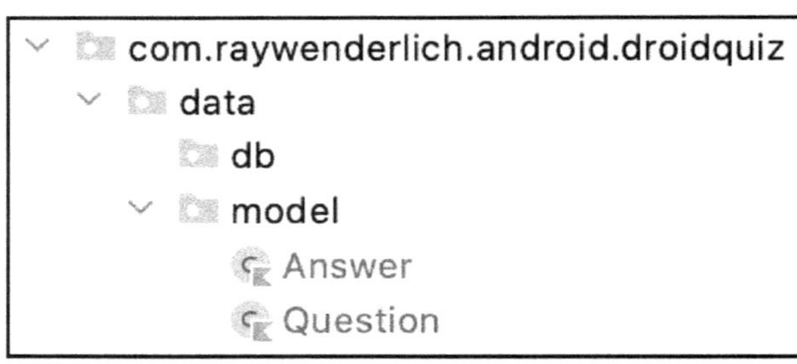

Project Structure

Now, create a new class under the **db** package and name it **QuizDatabase**. Replace everything inside with the following:

```
@Database(entities = [(Question::class), (Answer::class)],
version = 1)
abstract class QuizDatabase : RoomDatabase()
```

Similar to your entities, Room uses `@Database` to define which class should be used to generate your database tables, connections and queries.

`@Database` should always include at least two properties:

- `entities`: These should include an array of all the the entities associated with your database.
- `version`: This is the current version of your database, which is used to migrate everything once things change. You'll learn more about the importance of versions in "Chapter 11: Data Migration".

> **Note**: It's very important that you declare your class as an abstract class that extends from `RoomDatabase` or Room will throw an error.

There are many ways to get an instance of your database at runtime, but, for this app, you'll create a property inside your `Application` class.

Create a new class under the root package of your project — **droidquiz** — and name it **QuizApplication**.

Replace the class declaration with the following:

```
//1
class QuizApplication : Application() {

  private val DB_NAME = "quiz_database"

  companion object {
    lateinit var database: QuizDatabase // 2
      private set
  }

  override fun onCreate() {
    super.onCreate()
    database = Room
      .databaseBuilder(
        this,
        QuizDatabase::class.java,
        DB_NAME
      ) // 3
      .build()
  }
}
```

Taking each commented section in turn:

1. Makes this class extend `Application`, so that it runs with the app launch.
2. Creates a `database` property that will hold a reference to your Room database. Note that the property has a private setter. This ensures that the property can be initialzied only inside `QuizApplication`.
3. `databaseBuilder()` creates an instance of your Room database at runtime. The first parameter accepts a `Context` instance. The second parameter expects the class that you annotated as your Room database. The third parameter allows you to define a name for your SQLite database.

Now, open **AndroidManifest.xml** file and add your `QuizApplication` class to the `application` tag:

```
android:name=".QuizApplication"
```

Finally, build and run to verify that everything is still working properly.

Final Screen.

While the changes are still not visually noticeable since you haven't added any DAOs, you have already created your first SQLite tables using Room entities. Good job!

If you compare it to the very first implementation you've had with writing your SQLite helper, you understand how and why Room is becoming more and more popular among Android developers.

Key points

- Tables are structures similar to spreadsheets or two-dimensional arrays that let you store **records objects**, as **rows** with one or more **fields** defined as **columns**.
- `@Entity` declares that the annotated class is a Room entity.
- `@PrimaryKey` allows you to define a primary key for your table to **uniquely differentiate data**.
- `@ColumnInfo` lets you change the names for your columns, so you can use **different naming conventions** in Kotlin and SQL.
- `@Ignore` tells Room to ignore a certain property from your class so it does not get converted into a column in the database.
- `@Embedded` can be used on an entity's field to tell Room that the properties on the annotated object should be represented as columns on the same entity. This way you can **organize your data** clearly while writing the same SQL.

Where to go from here?

In this chapter, you learned a lot about SQLite tables, Room and entities. If you want to learn more about entities, I suggest the following resources:

- This official Android developer's guide page, "Defining Data Using Room Entities," on how to define data using Room entities, which you can find here: https://developer.android.com/training/data-storage/room/defining-data.
- This official Android developer's guide page, "Entity," which you can find here: https://developer.android.com/reference/androidx/room/Entity.

In the next chapter, you're going to learn even more about Room entities by creating your first relations.

Chapter 8: Mastering Relations

By Subhrajyoti Sen

In the previous chapter, you learned all you need to know about tables, entities and annotations. You also learned how to create your database and how to get a runtime instance of it by using `Room.databaseBuilder()`.

In this chapter, you'll learn even more about entities by creating relations between them using foreign keys and `@Relation`. Along the way, you'll learn:

- How to create a **relationship** using primary keys and foreign keys.
- How to define a **one-to-many relationship** in Room.
- How to represent different kinds of relationships using **entity-relationship diagrams**.
- How to use `@Embedded`.
- How to use `@ForeignKey`.
- How to use `@Relationship`.

> **Note**: This chapter assumes you have basic knowledge of Kotlin and Android. If you're new to Android, check out our Android tutorials (https://www.raywenderlich.com/category/android). If you know Android but are unfamiliar with Kotlin, take a look at Kotlin For Android: An Introduction (https://www.raywenderlich.com/174395/kotlin-for-android-an-introduction-2).

Getting started

If you are following along with your own app, open it up. If not, don't worry. You can use the **starter** project for this chapter, which you can find in the attachments. Now, open the app in Android Studio 4.2.1 or greater by going to **File ▸ Open**, and selecting the **starter** project directory.

Once the starter project finishes loading and building, run the app on a device or emulator.

The DroidQuiz Application.

Great! The app is working as expected.

The code is basically the same as the previous chapter. But, if you are just getting started, here is a quick recap of the packages and the code:

- The **data** package contains the **db** and **model** packages. The **db** package contains the class that creates your Room database, while **model** contains all of the code for the entities created in the previous chapter.
- The **view** package contains the code for all of the activities of your app.

You're no doubt eager to start writing some code. But, before that, you'll need to learn a bit of theory first!

Relations and entity-relationship diagrams

In this chapter, you'll create a relation between two entities that you created in the previous chapter — `Question` and `Answer`. The only problem is that relationships are always hard to understand even if it's just between two single tables. Therefore, in this section, we are going to talk about a little tool that will help you to better understand the different kinds of relations between — **entity-relationship diagrams**.

You might have heard of entity-relationship diagrams before. They are quite common in software design and it's one of the first things they teach in college in courses such as **Databases 101** or **Introduction to Relational Databases**. An entity-relationship diagram, ER diagram or **ERD** is a kind of flowchart that illustrates the relationships between the components of a system representing something like a school or a company using a set of symbols that include rectangles, ovals and connecting lines.

ER diagrams are commonly created during the initial design of a database schema to determine the tables, their fields and the nature of the relationship between them.

Many different ERD notations have been created over the years to serve different purposes. The notation that we are using in this section is called **Crow's Foot** notation. Although ER diagrams may have different elements depending on the notation system, they usually share similar components that include the following:

Entity

Represents a component, object or a concept of a system. Concepts described by an entity can be concrete, such as a student or a car, or abstract, such as an event or a schedule. Entities are translated as tables when creating your database schema. They are commonly illustrated as rectangles in most ER diagrams, as shown on the Image below.

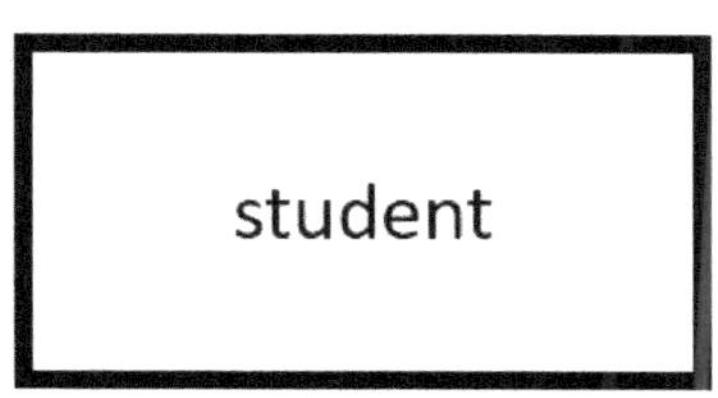

The Student Entity.

Entities in the Crow's Foot notation also include a list of attributes or properties that define them. For a user entity, its attributes could be username, password and email. They are listed in the rectangle as shown below:

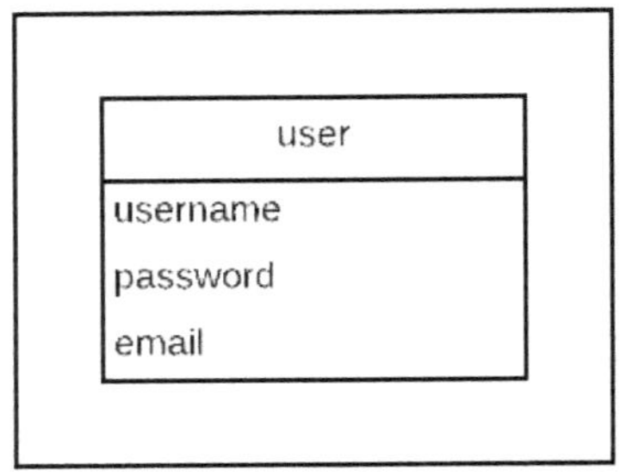

The User Entity.

Relationship

A relationship tells you how two entities interact with each other and it's usually represented as a verb surrounded by a diamond. For example, think about a student entity and a class entity. Their relationship could be described as follows:

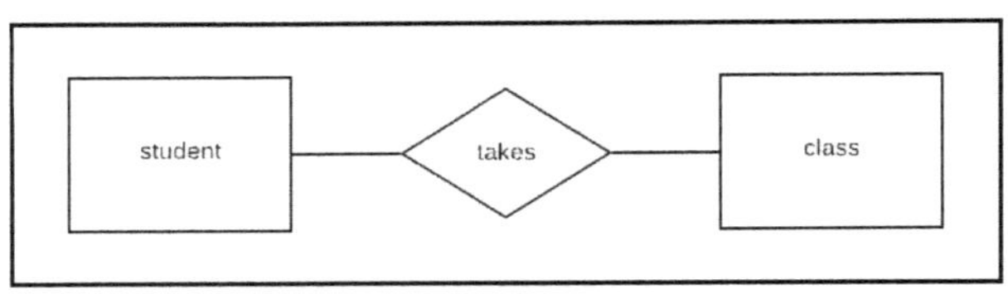

Relation between Entities.

In this ER diagram, the relationship is described as "takes" and you could read it left to right:

A student takes a class.

Or right to left:

A class is taken by a student.

> **Note**: Not all ER diagrams illustrate the relationship between their entities since it is often easy to infer from the context. In Crow's Foot notation, it is usually omitted.

Cardinality

Last but not least, **cardinality** tells you the kind of relationship two entities have. There are three main cardinal relationships:

One-to-one: When one entity can only be related to one and only one instance of the other entity. For example, a department on a company can only have one head of department, and that head of department can only lead one department.

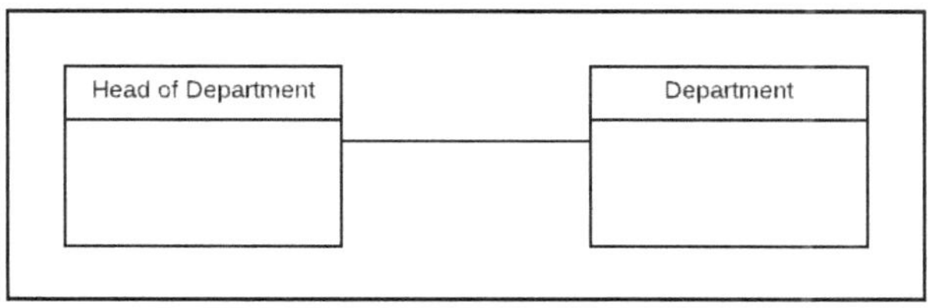

One-to-One Relation.

One-to-many: When one entity can be related to many instances of another entity. For example, a teacher can teach many classes in a single semester, but a class can only have one teacher.

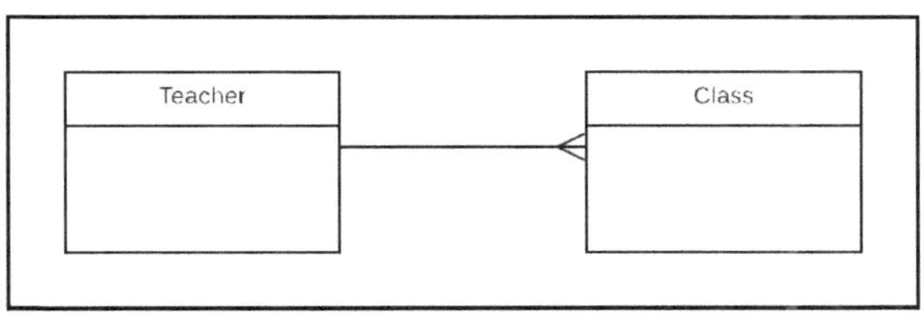

One-to-Many Relation.

Many-to-many: When many instances of an entity can also be related to many instances of another entity. For example, a book (like this one) can have many authors, and an author can write many books.

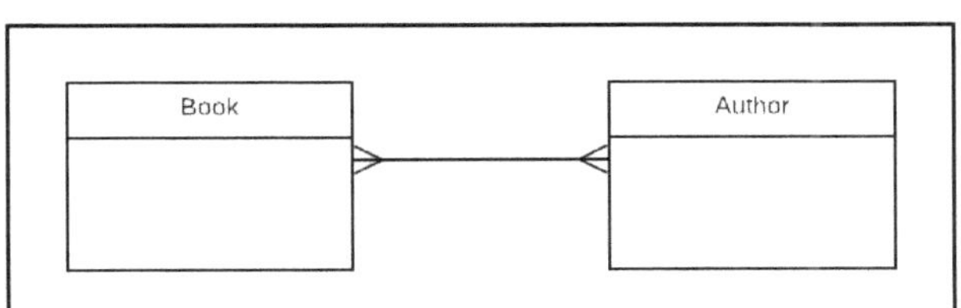

Many-to-Many Relation.

Cardinalities can also have constraints that indicate the minimum and maximum numbers in the relationships: **One and only one**, **zero or one**, **zero or many** and **one or many**.

Here is the full list of cardinalities and constraints that you can find:

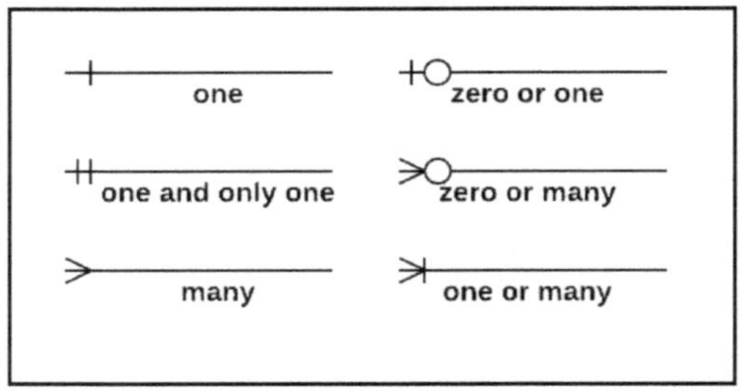

ER Cardinalities.

Now that you know how ER diagrams work, you'll now learn how to create relationships using **Roms Entities**.

Creating your relations

As briefly mentioned in the previous chapter, you'll only need to create one relationship between the entities in your app, and its ER diagram looks like this:

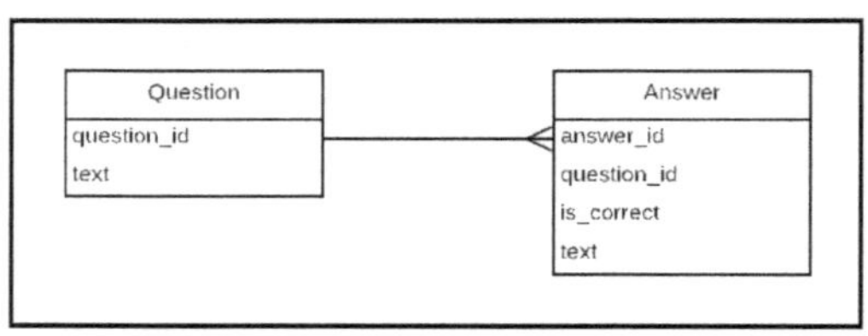

One-to-Many relation between Question and Answers.

Why don't you use your recently acquired knowledge to guess which kind of relationship is this?

Well, if you said "a one-to-many relationship" you are correct.

With the above ER diagram, you are saying: "One question can have one or more answers and each answer can only be related to one and only one question". Just think about it and it makes a lot of sense since each question of the DroidQuiz app will have at least one correct answer and two incorrect answers. The beauty of this design is that you can easily expand it or modify it to have something like two correct answers and two incorrect answers or 3 correct answers and 2 incorrect answers... You get the point.

Now, you'll see how easy it is to define foreign keys and one-to-many relationships between your Room entities. In fact, you can do it by adding a single line of code.

Defining a foreign key

Open **Answer.kt** under the **data ▸ model** package.

The `Answer` entity already has a `question_id` field that you can use as a foreign key that points to the `question_id` field of your `Question` entity. The problem is that you still haven't told Room that this is actually a *foreign key*. For this, you need to use the `foreignKeys` property of `@Entity` to define the relationships.

Add a `foreignKeys` property to `@Entity` of your `Answer` class like this:

```
@Entity(tableName = "answer",
  foreignKeys = [           // 1
    ForeignKey(entity = Question::class,                // 2
      parentColumns = ["question_id"],             // 3
      childColumns = ["question_id"],              // 4
      onDelete = CASCADE)               // 5
  ])
```

Also add the following imports:

```
import androidx.room.ForeignKey
import androidx.room.ForeignKey.CASCADE
```

Taking each commented section in turn:

1. `foreignKeys` allows you to define a relationship between this and another entity. This property accepts an array of `ForeignKey` objects that you can use to define foreign key constraints.
2. The first parameter in the constructor of a `ForeignKey` object accepts the entity to which this entity is related. In this case, you are passing the `Question` class since you want to create a foreign key constraint to the `Question` entity.
3. `parentColumns` accepts the column names in the parent entity as an array. Since you want to match each answer to a single question, you're passing the primary key of your Question entity: `question_id`.
4. `childColumns` accepts the column names in the current entity to use as foreign keys.
5. `onDelete` tells Room what to do in case the parent entity is deleted from the database. For example, what would happen to your answers if the respective question is deleted?

There are several options for `onDelete`:

1. **CASCADE**: If a record is deleted from the parent entity each row in the child entity that was associated with the parent entity is also deleted. For this app, you're using this option since you want to delete the answers if the question is deleted.
2. **NO_ACTION**: If the parent record is deleted or modified, no action is taken.
3. **RESTRICT**: This constraint means that, if a record in the parent entity has one or more records mapped to it in the child entity, the app is prohibited from deleting or updating the parent record.
4. **SET_DEFAULT**: If the parent record is deleted, the foreign key in the child record gets a default value.
5. **SET_NULL**: If the parent record is deleted or updated, the foreign key in the child record gets a `NULL` value.

Defining an index

One important thing to remember is that, if you define a foreign key constraint, SQLite requires that you create a **unique index** in the parent entity for the mapped columns. It's also recommended in the documentation that you create an index on the child table to avoid full table scans when the parent table is updated. If you don't, Room will throw a compile time warning.

Therefore, modify your annotation like this:

```
@Entity(tableName = "answer",
  foreignKeys = [
    ForeignKey(entity = Question::class,
      parentColumns = ["question_id"],
      childColumns = ["question_id"],
      onDelete = CASCADE)
  ],
  indices = [Index("question_id")])     // only this line
changes
```

You'll need to add the import for `androidx.room.Index`, or you can just import `andoidx.room.*`.

In the code above, the `indices` property allows you to define an index for one or more columns in your entity by passing an array with the column names. This takes care of the index for the child entity. Now you need to define it for the parent entity.

Open **Question.kt** and modify `@Entity` like below:

```
@Entity(tableName = "question", indices =
[Index("question_id")])
```

Again, you'll need to add the import for `androidx.room.Index`.

Just like the `Answer` entity, this code is telling Room that you want to create an index for the `question_id` primary key field.

Using @Relation

Now, say you want to retrieve a list of all the questions with their respective answers. To do this, you would need to write two different queries: One to retrieve the list of all the questions and another to retrieve the answers based on the `question_id` value. Your DAO would look like this:

```
@Query("SELECT * FROM question ORDER BY question_id")
fun getAllQuestions(): LiveData<List<Question>>

@Query("SELECT * FROM answer WHERE question_id = :questionId")
fun getAnswersForQuestion(questionId: Int): List<Answer>
```

While the above approach isn't bad, Room offers a better way to work with **one-to-many** relations: `@Relation`.

`@Relation` is a very handy annotation that automatically retrieves records from related entities. You can apply it to a `List` or `Set` of objects and Room will take care of the rest for you. To see `@Relation` in action, find **QuestionAndAllAnswers.kt** under the **data ▸ model** package. Add the following code to the class:

```
@Embedded        // 1
var question: Question? = null

@Relation(
  parentColumn = "question_id",      // 2
  entityColumn = "question_id"
)
var answers: List<Answer> = ArrayList()      // 3
```

Step by step:

1. Since you want to be able to access all the fields in the `Question` entity, you are using `@Embedded` to retrieve all the properties from that entity. If you need a reminder of how annotations like `@Embedded` work, take a look at the **Tables and Entities** section of the previous chapter.
2. `@Relation` accepts at least two parameters:

- `parentColumn` indicates the primary key of the parent entity.
- `entityColumn` indicates the field (usually the foreign key) on this entity that maps to the primary key of the parent entity.

3. The `answers` list will contain the `Answer` objects related to the `question` property.

> **Note**: It's important to remember that `@Relation` can only be used in Pojo classes. Entities in Room can't have relations.

And that's it! Build and run the app again to verify everything is still working fine.

The final DroidQuiz application.

While the app has not visually changed, you now have a good foundation about how Room works and your Database is almost ready.

In the next chapter, you'll learn how to interact with your **Entities** by creating your first **Database Access Objects**.

Key points

- An entity relation diagram, ER diagram or **ERD** is a kind of flowchart that illustrates the relation between the components of a system.
- Entities represent a component, object or concept of a system. They are usually translated as tables in your database.
- Entities in the Crow's Foot notation also include a list of attributes or properties that define them.
- An attribute that can uniquely identify a record of your entity is known as a key attribute and they usually become primary keys in your database.
- A relationship tells you how two entities interact with each other and it is usually represented as a verb.
- The cardinality of an ERD tells you the kind of relationship that two entities have.
- **One-to-one relation:** When one entity can only be related to one and only one instance of the other entity.
- **One-to-many relation:** When one entity can be related to many instances of another entity.
- **Many-to-many relation:** When many instances of an entity can also be related to many instances of another entity.

Chapter 9: The DAO Pattern

By Subhrajyoti Sen

In the previous chapter, you learned about different kinds of relations, such as **one-to-one**, **one-to-many** and **many-to-many**. You also learned how to create them using annotations.

In this chapter, you'll learn how to retrieve, insert, delete and update data from your database using **Database Access Objects (DAO)**.

Along the way, you will also learn:

- What DAOs are and how they work.
- How to create DAOs using Room annotations.
- How to prepopulate the database using a provider class.
- How to perform **INSERT INTO** queries using `@Insert` annotated methods.
- How to perform **DELETE FROM** queries using `@Delete`annotated methods.
- How to use `@Query` to read data from the database.

Ready? Dive in!

Getting started

Download the starter project attached to this chapter and open it using **Android Studio 4.2** or above. Once Gradle finishes building your project, take some time to familiarize yourself with the code. If you have been following along, to this point, you should already be familiar with the project since it is the same as the final project from the last chapter. If you are just getting started, here is a quick recap of the code:

- The **data** package contains two packages: **db** and **model**. The **db** package contains the `QuestionDatabase` class, which defines your Room database. The **model** package contains your entities: `Question` and `Answer`.
- The **view** package contains all your activities: `SplashActivity`, `MainActivity`, `QuestionActivity`, and `ResultActivity`.

Now, build and run the app to verify that everything is working properly.

The Main screen.

Cool! Now you are ready to start creating some Database Access Objects to manipulate the data.

Using DAOs to query your data

Database Access Objects are commonly known as **DAOs**. DAOs are objects that provide access to your app's data, and they are what make Room so powerful since they abstract most of the complexity of communicating to the actual database. Using DAOs instead of query builders or direct queries makes it very easy to interact with your database. You avoid all the hardship of debugging query builders, if something breaks, and we all know how tricky SQL can be! They also provide a better **separation of concerns** to create a more structured application and improve its testability.

In Room, the DAOs are defined as **interfaces** or **abstract classes**. The only difference between both implementations is that the abstract class can *optionally* accept a `RoomDatabase` instance, as a constructor parameter. They are also convenient for defining large database transactions, using `@Transaction` on a method, and calling multiple different methods within.

If you are wondering why DAOs are defined as abstract classes or interfaces, it's because Room takes care of creating each DAO implementation at compile-time, by generating the business logic code for your definitions.

> **Note**: Remember that Room does not support database access on the main thread by default since performing long-running operations such as database transactions might cause your app to freeze or crash. If you still want to take this risk, you'll need to explicitly call `allowMainThreadQueries()` on your database builder.

But, alright, that's enough theory. Think about all the operations that you will need to perform on your database to make the DroidQuiz app work:

- You'll need to **get the list of all the questions** currently stored in your database.
- You'll also need to be able to **create new questions** when your app is created.
- Finally, you'll have to **delete questions** at some point.

With the above in mind, create a DAO in your project that performs **CREATE**, **READ**, and **DELETE** queries in your database. You'll see how easy it is to create DAOs in Room.

Create a new interface under the **db** package and name it **QuizDao**. To turn your new interface into a DAO, simply add the `@Dao` annotation like below:

```
@Dao
interface QuizDao {
}
```

Now, add the following code to the interface:

```
@Insert(onConflict = OnConflictStrategy.REPLACE)
fun insert(question: Question)

@Insert(onConflict = OnConflictStrategy.REPLACE)
fun insert(answer: Answer)
```

`@Insert` is a shortcut that allows you to automatically create an **INSERT INTO** query, that creates a new record in the appropriate table, with the object passed as a parameter. In this case, the first method is going to create a new record in your **Question** table using the `question` object passed as a parameter and the second method is going to create a new record in your **Answer** table.

You might have also noticed the `onConflict` parameter. It allows you to define an `OnConflictStrategy`, which will be used to specify what happens in case there is a conflict when creating a new entry. There are several options:

- **ABORT** is the default option and instructs Room to abort the transaction, return an error and roll back any changes made by the current SQL statement.
- **IGNORE** makes the transaction ignore the conflict and continue as expected.
- **REPLACE** replaces the old data with the new values and continues the transaction.

That's all you need to create a DAO to insert new questions and answers into your Database. Now, create the method to delete questions.

Add the following method to the same class:

```
@Query("DELETE FROM question")
fun clearQuestions()
```

That code uses @Query to execute a **DELETE FROM** query in your question table. Since there is no **WHERE** clause, this will just delete all the records in your question table, which is what you'll need later.

> **Note**: Notice how, if you examine the query String, there's some degree of autocomplete available. Room knows which entity definitions you've created and which fields exist within them. You can use this to write queries and to easily connect to those definitions, knowing that autocomplete is here to help you write them.

Room also offers @Delete to automatically create **DELETE FROM** queries. A method annotated with @Delete will delete its parameter objects from the database. For example, if you wanted to delete a single question from your database, you could do something like this:

```
@Delete
fun deleteQuestion(question: Question)
```

> **Note**: If you want to learn more about @Delete, you can check out the official documentation here: https://developer.android.com/reference/androidx/room/Delete.

Finally, add the following methods:

```
@Query("SELECT * FROM question ORDER BY question_id") // 1
fun getAllQuestions(): List<Question>

@Transaction // 2
@Query("SELECT * FROM question") // 3
fun getQuestionAndAllAnswers(): List<QuestionAndAllAnswers>
```

Just like deleteQuestion(), the above methods use @Query to create SQL statements.

Taking each commented section in turn:

1. This statement is retrieving all the question records in your database and **ordering** them by `question_id`. The response is returned as a `List` of `Question` objects.
2. `@Transaction` tells Room that the following SQL statements should be executed in a **single transaction**. This is especially useful when you want to query multiple tables like in the case of your one-to-many relation between the `questions` table and the `answers` table.
3. Finally, you're creating a select statement to retrieve all the questions from your `questions` table. Notice that this method is returning a list of your `QuestionAndAllAnswers` class so Room will immediately take the answers associated with each question and store them inside the properties of your class.

And that's it! Those are all the DAO definitions you will need.

For this app, you won't be doing any updates to the data; therefore, you didn't use `@Update`. With `@Update`, the implementation of the annotated method will simply update its parameters in the database if they already exist or won't create any if they don't. But since you're using the `OnConflictStrategy.REPLACE` when inserting data anyways, you have a way to update the data, after all.

Now, to provide the `QuizDao` instance for usage, you simply need to add a function to `QuizDatabase`. Open **QuizDatabase.kt**, and add the following code within:

```
abstract fun quizDao(): QuizDao
```

Your code should now look like this:

```
@Database(
    entities = [(Question::class), (Answer::class)],
    version = 1
)
abstract class QuizDatabase : RoomDatabase() {

    abstract fun quizDao(): QuizDao
}
```

Now, when you need to access `QuizDao`and its functions, you simply have to retrieve it from the `QuizDatabase` instance you create on app startup.

Creating a provider class

Now that your DAO methods are ready, you'll create a provider class, that you will need later on, to prepopulate your database. Create a new class under the **data** package, name it **QuestionInfoProvider** and add the following method:

```
private fun initQuestionList(): MutableList<Question> {
  val questions = mutableListOf<Question>()
  questions.add(
      Question(
          1,
          "Which of the following languages is not commonly used
to develop Android Apps")
  )
  questions.add(
      Question(
          2,
          "What is the meaning of life?")
  )
  return questions
}
```

This method creates `MutableList` of two questions with the respective `id` and `text` fields. You'll use these questions later when prepopulating your database.

But you will also need to have answers for the above questions, so add the following method:

```
private fun initAnswersList(): MutableList<Answer> {
  val answers = mutableListOf<Answer>()
  answers.add(Answer(
      1,
      1,
      true,
      "Java"
  ))
  answers.add(Answer(
      2,
      1,
      false,
      "Kotlin"
  ))
  answers.add(Answer(
      3,
      1,
      false,
      "Ruby"
  ))
  answers.add(Answer(
```

```
        4,
        2,
        true,
        "42"
    ))
    answers.add(Answer(
        5,
        2,
        false,
        "35"
    ))
    answers.add(Answer(
        6,
        2,
        false,
        "7"
    ))
    return answers
}
```

Just like `initQuestionsList()`, this method is creating `MutableList`, but with `Answer` objects. Each answer corresponds to a `Question` object of the previous method, using the `questionId` property to match each of them.

Now, add the following properties at the top of your class:

```
val questionList = initQuestionList()
val answerList = initAnswersList()
```

The above properties are immediately initialized with the list of questions and answers that `initQuestionList()` and `initAnswersList()` return.

Finally, make this class a singleton by changing the `class` keyword to `object`:

```
object QuestionInfoProvider { ...}
```

The reason you use the object keyword is to make this class a singleton so that we never really have to instantiate this class ourselves since you are only interested in the utilities that this class provides.

And that's it! Build and run your app to verify that it is still working as expected.

Verifying that the app is working fine.

Sweet! Although the UI is still not working, your database and DAOs are pretty much ready to use. You'll connect the business logic in the following chapters.

Testing your database

Although your app's UI isn't working yet, you can still interact with your database by performing some tests such as adding or deleting questions to verify its functionality.

Now, to test your database, you could start writing code in your activities that insert or delete data and print the results. You could also wait until you have all your `ViewModels` and wire it to your UI. The problem with this approach is that you might end up with a ton of code that you'll have to delete at the end anyway. Also, you might forget to delete some of your `print()` statements and expose sensitive data from your users.

To avoid the above issues, you are going to use a very useful testing framework for Andriod named **Espresso**.

In your project, there's a **com.raywenderlich.android.droidquiz** package with **(androidTest)** next to it.

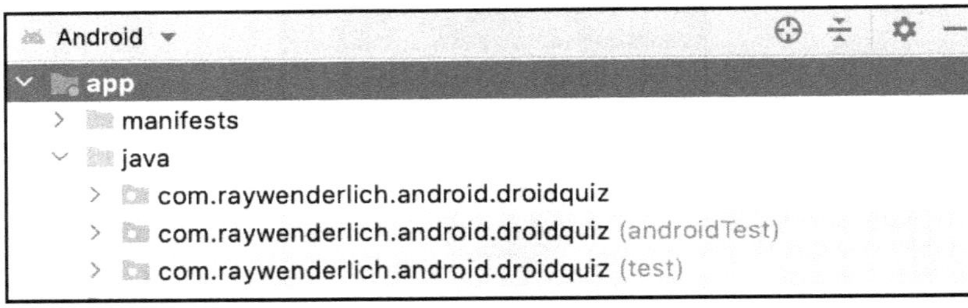

The androidTest package.

Under this package, create a new class named **QuizDaoTest** and add the following code to it:

```
@RunWith(AndroidJUnit4::class)
class QuizDaoTest { // 1
  @Rule
  @JvmField
  val rule: TestRule = InstantTaskExecutorRule() // 2

  private lateinit var database: QuizDatabase // 3
  private lateinit var quizDao: QuizDao // 4
}
```

While adding the import for `AndroidJUnit4`, use `androidx.test.ext.junit.runners.AndroidJUnit4`.

Briefly, the code above does the following:

1. Creates a test class for your `QuizDao` named `QuizDaoTest`.
2. Specifies that all tasks executed using Google's Architecture Components should be executed synchronously on the **main thread**. This is very important since unit tests should be executed sequentially and synchronously.
3. Creates a `lateinit var` that will hold a reference to your Room database.
4. Creates a `lateinit var` that will hold a reference to your `QuizDao`.

Next, add the following code:

```
@Before
fun setUp() {
  val context =
InstrumentationRegistry.getInstrumentation().context // 1
  try {
```

```
      database = Room.inMemoryDatabaseBuilder(
          context,
          QuizDatabase::class.java) //2
        .allowMainThreadQueries() //3
        .build()
    } catch (e: Exception) {
      Log.i(this.javaClass.simpleName, e.message ?: "") //4
    }
    quizDao = database.quizDao() //5
  }
```

When adding the import for `InstrumentationRegistry`, use `androidx.test.platform.app.InstrumentationRegistry`.

`@Before` is used to specify a method that should be executed before any test is run. Here's what's happening in the previous code:

1. Gets the context for this test and assigns it to `context`.
2. Creates an in-memory version of your database. This means that all data will safely be deleted at the end of your test.
3. `allowMainThreadQueries()` allows you to execute queries on the main thread. You need to call this method on your database builder, or Room will throw an error.
4. Logs an exception if the database can't be built.
5. Initializes your `QuizDao`.

Next, add the following code:

```
  @Test
  fun testInsertQuestion() {
    // 1
    val previousNumberOfQuestions = quizDao.getAllQuestions().size
    //2
    val question = Question(1, "What is your name?")
    quizDao.insert(question)
    //3
    val newNumberOfQuestions = quizDao.getAllQuestions().size
    //4
    val changeInQuestions = newNumberOfQuestions -
  previousNumberOfQuestions
    // 5
    Assert.assertEquals(1, changeInQuestions)
  }
```

When adding the import for `Assert`, use `org.junit.Assert`.

`@Test` specifies that this method is a test that you want to execute. Here's what is going on:

1. Calls `getAllQuestions()` of your DAO and store the size of currently available questions.
2. Creates a `Question` and inserts it into your database.
3. Gets the new amount of questions from the database.
4. Calculates the delta from the new and previous amount of questions in the database.
5. Uses `assert()` to let the test know you're expecting only one new question in the database. If the assertion fails, it means the `Question` object you created wasn't stored in the database, or it was stored more than once.

Next, add the following method:

```
@Test
fun testClearQuestions() {
  for (question in QuestionInfoProvider.questionList) {
    quizDao.insert(question)
  }
  Assert.assertTrue(quizDao.getAllQuestions().isNotEmpty())
  Log.d("testData", quizDao.getAllQuestions().toString())
  quizDao.clearQuestions()
  Assert.assertTrue(quizDao.getAllQuestions().isEmpty())
}
```

This test simply verifies the correct functionality of `clearQuestions()` by inserting and deleting all the question records in `QuestionInfoProvider`. It also logs the data saved, so you can see the data does exist within the database.

Finally, add the following method:

```
@After
fun tearDown() {
  database.close()
}
```

Contrary to `@Before` that specifies methods that should be executed before any test is run, `@After` specifies which methods should be executed after each of the tests has concluded. Generally speaking, methods annotated with `@After` are used to release resources allocated with `@Before`. In this case, you are closing the connection to your database.

When you run an Espresso test, it'll install your app on a device or emulator, then execute all the code in your tests. Under the **com.raywenderlich.android.droidquiz** with the **(androidTest)** notation, right-click your `QuizDaoTest` and select **Run 'QuizDaoTest'**. You can also click the green arrow next to the test class name, or click the arrow next to an individual test.

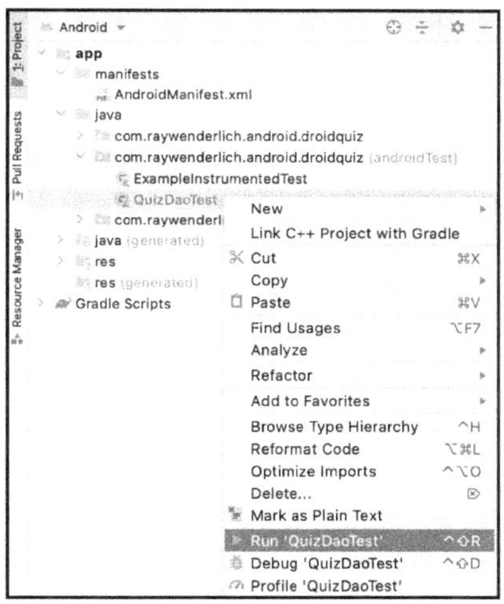

Running the Instrumenttion Test.

When asked to select a deployment target select your emulator and click **OK**.

Your project will build, install, and execute all your tests. If you followed every step properly all the tests should pass.

You have now interacted with your database without adding a single line of code to your activities. You also know that your DAOs work as expected and can confidently proceed to focus on the other layers of your architecture such as your **ViewModels** and **Views**.

If you need even more proof of the awesome work you did in this chapter, you can add some `Log.d()` statements to the tests, to print out the data being read from the in-memory database. But the tests should be proof enough!

Key points

- **Database Access Objects** are commonly referred to as **DAOs**.
- DAOs are objects that provide access to your app's data by abstracting most of the complexity behind **querying and updating** your database.
- In Room, DAOs can be defined as **interfaces** or **abstract classes**.
- `@Insert` is a marker, which allows you to automatically create an **INSERT INTO** query.
- `@Insert` can take an `OnConflictStrategy` parameter, that allows you to specify what happens in case there is a conflict when creating a new database entry.
- `@Query` allows you to perform any kind of **queries** in your database. You can also use **autocomplete**, to easily connect to **entities** and their **property definitions**.
- `@Transaction` tells Room that the following SQL statements should be executed in a **single transaction**.
- `@Delete` allows you to automatically create **DELETE FROM** queries, but it requires a parameter to be removed; e.g., a `Question` object.
- `@Update` updates a record in the database **if it already exists**, or omits the changes, if it doesn't, leaving the database **unchanged**.
- Writing tests with **Espresso** is a good way to see if your database code works properly.
- You can run Espresso tests, **without manually going through the app**, in less than a few seconds.
- Inserting the data and reading from the databse in Espresso is safe, because you can work with an **in-memory** version of the database.
- In-memory databases **clear up after tests end**, so there's no need to do extra cleanup, other than to `close()` the database, to avoid leaks.

Where to go from here?

You now know how to create DAOs to interact with your database. You can download the final project by opening the attachment on this chapter, and if you want to learn more about DAOs in Room, you can explore the following resources:

- Google's guide, "Accessing data using Room DAOs" (https://developer.android.com/training/data-storage/room/accessing-data).
- The official documentation about Room DAOs (https://developer.android.com/reference/androidx/room/Dao).

In the next chapter, you are finally going to see your UI working by integrating your Room database and DAOs with other architecture components such as **LiveData** and **ViewModels**.

Chapter 10: Using Room with Android Architecture Components

By Subhrajyoti Sen

In the previous chapters, you learned how to create the most important components of a Room Database: your **Data Access Objects (DAOs)** and your **Entities**.

While having your DAOs and entities is usually enough to interact with your database, you still need a way to display all the information to the user, all the while handling the lifecycle of the app and configuration changes. This is where Android Architecture Components such as **ViewModel** and **LiveData** come to the rescue!

In this chapter, you'll learn:

- What **LiveData** and **ViewModel** are, and how to use them.
- How to make your DAOs return LiveData instead of simple data objects.
- How to create `ViewModels` that are **lifecycle-aware** and **observe** them in your activities.
- How to create a **Repository** that acts as a bridge between your ViewModels and your DAOs.
- How to **prepopulate** your database using a provider class.

> **Note**: This chapter assumes you have basic knowledge of Kotlin and Android. If you're new to Android, check out our Android tutorials here: https://www.raywenderlich.com/category/android. If you know Android but are unfamiliar with Kotlin, take a look at, "Kotlin For Android: An Introduction," here: https://www.raywenderlich.com/174395/kotlin-for-android-an-introduction-2.

Getting started

Start by opening the **starter** project using **Android Studio 4.2**, or greater, by going to **File ▸ Open** and selecting the starter project directory.

If you have been following along until this point, you should already be familiar with the code since it is the same as the final project from the last chapter. But, if you are just getting started, here is a quick recap:

- The **data** package contains two packages: **db** and **model**. **db** contains the `QuizDatabase` class and your DAOs. **model** contains your entities: `Question` and `Answer`.
- The **view** package contains all the activities for your app: `SplashActivity`, `MainActivity`, `QuestionActivity` and `ResultActivity`.

Build and run the app on a device or emulator.

The Main Screen.

Looks like everything is working as expected. You're ready to start working on connecting Room to your app. But, first, you need to learn about **LiveData**.

Using LiveData with a Repository

To use `LiveData`, you first need to learn what it is. To put it simply, `LiveData` is an **observable piece of data**, which is **aware of the Android lifecycle**. You could, for simplicity's sake, think of an **Observable** from Reactive Extensions, but which also listens to the Android lifecycle. As such, you can listen to its updates, by adding `Observers`.

Furthermore, by knowing the lifecycle state at all times, it has smart internal mechanisms, which stop potential observers from being updated, unless the lifecycle is *active* — your app and the screen with `LiveData` objects are visible. Because of this, you can easily avoid updating the UI, when the app is not active — e.g. when it's in the background.

According to the documentation, there are six main advantages of using LiveData vs other similar libraries:

- **Ensures your UI matches your data state**: Since LiveData implements the observer pattern, you can be sure that your UI widgets such as `Buttons`, `ListViews`, `RecyclerViews` or `TextViews` will always be updated with the **latest information**.
- **No memory leaks**: Since LiveData observers are bound to the lifecycle of other components, they will be destroyed as soon as the associated component is destroyed.
- **No crashes due to stopped activities**: When an `Activity` becomes *paused* or *stopped* it won't receive any new `LiveData` notifications.
- **No more manual lifecycle handling**: Google made sure that `LiveData` is lifecycle-aware by default, so you don't have to manually control them.
- **Proper configuration changes**: Since `LiveData` is lifecycle-aware, and it caches the latest piece of data emitted, your Android components will receive the last emitted state, after configuration changes.
- **Sharing resources**: `LiveData` can be extended to wrap system services, so they can be shared in your app.

It sounds awesome, right? Well, you're going to use it to wrap the results of your DAO queries, and as such, every `Activity` and `Fragment` you use will automatically be notified of any changes. But, to do this, you need to add the LiveData dependency to your project, and change the DAO definitions, to return `LiveDatas`.

Adding LiveData to the project

Add the following dependencies to the app `build.gradle` file:

```
// architecture components
implementation "androidx.arch.core:core-common:2.1.0"
implementation "androidx.lifecycle:lifecycle-common:2.3.1"
implementation "androidx.lifecycle:lifecycle-extensions:2.2.0"
implementation "androidx.lifecycle:lifecycle-viewmodel-
ktx:2.3.1"
```

By adding the `core` and `lifecycle` dependencies, you add some of Android Jetpack's fundamental components, which are related to the Android lifecycle. This also includes the `LiveData` component, so you can use it, without changing anything.

Now, open **QuizDao.kt** inside the **data > db** package. Take a look at `getAllQuestions()` and `getQuestionAndAllAnswers()`:

```
@Query("SELECT * FROM question ORDER BY question_id")
fun getAllQuestions(): List<Question>

@Transaction
@Query("SELECT * FROM question")
fun getQuestionAndAllAnswers(): List<QuestionAndAllAnswers>
```

Right now, these methods are just returning a simple `List` but how do you make them return a `LiveData` object instead? Well, it's very easy! You just need to change your method signatures to this:

```
@Query("SELECT * FROM question ORDER BY question_id")
fun getAllQuestions(): LiveData<List<Question>>

@Transaction
@Query("SELECT * FROM question")
fun getQuestionAndAllAnswers():
LiveData<List<QuestionAndAllAnswers>>
```

As previously mentioned, `LiveData` is an observable wrapper around a piece of data. Because of this, you can hold anything within it, like a list, array or a list of nested lists, you get the point!

So, to use `LiveData`, you need to wrap the object that you want to observe for changes, which in this case are the results of `getAllQuestions()` and `getQuestionsAndAllAnswers()`. Now, every time the data in Room changes, for example by adding a new `Question` object, your `LiveData` and its observers will be notified, with the new information. But, if you keep calling to the DAO, you'll always get a new `LiveData`, and this defeats the purpose of Room being observable.

Additionally, you should never talk to the DAOs directly, because it's easier to modify the code for internal database communication if you wrap it around another layer of abstraction. For this reason. you'll create a **Repository** that acts as a bridge between your DAOs and the `ViewModels`, which you'll define later.

Creating a quiz repository

Create a new Kotlin interface under the **data** package and name it **QuizRepository**. Add the following code, also importing the missing classes:

```
interface QuizRepository {

  fun getSavedQuestions(): LiveData<List<Question>>

  suspend fun saveQuestion(question: Question)

  suspend fun saveAnswer(answer: Answer)

  fun getQuestionAndAllAnswers():
LiveData<List<QuestionAndAllAnswers>>

  suspend fun deleteQuestions()
}
```

The above interface defines the methods that you'll need in your repository. By using an interface you make it much easier to change the implementation of your code if you later decide that you need another database implementation rather than Room.

Now, create a new Kotlin class under the **data** package and name it **Repository**. Make your class implement the **QuizRepository** interface:

```
class Repository: QuizRepository {
}
```

Override all the functions in the interface to implement them. You can press **Ctrl + I** and Android Studio should display a list of all the missing members. Select all of them and press **OK**.

Next, add the following properties at the top of your class:

```
private val quizDao: QuizDao by lazy {
  QuizApplication.database.quizDao()
}
private val allQuestions by lazy {
  quizDao.getAllQuestions()
}
private val allQuestionsAndAllAnswers by lazy {
  quizDao.getQuestionAndAllAnswers()
}
```

You create two `LiveData` values, to observe and react to the data within the database, and all the changes. `allQuestions` will hold a reference to all the questions currently stored in your database.

Once again, since this is `LiveData`, your observers will be notified each time a new record is added or updated in the `questions` table. `allQuestionsAndAllAnswers` holds a `LiveData` list of `QuestionAndAllAnswers`. This property will be useful when displaying a question and its answers to your users.

Now, implement `saveQuestion()` and `saveAnswer()` as follows:

```
override suspend fun saveQuestion(question: Question) {
  quizDao.insert(question)
}

override suspend fun saveAnswer(answer: Answer) {
  quizDao.insert(answer)
}
```

The above code uses `insert()` of your `quizDao` to create new `Question` and `Answer` records in your database. You are using a suspend function because you don't want to block the main thread by executing long-running operations on it.

> **Note**: If you are new to suspend functions, check out the Kotlin Coroutines Tutorial for Android: Getting Started at https://www.raywenderlich.com/1423941-kotlin-coroutines-tutorial-for-android-getting-started.

Next, add this line to `deleteQuestions()` :

```
quizDao.clearQuestions()
```

Just like `saveAnswer()` and `saveQuestion()`, this method uses a suspend function to execute one of your DAO's methods: `clearQuestions()`. As the name implies, `deleteQuestions()` will delete all the questions in your database.

Finally, implement the remainder of the code like this:

```
override fun getSavedQuestions() = allQuestions

override fun getQuestionAndAllAnswers() =
allQuestionsAndAllAnswers
```

Once again, because you're using `LiveData`, if you ever need to access fresh information from the database, you simply have to observe the preloaded `LiveDatas` in your repository. And that is all you need to create a repository that interacts with your database using your Data Access Objects.

At this point, you might be wondering: *Why do I need to define a repository that interacts with my DAOs? Can't I simply use my DAOs inside my ViewModels?*

Well, you certainly can use your DAOs directly inside your ViewModels, but you also need to remember a very important principle in programming: **The Single Responsibility Principle**. The Single Responsibility Principle states that each class in your code should have a single responsibility or a single reason to change and that it should do it well. Just like in a company, you wouldn't want developers doing accounting stuff and you wouldn't want your accountants touching your code.

Also, by having each class focusing on a single task you'll make your code much easier to maintain and test.

All right, that's enough about LiveData. Next, you'll learn about ViewModel!

Creating ViewModels

The ViewModel is a part of the **Android Architecture Components** and it's designed to solve two common issues that developers often face when developing Android apps:

- **When an activity or fragment is destroyed, data is lost**: Most developers can restore simple data by saving it using `onSaveInstanceState()` and retrieving it from the `Bundle` in `onCreate()`. However, this is not always a good approach since `Bundles` are only suitable for small amounts of data that can be serialized and de-serialized. You shouldn't store *all the data* you're displaying and working with.

- **Separation of Concerns**: Activities and fragments usually have to execute different operations such as database transactions, HTTP requests, UI updates and more. It's better to separate `Views` from the business logic by delegating this task to a more appropriate class such as `ViewModels`.

But how does the ViewModel help solve these issues? Well, `ViewModel` is specifically designed to hold and manage data related to your user interface. Just like `LiveData`, `ViewModel` is lifecycle aware, which means that it can react to the state of your Android components. Furthermore, using factories, and dependency management, it can survive configuration changes such as screen rotations. Therefore you won't need to manually restore data using methods such as `onSaveInstanceState()`, you can simply retrieve everything you stored within the view model.

`ViewModel` sounds like the perfect choice to manage the questions and answers for your DroidQuiz app, right?

Create a new package named **viewmodel** under **drodquiz**. Create a new Kotlin class inside this package and name it **MainViewModel**.

Make `MainViewModel` extend the `ViewModel` abstract class by modifying your code like this:

```
class MainViewModel() : ViewModel() {

}
```

Now, since you are going to need your repository to interact with your database from your `ViewModel` classes, add the following parameter to the primary constructor of your class:

```
class MainViewModel(private val repository: QuizRepository) :
ViewModel() {

}
```

Finally, add the following code:

```
fun prepopulateQuestions() {
  viewModelScope.launch(Dispatchers.IO) {
    for (question in QuestionInfoProvider.questionList) {
      repository.saveQuestion(question)
    }
    for (answer in QuestionInfoProvider.answerList) {
      repository.saveAnswer(answer)
    }
  }
```

```
}

fun clearQuestions() {
  viewModelScope.launch(Dispatchers.IO) {
    repository.deleteQuestions()
  }
}
```

In the code above, `prepopulateQuestions()` creates new question and answer records in your database by using the sample data included in your `QuestionInfoProvider`, while `clearQuestions()` deletes all the questions in your database using `deleteQuestions()` on your `QuizRepository`. `viewModelScope` is a **CoroutineScope** that is tied to the lifecycle of the `ViewModel`, meaning that whenever `ViewModel` is destroyed, all work launched from `viewModelScope` will be automatically canceled. `Dispatchers.IO` specifies that the work should be performed on a background thread.

> **Note**: Here you are using a method in your `ViewModel` to prepopulate your database since it is very useful to learn how to perform delete and insert operations at any time. However, if you want to prepopulate your database with some default data, most of the time you'll probably use `addCallback()` on your database builder, which gives you a callback, for when the database is ready. Then, within the callback you can call your prepopulated code.

The `ViewModel` class for `MainActivity` is ready! Now, it's time to create one for your `QuestionActivity`. This will be slightly more complex, but don't worry, you'll be guided every step of the way.

Representing the state

`QuestionActivity` can have four different states at any given point:

- **Loading State**: Displayed when the list of questions is being loaded from your database and it's represented by a progress bar.

The Loading State.

- **Data State**: Displayed when you are ready to display a question to your user. This state is represented by a text and a group of radio buttons for the options.

The Data State.

- **Empty State**: Displayed when there are no questions in your database. This state is represented by an image and a text saying that there are no questions.

The Empty State.

- **Finish State**: A special state, sent from `ViewModel` when there are no more questions to be displayed. This state is only used by `QuestionActivity` to know when to navigate to `ResultActivity`.

To represent the above states you are going to create a sealed class that your **ViewModel** will update and `QuestionActivity` will observe using `LiveData`. In the end, you'll have an architecture like this.

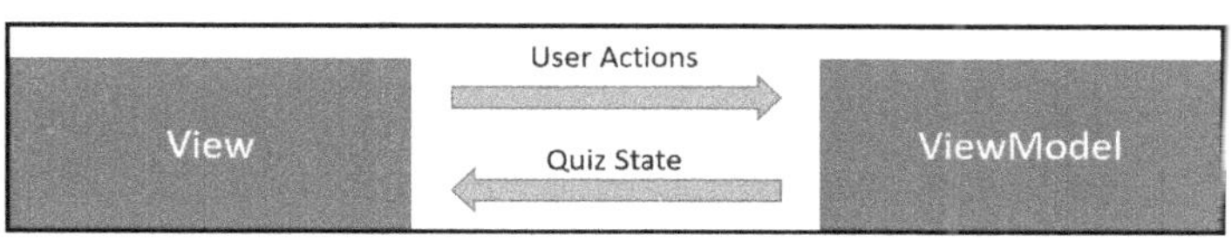

The MVVM Architecture.

Your Views will only be in charge of communicating the actions from the user to your ViewModel and rendering the data received. ViewModel will be in charge of communicating with the repository, handling the logic and sending UI-ready data to your View. Interesting huh? :]

Create a new Kotlin class under the **model** package and name it **QuizState**. Modify your class like below:

```
sealed class QuizState {
  object LoadingState : QuizState()
  data class DataState(val data: QuestionAndAllAnswers) :
QuizState()
  object EmptyState : QuizState()
  data class FinishState(val numberOfQuestions: Int, val score:
Int) : QuizState()
}
```

As you can see each of the aforementioned states is represented here. The DataState has a data attribute that contains a question and its associated answers. The FinishState class holds the number of questions in the quiz, within numberOfQuestions and the number of correct answers from the user within score. The other two states - LoadingState and EmptyState are simple objects, which represent events for the two cases.

Now, it's time to create your ViewModel.

Changing the state

Create a new class under the **viewmodel** package and name it **QuizViewModel**. Modify your class like below:

```
class QuizViewModel(repository: QuizRepository) : ViewModel() {
}
```

Just like before, you are making the QuizViewModel class extend from ViewModel() and have the repository property in the primary constructor.

Next, add the following properties to the top of your class:

```
private val questionAndAnswers =
MediatorLiveData<QuestionAndAllAnswers>() // 1
private val currentQuestion = MutableLiveData<Int>() // 2
private val currentState = MediatorLiveData<QuizState>() // 3
private val allQuestionAndAllAnswers =
repository.getQuestionAndAllAnswers() // 4
private var score: Int = 0 // 5
```

Step by step:

1. Represents the current `QuestionAndAnswers` that is going to be sent to `QuestionActivity` and displayed to the user.
2. `currentQuestion` is a helper property that helps you keep track of which question has to be displayed from the list of questions retrieved from the repository. For example, if `currentQuestion` is equal to 0 you are going to display the question with `question_id = 0`.
3. `currentState` contains the current `QuizState` that is going to be updated by your `ViewModel` and observed by `QuestionActivity`.
4. `allQuestionAndAllAnswers` contains a `LiveData` list of all the questions in your database.
5. `score` is another helper that holds the score of your user which is updated each time your user answers a question correctly.

Next, add the following methods:

```
fun getCurrentState(): LiveData<QuizState> = currentState

private fun changeCurrentQuestion() {
  currentQuestion.postValue(currentQuestion.value?.inc())
}
```

`getCurrentState()` will be used by your `MainActivity` to retrieve and observe the current `QuizState`. `changeCurrentQuestion()` simply adds one to the value of `currentQuestion`.

Next, add the following method:

```
private fun addStateSources() {
  currentState.addSource(currentQuestion)
{ currentQuestionNumber -> // 1
    if (currentQuestionNumber ==
allQuestionAndAllAnswers.value?.size) {

currentState.postValue(QuizState.FinishState(currentQuestionNumb
er, score))
    }
  }
  currentState.addSource(allQuestionAndAllAnswers)
{ allQuestionsAndAnswers ->
    // 2
    if (allQuestionsAndAnswers.isEmpty()) {
      currentState.postValue(QuizState.EmptyState)
```

```
    }
  }
  currentState.addSource(questionAndAnswers)
{ questionAndAnswers -> // 3

currentState.postValue(QuizState.DataState(questionAndAnswers))
  }
}
```

You'll call `addStateSources()` to add the sources which your `currentState` needs to observe: `currentQuestion`, `allQuestionAndAllAnswers` and `questionAndAnswers`. Taking each commented section in turn:

1. If `currentQuestion` is equal to the number of questions in your database it means that your user has finished answering the questions in your quiz, so you'll change the value of `QuizState` to `FinishState`.
2. If the list of questions retrieved from the database is empty you'll change the value of `QuizState` to `EmptyState`.
3. This is the `questionAndAnswers` that you'll send to the `QuestionActivity` in `DataState`.

Now, add the following method:

```
 private fun addQuestionSources() {
  questionAndAnswers.addSource(currentQuestion)
{ currentQuestionNumber ->
    val questions = allQuestionAndAllAnswers.value

    if (questions != null && currentQuestionNumber <
questions.size) {

questionAndAnswers.postValue(questions[currentQuestionNumber])
    }
  }

  questionAndAnswers.addSource(allQuestionAndAllAnswers)
{ questionsAndAnswers ->
    val currentQuestionNumber = currentQuestion.value

    if (currentQuestionNumber != null &&
questionsAndAnswers.isNotEmpty()) {

questionAndAnswers.postValue(questionsAndAnswers[currentQuestion
Number])
    }
  }
}
```

This method adds two different sources to your `questionAndAnswers`: `currentQuestion` and `allQuestionAndAllAnswers`. Observing `currentQuestion` will help you update the current `allQuestionAndAllAnswers` that will be sent to the `QuestionActivity` using a `Data`. Observing `allQuestionAndAllAnswers` will tell your `questionAndAnswers` when the list of questions has been properly retrieved from your database.

Next, add the following methods:

```
fun nextQuestion(choice: Int) { // 1
  verifyAnswer(choice)
  changeCurrentQuestion()
}

private fun verifyAnswer(choice: Int) { // 2
  val currentQuestion = questionAndAnswers.value

  if (currentQuestion != null &&
currentQuestion.answers[choice].isCorrect) {
    score++
  }
}
```

Step by step:

1. This method will be called when the user presses **NEXT** and will call `verifyAnswer()` and `changeCurrentQuestion()`.

2. `verifyAnswer()` checks if the answer selected by the user is correct and will increase the `score` value accordingly.

Finally, add the following `init` block, under your class properties, to set up your `ViewModel`:

```
init {
  currentState.postValue(QuizState.LoadingState)
  addStateSources()
  addQuestionSources()
  currentQuestion.postValue(0)
}
```

Here, you are initializing the `QuizState` as `LoadingLoadingState` and `currentQuestion` with a value of zero (`0`). You are also calling `addStateSources()` and `addQuestionSources()` as soon as your **ViewModel** is created.

And that's it! Your `ViewModels` are ready. Now, you need to create your `Views`.

Defining your Views

As mentioned at the beginning of this chapter, the `ViewModel` is scoped to the lifecycle of an `Activity` or `Fragment` which means that it will live as long as its scope is still alive.

Getting access to a ViewModel

To create a `ViewModel` you usually call the `ViewModelProviders.of(Scope).get(Type)` which contains several utility methods that help you attach a `ViewModel` to a certain lifecycle and keep track of its state. This is how the code would look:

```
viewModel =
ViewModelProvider(this).get(MainViewModel::class.java)
```

The only problem with the above approach is that the `ViewModelProvider` is responsible for creating our `ViewModels` and, as such, it can't call their custom constructors. By default, `ViewModelProvider` will always call the empty constructor using `get()`. This is a problem because you need to pass the repository as a parameter.

There are several approaches to solve the above problem but the usual way of doing it is to create a factory for the `ViewModel` and to pass it to `ViewModelProvider`. To keep things short and to the point, a couple of extension functions for the `Activity` and `Fragment` classes have already been prepared for you that automatically take care of doing all of this for you. If you want to take a look at the source code just open **Utils.kt** under the root package.

Open **MainActivity.kt** and add the following property at the top of your class:

```
private val viewModel by lazy { getViewModel
{ MainViewModel(Repository()) } }
```

The above code uses lazy initialization to create your `MainViewModel` using `getViewModel()` which automatically takes care of the initialization and creation logic of the `ViewModels` using a `ViewModelFactory`.

Next, you need to set up menu actions for the user.

Interacting with the ViewModel

Add the following methods to `MainActivity`:

```
private fun prepopulateQuestions() =
viewModel.prepopulateQuestions() // 1

private fun clearQuestions() = viewModel.clearQuestions() // 2

override fun onOptionsItemSelected(item: MenuItem): Boolean { //
3
  when (item.itemId) {
    R.id.prepopulate -> prepopulateQuestions()
    R.id.clear -> clearQuestions()
    else -> Toast.makeText(this, "error",
Toast.LENGTH_SHORT).show()
  }
  return super.onOptionsItemSelected(item)
}
```

Step by step:

1. `prepopulateQuestions()` uses your `viewMode` instance to prepopulate your Room database with sample question and answer records.

2. `clearQuestions()` uses your `viewModel` instance to clear all the rows in your database.

3. Here, you are adding the appropriate actions to your `Activity`'s action bar. If the user taps on the **prepopulate** button, you're going to call `prepopulateQuestions()`. If the user taps the **clear** button, you'll call `clearQuestions()`.

And that is all you need to do in your `MainActivity`! Now, you need to set up the `ViewModel` for `QuestionActivity`.

Open **QuestionActivity.kt** and add the following property for your `QuizViewModel`:

```
private val viewModel by lazy { getViewModel
{ QuizViewModel(Repository()) } }
```

Just like `MainActivity`, you are using lazy initialization and `getViewModel()` to create an instance of your `QuizViewModel` when `QuestionActivity` is created for the first time.

Now that your `ViewModel` is set up, you only need to create some methods that handle the different states provided by your `QuizState` and render them to the screen. Since all the logic is handled in your `ViewModel`, this should be pretty easy.

Add the following code:

```
private fun render(state: QuizState) {
  when (state) {
    is QuizState.EmptyState -> renderEmptyState()
    is QuizState.DataState -> renderDataState(state)
    is QuizState.FinishState ->
goToResultActivity(state.numberOfQuestions, state.score)
    is QuizState.LoadingState -> renderLoadingState()
  }
}
```

`render()` will be in charge of calling the appropriate methods depending on `QuizState` using a `when` expression.

Now, add the following code to handle your states:

```
private fun renderDataState(quizState: QuizState.DataState)
{ //. 1
  binding.progressBar.visibility = View.GONE
  displayQuestionsView()
  binding.questionsRadioGroup.clearCheck()
  binding.questionTextView.text = quizState.data.question?.text
  binding.questionsRadioGroup.forEachIndexed { index, view ->
    if (index < quizState.data.answers.size)
      (view as RadioButton).text =
quizState.data.answers[index].text
  }
}

private fun renderLoadingState() { // 2
  binding.progressBar.visibility = View.VISIBLE
}

private fun renderEmptyState() { // 3
  binding.progressBar.visibility = View.GONE
  binding.emptyDroid.visibility = View.VISIBLE
  binding.emptyTextView.visibility = View.VISIBLE
}
```

These are all the methods that `render()` will use to display different kinds of screens to the user. Taking each commented section in turn:

1. `renderDataState()` displays a question to your user using`data` of your `QuizState.Data`.
2. `renderLoadingState()` displays a progress bar.
3. `renderEmptyState()` displays an image and text saying that there are no questions in the database.

Now, add the following methods:

```
fun nextQuestion() { // 1
  val radioButton =
findViewById<RadioButton>(binding.questionsRadioGroup.checkedRad
ioButtonId)
  val selectedOption =
binding.questionsRadioGroup.indexOfChild(radioButton)
  if (selectedOption != -1) {
    viewModel.nextQuestion(selectedOption)
  } else {
    Toast.makeText(this,
getString(R.string.please_select_an_option),
Toast.LENGTH_SHORT).show()
  }
}

private fun displayQuestionsView() { // 2
  binding.questionsRadioGroup.visibility = View.VISIBLE
  binding.questionTextView.visibility = View.VISIBLE
  binding.button.visibility = View.VISIBLE
}

private fun goToResultActivity(numberOfQuestions: Int, score:
Int) { // 3
  val intent = Intent(this, ResultActivity::class.java).apply {
    addFlags(Intent.FLAG_ACTIVITY_NEW_TASK)
    addFlags(Intent.FLAG_ACTIVITY_CLEAR_TASK)
    putExtra(SCORE, score)
    putExtra(NUMBER_OF_QUESTIONS, numberOfQuestions)
  }

  startActivity(intent)
}
```

Briefly:

1. `nextQuestion()` calls your `ViewModel`'s `nextQuestion()` passing the index of the selected radio button as a parameter. It will be called every time the user taps **NEXT**. The `OnClickListener` is bound within the XML to `nextQuestion()`.

2. `displayQuestionsView()` makes your `questionsRadioGroup`, `questionTextView` and `button` widgets visible, so you can display a question to your user.

3. `goToResultActivity()` creates an `Intent`object to start `ResultActivity` and passes the `score` and `numberOfQuestions` values as extras.

To define `SCORE` and `NUMBER_OF_QUESTIONS`, add the following code to the bottom of your class:

```
companion object {
  const val SCORE = "SCORE"
  const val NUMBER_OF_QUESTIONS = "NUMBER_OF_QUESTIONS"
}
```

The code above defines two string constants that will act as keys in `Bundle` being passed to `ResultActivity`.

Next, add the following code:

```
private fun getQuestionsAndAnswers() {
  viewModel.getCurrentState().observe(this) {
    render(it)
  }
}
```

This method simply calls `getCurrentState()` to get the `QuizState` value of your `ViewModel`. Since `QuizState` is a `LiveData` value you can observe it using `observe()` and each time its value changes you'll call `render()` passing a new `QuizState` as a parameter.

Finally, add the following line inside onCreate():

```
binding.button.setOnClickListener { nextQuestion() }
getQuestionsAndAnswers()
```

In the code above, you set a click listener on the **NEXT** button which invokes nextQuestion() when clicked. Since you immediately want to start observing the QuizState value, onCreate() is the best place to call getQuestionsAndAnswers().

The last step to finish building your app is to display the quiz results to your user.

Open **ResultActivity.kt** under the **view** package. Add the following code inside onCreate(), importing scoreTextView from **activity_result.xml**:

```
val score = intent.extras?.getInt(QuestionActivity.SCORE)
val numberOfQuestions =
intent.extras?.getInt(QuestionActivity.NUMBER_OF_QUESTIONS)
binding.scoreTextView.text =
String.format(getString(R.string.score_message), score,
numberOfQuestions)
```

That's it! Build and run your app to see it in action.

The Start Screen shows properly.

Click **START** to see the empty screen layout.

The Empty Screen.

Now, go back to the main screen and click **prepopulate** in your action bar:

The Prepopulate Menu Option.

Click **START** and you'll see your question and answers displayed.

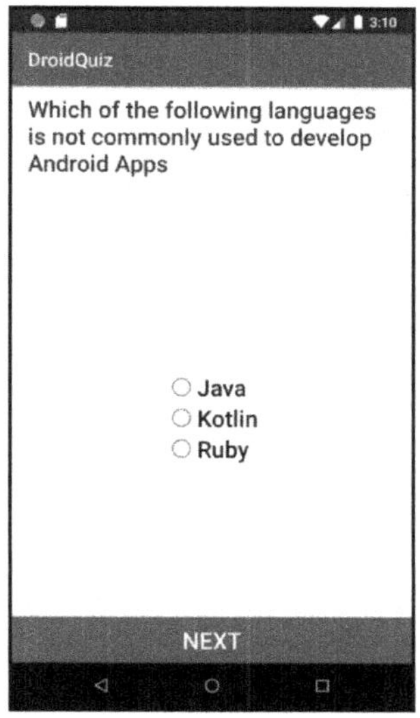

The Question & Answers Screen.

Answer the questions and take a look at the final screen to see your score!

The Results Screen.

Sweet! Your app is now working and displaying your Question and Answers!

Key points

- `LiveData` is a data holder class, as a `List`, that can be observed for changes by an `Observer`.
- `LiveData` is lifecycle-aware, meaning it can observe the lifecycle of Android components like the `Activity` or `Fragment`. It will only keep updating observers if its component is still active.
- `ViewModel` is part of the **Android Architecture Components** and it's specifically designed to manage data related to your user interface.
- A **Repository** helps you separate concerns to have a single entry point for your app's data.
- You can combine `LiveDatas` and add different `sources`, to take action if something changes.

Where to go from here?

I hope you enjoyed this chapter! If you had trouble following along, you can always download the final project attached to this chapter.

So far, you have only learned about three of the Android Architecture Components classes: **LiveData**, **ViewModel** and **Room**. However, there are many other classes that Google provides. If you want to learn about them, you can use the following resources:

- This tutorial about MVVM and Databinding with Android Design Patterns: https://www.raywenderlich.com/636803-mvvm-and-databinding-android-design-patterns.
- This tutorial about the Paging Library which helps create Lists on Android: https://www.raywenderlich.com/6948-paging-library-for-android-with-kotlin-creating-infinite-lists.
- This tutorial about the WorkManager architecture component in which you'll learn how to create and manage background tasks: https://www.raywenderlich.com/6040-workmanager-tutorial-for-android-getting-started.

See you in the next chapter!

Chapter 11: Data Migration

By Subhrajyoti Sen

In the last chapter, you finally learned how to integrate your Room components with other architecture components like LiveData and ViewModel to make your app display a nice set of questions to your users.

But what happens if you want to modify your database schema to organize questions by category or difficulty?

Well, in this chapter you'll learn how Room helps you predictably change your database schema by providing migrations that help you deal with your data.

Along the way you'll learn:

- How to create a **migration**.
- How to add a migration to your database.
- How to perform SQLite queries.
- How to fall back to a destructive migration.

Ready? It's time to get started.

Getting started

To begin, open the **starter** project in Android Studio 4.2 or greater by going to **File ▸ Open** and selecting the project from this chapter's attachments.

If you've been following along up to this point, you should already be familiar with the code. If you're just getting started, here's a quick recap:

- The **data** package contains two packages: **db** and **model**. **db** contains `QuestionDatabase`, which implements your Room database. The **model** package contains your entities, `Question` and `Answer`. It also includes `Repository`, which helps your `ViewModels` interact with your DAOs.
- The **view** package contains all your activities: `SplashActivity`, `MainActivity`, `QuestionActivity` and `ResultActivity`.
- The **viewmodel** package contains `ViewModels` of your classes: `MainViewModel` and `QuestionViewModel`.

Build and run the app on a device or emulator.

The Main Screen.

Important: Prepopulate the database and then tap **START** to start a quiz.

Cool! Now, it's time to start working with migrations.

Migrations

Before creating your first migrations with Room, you need to learn what migrations are, right?

Simply put, a **database or schema migration** is the process of moving your data from one database schema to another. There are many reasons why you might want to move your data to another database schema. For example, you might need to add a new table because you want to implement a new feature. Some data isn't available and some columns of your database can be removed. Or, the API you're invoking provides different information and you want to add some new columns to an existing table. Or, another table can be removed because part of an A/B test and you need to save space.

The process of migrating your data from one schema to another could be as simple as copying data from one table to another or as complex as reorganizing your entire database. Either way, properly planning your migrations comes with benefits:

- **Reversible**: Sometimes, you might want to roll back your changes and return to an old schema. Without migrations, this process might be a complete nightmare. You'd have to manually apply all the changes, and you might not even remember how your old database looked.
- **No data loss**: With migrations, it's much easier to move your data from one schema to another in a predictable manner without losing data.

Understanding Room migrations

SQLite handles database migrations by specifying a version number for each database schema you create. In other words, each time you modify your database schema by creating, deleting or updating a table, you have to increase the database version number and modify `SQLiteOpenHelper.onUpgrade()`. `onUpGrade()` will tell SQLite what to do when one database version changes to another.

For example, say one of your users still has database version 1 but a new update of your app now uses database version 2. SQLite would realize that the current database version is obsolete and needs an upgrade. Then, SQLite would look for `SQLiteOpenHelper.onUpgrade(db, 1, 2)` and trigger its body to migrate to the new schema. If `SQLiteOpenHelper.onUpgrade(db, 1, 2)` doesn't exist, it will trigger an error.

Room migrations work in a very similar way. The difference is that Room provides an abstraction layer on top of the traditional SQLite methods with a `Migration` class.

`Migration(startVersion, endVersion)` is the base class of a database migration; it can move between *any* two versions defined by the `startVersion` and `endVersion` parameters. The reason for emphasizing *any* is because you don't necessarily need to specify a sequential migration. For example, say Room opens database version 2 and the latest version is 5. Normally, Room would execute migrations in this order:

`Migration(2, 3)`

`Migration(3, 4)`

`Migration(4, 5)`

The beauty of Room is that you can also specify a migration that goes directly from version 2 to version 5 like this: `Migration(2, 5)`, which makes the migration process much faster. Of course, there won't always be a direct path from migration X to migration Y, so executing all your migrations one by one might be necessary, but it's usually a good practice to specify a direct migration if possible.

If you don't specify an appropriate migration for the current database version, Room will throw a runtime error and the app will crash.

> **Note**: You can also call `fallbackToDestructiveMigration()` when building your database. This will tell Room to destructively recreate tables if you haven't specified a migration. The advantage is that you won't need to create any migrations and your app won't crash. The disadvantage is that you'll delete your data every time you specify a new database version.

Now that you know the theory, you can move on to creating your first Room migrations!

Exporting schemas

It's considered good practice to start exporting the schema before you start writing your first migration. The **export** is a **JSON representation** of the database schema. This representation comes in very handy when you want to understand the changes taking place over various database versions.

Open **QuizDatabase.kt** and set the `exportSchema` attribute of `@Database` to true as follows:

```
@Database(entities = [(Question::class), (Answer::class)],
  version = 1,
  exportSchema = true
)
```

Next, you have to specify the directory to store the schemas in. Add the following code inside `defaultConfig` of the app-module **build.gradle**:

```
kapt {
  arguments {
    arg("room.schemaLocation", "$projectDir/schemas".toString())
  }
}
```

The code above passes an argument to the Kotlin annotation processer that sets the location of the schema to the **schemas** directory inside the project directory, which in this case is **app**.

Build the app. Once the build is complete, you'll find the schema export at **app/schemas/com.raywenderlich.android.droidquiz.data.db.QuizDatabase/1.json** where 1 represents the database version. Whenever you'll change the database version and build the project, the new schema will be exported.

Creating Room migrations

Right now, you have a very nice app that displays a series of random questions to your users. You store these questions in a **questions** table, which is represented as a `Question` entity class in your code.

But what happens if you want to add difficulty levels like easy, medium and hard?

Well, right now your question table doesn't have an attribute to classify questions based on their difficulty. So your first step is to add a new column to provide that functionality to your users. Here's how you do that:

Open **Question.kt** under the **data ▸ model** package. You want to represent the difficulty in terms of numbers such as 1, 2 or 3, where 1 is the lowest difficulty and 3 is the highest. To represent this concept, modify your question class to add a `difficulty` property like so:

```
@Entity(tableName = "questions", indices =
[Index("question_id")])
data class Question(
  @PrimaryKey(autoGenerate = true)
  @ColumnInfo(name = "question_id")
  var questionId: Int,
  val text: String,
  val difficulty: Int = 0   // Only this line changes
)
```

This property will represent the difficulty of the question and will have a default value of 0.

Now, build and run the app and press **START** to see if it works. And the app crashed!

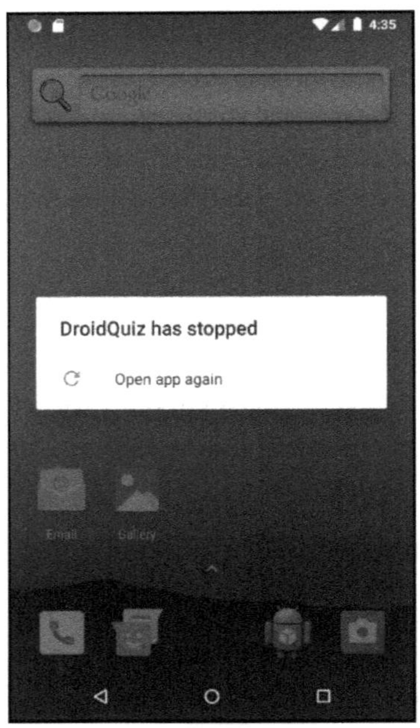

A Dialog informing that the app crashed.

Open the logcat console and take a look at the error displayed.

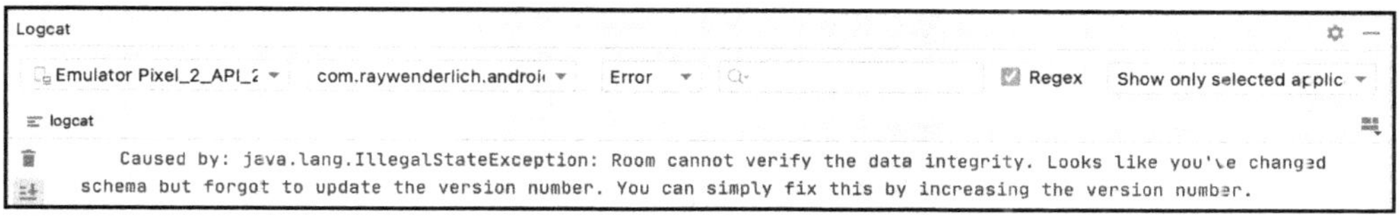

The App Crash error.

> **Note**: If the app didn't crash, you might have forgotten to press **START** earlier, when you ran the app before modifying. If the app crashed but you got a different error message, try uninstalling the app from your device or emulator and repeating the steps above.

Did you expect that crash?

Upgrading the database version

Each time you change the database schema, you need to change the database version. This will help Room know which migrations to run when building the database.

The error seems simple enough to fix, right? According to the Logcat console, you just need to increase the version number, so try that now.

Open **QuizDatabase.kt** under the **data ▸ db** package and increase the database version by changing the `version` parameter value to 2 in the `@Database` notation:

```
@Database(
  entities = [(Question::class), (Answer::class)],
  version = 2, // version change
  exportSchema = true
)
```

Build and run the app again and press **START**. And the app crashes again!

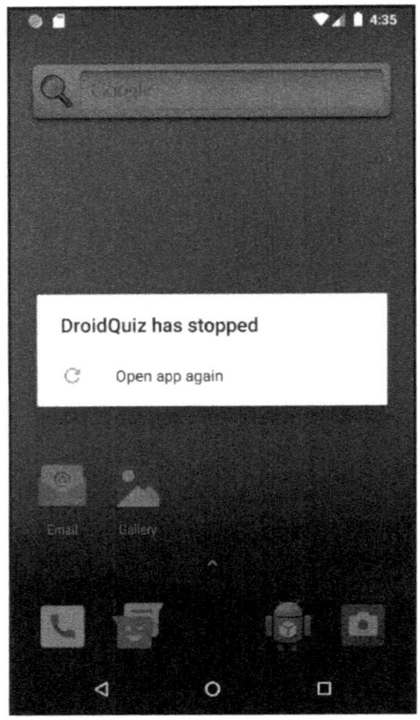

App has crashed again.

Open the Logcat console to see the problem.

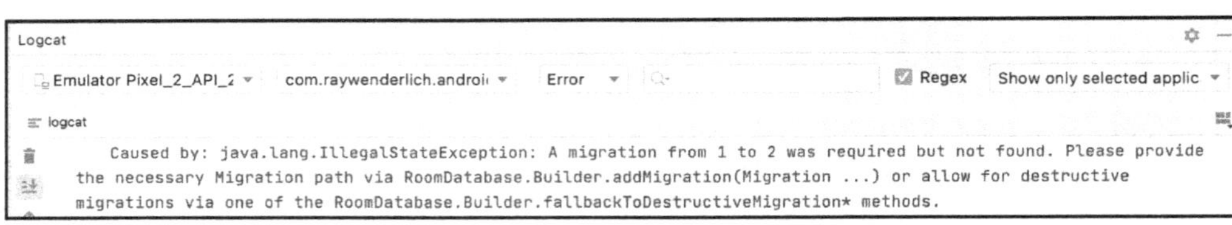

The App Crash error.

It looks like you're making some progress since the error is different now. The error indicates that Room doesn't know how to change the database schema from 1 to 2, so it's giving you two options:

- Create a migration that goes from database schema 1 to 2.
- Call `fallbackToDestructiveMigration()` when building your database.

The second option is the easiest one to implement since you only need to add a single line of code. The only problem with this approach is that you'll lose all your data when changing the schema from version 1 to 2. This is fine for your app since you have a handy button to populate your database in the main menu, but it might not be a good idea for other projects where you want to preserve user data.

With the above in mind, you're going to follow the first approach and create a new migration.

Implementing a migration

Create a new package under the **db** package and name it **migrations**.

Inside **migrations**, create a new class and name it **Migration1To2**. Make your class extend `Migration` like this:

```
class Migration1To2 : Migration(1, 2) {
}
```

The first parameter in the constructor represents the start version of the database. The second one represents the end version after you've applied this migration.

Next, press **Control + I** (*implement methods*) so Android Studio displays all missing members. Select all of them and press **OK**. Your class should now have `migrate()` :

```
class Migration1To2 : Migration(1, 2) {
  override fun migrate(database: SupportSQLiteDatabase) {
    TODO("not implemented") // To change body of created
functions use File | Settings | File Templates.
  }
}
```

Inside `migrate()`, you should execute all the queries you need to properly change the database schema to the version indicated in the constructor.

Now, since the change is a very simple one, you'll only need to execute a single **ALTER** query to change your **questions** table.

Modify `migrate()` as follows:

```
override fun migrate(database: SupportSQLiteDatabase) {
  database.execSQL("ALTER TABLE questions ADD COLUMN difficulty
INTEGER NOT NULL DEFAULT 0")
}
```

`database.execSQL()` executes the query passed as a parameter. Here, you're executing an **ALTER TABLE** query in your **questions** table that adds a new **difficulty** column that only accepts integers. It has a default value of 0.

Now that you've defined your migration, you need to tell Room to execute it before building your database.

Open **QuizDatabase.kt** and add the following companion object to the bottom of your class:

```
companion object {
  val MIGRATION_1_TO_2 = Migration1To2()
}
```

You'll use this companion object to store a reference to all the migrations that you'll define later.

Now, open **QuizApplication.kt** and modify your database builder inside `onCreate()` as follows:

```
database = Room.databaseBuilder(this, QuizDatabase::class.java,
"question_database")
    .addMigrations(QuizDatabase.MIGRATION_1_TO_2) // Only this
line changes
    .build()
```

`addMigrations()` accepts one or more migration objects. Room will use these migrations to bring the database to the latest version.

Build and run your app and press **START** to verify that your migration works properly:

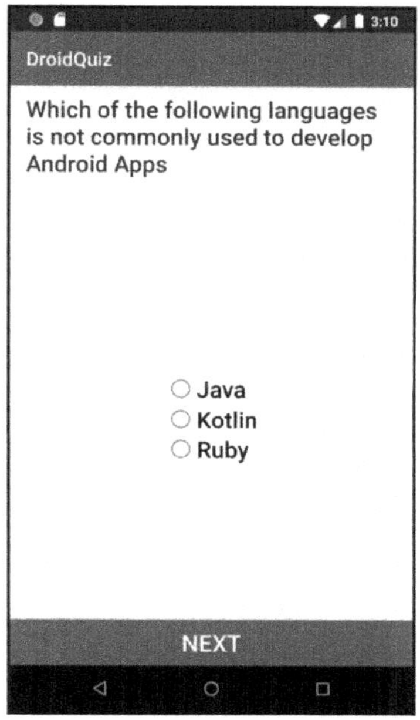

Migration works correctly.

Sweet! It looks like your app works now.

Until now, the changes that you've made to your database schema have been really simple, since you only needed to add a new column to your table.

Changing column type in the schema

What happens if you need to modify a previously created column?

Well, it turns out that the **ALTER TABLE** statement is very limited; the only operations that you can perform with it are **RENAME TABLE**, **RENAME COLUMN** and **ADD COLUMN**.

If you want to perform complex schema changes such as changing the type affinity of a column, you'll need to use more than one query. But don't worry, the following steps summarize the process:

1. Create a new temporary table with the new schema.
2. Copy the data from the original table to the temporary table.
3. Drop the original table.
4. Rename the temporary table with the same name as the original table.

To illustrate this process, imagine you want to modify the type affinity of the difficulty column to TEXT instead of INTEGER so that you can store the operating system that the question refers to.

To do this, open **Question.kt** and modify the category property:

```
@Entity(tableName = "questions", indices =
[Index("question_id")])
data class Question(
  @PrimaryKey(autoGenerate = true)
  @ColumnInfo(name = "question_id")
  var questionId: Int,
  val text: String,
  val difficulty: String = "0", // Only this line changes
)
```

The code above changes the data type of `difficulty` from `Int` to `String`.

Now, create a new class under the **migrations** package and name it **Migration2To3**. Add the following code to the file:

```
class Migration2To3 : Migration(2, 3) {
  override fun migrate(database: SupportSQLiteDatabase) {
    database.execSQL(
      "CREATE TABLE question_new (question_id INTEGER NOT NULL,
" +
            "text TEXT NOT NULL, " +
            "difficulty TEXT NOT NULL, " +
            "PRIMARY KEY (question_id))"
    ) //1

    database.execSQL("CREATE INDEX
index_question_new_question_id ON question_new(question_id)") //
2

    database.execSQL(
      "INSERT INTO question_new (question_id, text, difficulty)
" +
```

```
        "SELECT question_id, text, difficulty FROM questions'
    )//3

    database.execSQL("DROP TABLE questions") //4

    database.execSQL("ALTER TABLE question_new RENAME TO
questions") //5

  }
}
```

Briefly:

1. Creates a new temporary table with the new schema called **question_new**.
2. Adds an index to the **question_id** column of your **question_new** table.
3. Retrieves all the data from your original **questions** table using a **SELECT** statement and adds it to your **question_new** table using an **INSERT INTO** statement.
4. Drops the original question table using a **DROP TABLE** statement.
5. Renames your **question_new** table to **questions** using an **ALTER TABLE** with a **RENAME TO** statement.

Open **QuizDatabase.kt** and modify `QuizDatabase` like this:

```
@Database(
  entities = [(Question::class), (Answer::class)],
  version = 3, // Changes the db version
    exportSchema = true
)
abstract class QuizDatabase : RoomDatabase() {
  abstract fun quizDao(): QuizDao

   companion object{
    val MIGRATION_1_TO_2 = Migration1To2()
    val MIGRATION_2_TO_3 = Migration2To3() // Adds a reference
to your new migration
  }
}
```

Just like before, you've changed the database version to 3 and created a reference to your new migration inside the companion object.

Finally, add your new migration to your database by opening the **QuizApplication.kt** file and changing your database builder inside `onCreate()`:

```
database = Room.databaseBuilder(this, QuizDatabase::class.java,
DB_NAME)
  .addMigrations(QuizDatabase.MIGRATION_1_TO_2,
QuizDatabase.MIGRATION_2_TO_3)
  .build()
```

Build and run, then press **START**.

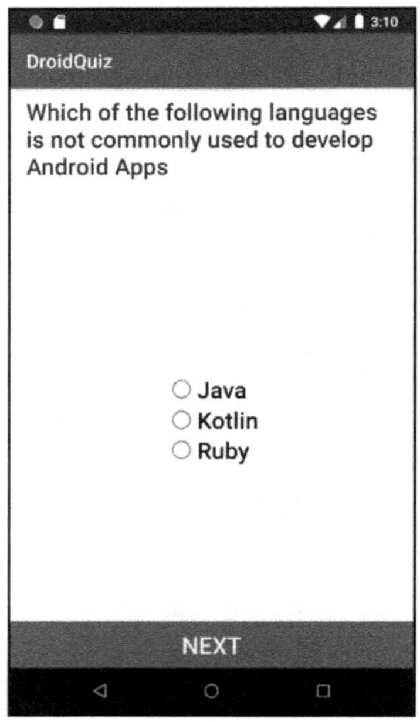

Second migration works correctly.

Creating a direct migration

You might have noticed that you now have two different migrations for three different versions of your database. If one of your users had the first version of your database installed and wanted to update the app to the latest version, Room would execute each migration one by one. Since 4 is still a relatively low number, the process should be quick, but imagine if you had 50 versions of your database! It would be much better to have a shortcut right?

Well, Room allows you to define a migration path that starts from and goes to any version of your database. To illustrate this concept, define a migration that goes from database version 1 to 3.

Create a new class under the **migrations** package and name it **Migration1To3**. Replace everything inside the class with the following:

```
class Migration1To3 : Migration(1, 3) {
  override fun migrate(database: SupportSQLiteDatabase) {
    database.execSQL("ALTER TABLE questions ADD COLUMN
difficulty TEXT NOT NULL DEFAULT '0'")
  }
}
```

The above simply executes two **ALTER TABLE** statements to add difficulty and category columns. Since these columns didn't exist in the version 1 database, we don't have to worry about the more complex SQL for the migration in the prior step.

Open **QuizDatabase.kt** and add the following line to the **companion object** to create a reference to your new migration:

```
val MIGRATION_1_TO_3 = Migration1To3()
```

Now, go to **QuizApplication.kt** and add your new migration to the database builder:

```
database = Room.databaseBuilder(this, QuizDatabase::class.java,
DB_NAME)
  .addMigrations(
    QuizDatabase.MIGRATION_1_TO_2,
    QuizDatabase.MIGRATION_2_TO_3,
    QuizDatabase.MIGRATION_1_TO_3
  )
  .build()
```

Cool! You now have a migration that goes directly from database version 1 to 3. If you build the app, the migration won't execute since your app is already on database version 3, but you can now be sure that all your users on database version 1 will properly migrate to the new version when they update the app.

Automated migrations

The migrations that you wrote in the previous section can seem like a lot of code to achieve simple changes. Luckily, from version 2.4.0-alpha01 onwards, Room supports automatic migrations.

Automatic migrations work great only for simple schema changes like:

- Deleting a column (`@DeleteColumn`)
- Deleting a table (`@DeleteTable`)
- Renaming a column (`@RenameColumn`)
- Renaming a table (`@RenameTable`)

In the points above, you can see their related annotations. In this section, you'll use `@RenameColumn` but the procedure to use the other annotations is quite similar.

Consider that you want to rename the `difficulty` attribute to something like `challengeLevel`.

Create a new file inside **migrations** and name it **Migration3To4**. Adding the following code to it:

```
@RenameColumn(
  tableName = "questions",
  fromColumnName = "difficulty",
  toColumnName = "challengeLevel"
)
class Migration3To4 : AutoMigrationSpec
```

The code above does a couple of things:

1. Automated migrations extend `AutoMigrationSpec` instead of `Migration`.
2. `@RenameColumn` specifies the original name of the column as well as the table name, and also the new column name.

Next, open **QuizDatabase.kt** and add the following paramter to `@Database`:

```
autoMigrations = [
  AutoMigration(
    from = 3,
    to = 4,
    spec = Migration3To4::class
  )
]
```

In the code above, `autoMigrations` takes an array of automated migrations and starts applying them one by one.

Also, change the database version to **4**.

Your `@Database` should now look like the following:

```
@Database(entities = [(Question::class), (Answer::class)],
  version = 4,
  exportSchema = true,
  autoMigrations = [
    AutoMigration(
      from = 3,
      to = 4,
      spec = Migration3To4::class
    )
  ]
)
```

Build and run the app. Click **START**. You will notice that the app runs fine, verifying that the migration was successful.

Room internally uses the exported schemas to figure out the changes needed to make the migration work.

You have successfully added your first automated migration.

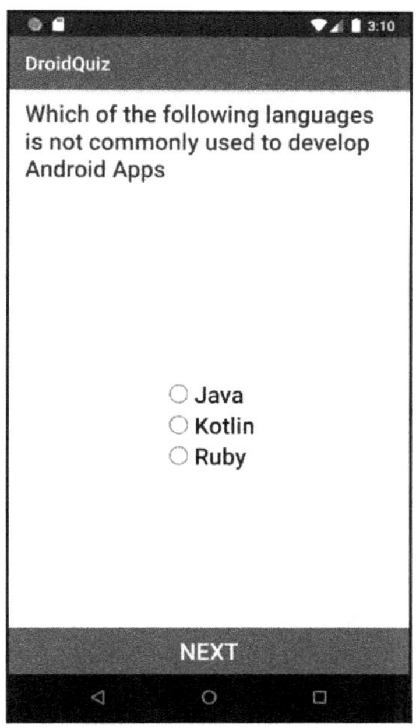

Migration worked correctly

Key points

- Simply put, a **database or schema migration** is the process of moving your data from one database schema to another.
- SQLite handles database migrations by specifying a version number for each database schema that you create.
- Room provides an abstraction layer on top of the traditional SQLite migration methods with `Migration`.
- `Migration(startVersion, endVersion)` is the base class for a database migration. It can move between *any* two migrations defined by the `startVersion` and `endVersion` parameters.
- `fallbackToDestructiveMigration()` tells Room to destructively recreate tables if you haven't specified a migration.

Where to go from here?

By now, you should have a very good idea of how Room migrations work. Of course, the process will differ from project to project, since the queries you'll need to execute will depend on your database schema, but the basic idea is always the same:

- Change the database version.
- Create a migration.
- Add the migration to your database builder.

If you want to learn more about Room migrations the official documentation at https://developer.android.com/training/data-storage/room/migrating-db-versions is always a good resource.

See you in the next *Room*, er, chapter!

Section 3: Using Firebase

Firebase is a mature suite of products that allow you to implement Android apps that persist information safely, securely and reliably. In this section, you'll learn the fundamentals and more advanced concepts of **Firebase**, including how to read and write to **Realtime Database**, how to use it in offline mode and everything you need to know about its usage and performance. You'll learn a few things about managing and securing data in **Cloud Firestore**. Finally, the last part of the section contains basics about **Cloud Storage**.

Chapter 12: Firebase Overview

By Fuad Kamal

Creating a successful mobile app isn't easy. Not only do developers need to focus on writing code and fixing bugs, they often need to manage a variety of tools and build complex infrastructures too. Factor in tight schedules and resource constraints, and you've got your work cut out!

Thankfully, though, Google understood the need for a simpler way to create high-quality apps, and in 2014 they acquired **Firebase**. More recently, Google announced that in October 2019, they will start to sunset their existing **Google Analytics** for mobile apps and is directing its users to use Firebase instead. With Firebase, developers got all of the existing functionality of Google Analytics, plus a lot more.

> **Note**: The Google Analytics referred to hereafter in this book is a new sub-feature of Firebase and not the legacy platform.

Firebase history

Initially, Firebase was a mobile backend service that let you build mobile apps without having to worry about managing your own backend. However, not too long after its release, developers wanted more, so Firebase expanded its initial feature set to include more features. With these new features, you can develop apps faster, increase your user base, make more money and ensure the delivery of high-quality apps. On top of all that, there's an analytics product that ties it all together.

> **Note**: Most modern mobile apps require a data access layer for things that can't be done solely on a device, like sharing and processing data from multiple users or storing large files. The remote server, typically known as the backend, is responsible for handling these backend services.

Why Firebase?

Firebase is known for its easy-to-use APIs, great documentation and fantastic developer support. In addition to that, it only takes a few minutes to integrate Firebase with your projects.

Today, apps are rarely developed for a single platform, and most mobile apps are developed for the two biggest: Android and iOS. For that reason, developers often look for cross-platform solutions.

Firebase is a cross-platform service that works on Android, iOS and the web. By using a cross-platform solution, developers are not spending as much time as they would if they needed to use a separate service for each one. Not to mention, there's no need for businesses to invest additional money in different platforms.

Another bonus to using Firebase is that its products are integrated into one set of tools. There's a single SDK, a console and one place to go for the documentation and support. Data between different Firebase products is shared where and when needed, which leads to even faster development.

Getting started

Firebase Console

Firebase Console is where you set up and manage your apps. From there, you can view all of your projects as well as create new ones.

To get started with Firebase, open your web browser and navigate to https://console.firebase.google.com.

If you're not already logged in, do so now.

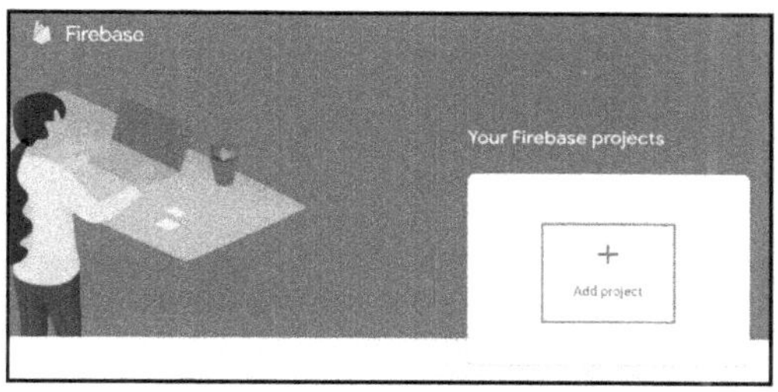

Firebase Console Main Screen.

To get started, you'll create a simple social media app that lets you share your thoughts with other app users.

First, you need to add your app to Firebase. Follow the steps:

1. Click **Add project**.
2. For the project name, enter **WhatsUp**.

Create Project Dialog.

3. Uncheck **Enable Google Analytics for this project**.
4. Click **Create project**.

Disable Google Analytics Switch.

Once your project is created, click **Continue**. Then you'll see the main screen.

Project Homepage.

That's it! You've successfully created your first Firebase project.

Now, click **Build** from the menu on the left and then select **Authentication**.

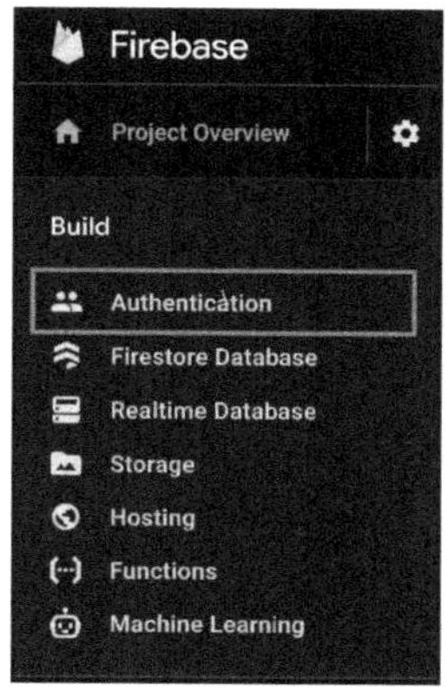

The Firebase Options Menu.

Next, you'll see the authentication screen. Click the **Sign-in method** tab.

Authentication Page.

Among the sign-in providers click **Google**. Enable **Google sign-in** and click save.

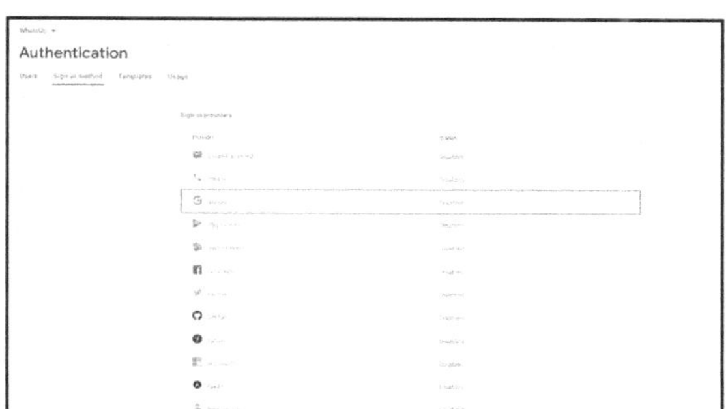

The list of sign-in providers.

This allows your app users to authenticate with their Google account.

Firebase analytics

To build a successful app, you need to clearly understand how your users behave and how they use your app. This is why analytics are so important.

There are many analytics categories that your app can use. This includes, in-app behavior analytics, which measures who your users are and what they are doing; attribution analytics, which you can use to measure the effectiveness of your advertising and other growth campaigns; push notifications analytics, crash reporting analytics and more.

Without Firebase, you may need to use multiple analytics libraries and tools to collect and save your analytics data. This becomes problematic when you need to share analytics data among those tools. Analytics for Firebase, however, is built to provide all of the data mobile app developers need in one place. Analytics integrates across Firebase features and provides you with two key capabilities: unlimited reporting for up to 500 distinct events and audience segmentation. With audience segmentation, you can create a custom audience that you target with new features or notification messages, for example. You can choose your custom audience base using parameters like device data or user properties.

Once you integrate your app with Firebase, analytics comes standard out-of-the-box.

Developing

Firebase offers many products that help you develop your app. Products that you'll use in this section of the book are Authentication, Realtime Database, Cloud Firestore and Cloud Storage. Now, you'll learn the basics of each one.

Authentication

Most apps need a way to identify a user so they can customize their experience and keep user data secure, while making authentication easy for both end-users and developers.

Firebase supports many different ways for your users to authenticate. **Firebase Auth** has built-in functionality for third-party providers such as Facebook, Twitter, Github or Google. If you want to authenticate users via an email address, you can do that, too.

You can present login functionality to the users in two different ways: using your own interface or taking advantage of Firebase's open source UI, which is also customizable. When the user authenticates, information about that user is returned to the device via a callback. You can then use that information to customize the experience for the specific user.

Firebase also manages user sessions, which means that users will remain logged in after the app restarts.

Realtime Database

Many apps need a way to store and share data from the server. When building your own backend, there are a few things that you need to manage, such as setting up and maintaining the database, real-time data synchronization and offline support. This can be tedious and time-consuming.

Firebase **Realtime Database** does it all for you, including storing and syncing data in real time. This allows users to access the data from any device.

Data is stored on the cloud, and whenever data is updated, all relevant devices get notified simultaneously within milliseconds.

Realtime Database is also optimized for offline use. It uses a local cache to store changes when the user loses network connection and when it comes back online local data gets automatically synchronized.

Realtime Database also takes care of security. You can use security rules to specify who has access to various pieces of data. Security rules are securely stored on the server.

Cloud Firestore

Cloud Firestore, like Realtime Database, is also used for saving the data to the cloud. It comes with the same feature set as Realtime Database, letting you store data in the cloud and sync data among different devices or share it with other users.

Cloud Firestore comes with client libraries, full offline mode support, a comprehensive set of security rules that help manage access to the data and a data browsing tool. It allows you to structure your data in a way that makes sense to you. It also automatically fetches changes from the server as they happen, or if you prefer, you can fetch them manually.

Cloud Firestore also integrates with other Firebase products like Authentication. You'll learn the differences between Realtime Database and Cloud Firestore as you progress through this book.

Cloud Storage

When it comes to storing and sharing pictures and similar files, Cloud Storage is crucial. Cloud Storage lets you upload user files to the cloud so they can be shared with others. If you want to share those files with specific users, you can leverage Firebase Authentication for that.

All network transfers are performed through a secure connection. If the connection breaks during network transfer, the transfer is paused and resumed once the network connection comes back online. This makes Cloud Storage ideal for large files or slow and unreliable network connections.

Other products

Firebase also offers other products for developing your app that aren't covered in this book. These include ML Kit, Cloud Functions and Hosting. You can learn more about them by reading the official Firebase page at https://firebase.google.com/products/.

Improving app quality

Firebase can help you improve the quality of your apps.

Before pushing your app to production, you need to test it. For that, Firebase provides you with **Test Lab**.

With so many different devices out there, you need to ensure that every feature of your app works as expected regardless of screen size or operating system version. Testing on every device is challenging since most developers don't have access to all available devices. Firebase Test Lab makes it possible to test your app with a variety of physical devices hosted in the cloud.

Bugs are frustrating for users and can cause them to uninstall the app and negatively impact its success. Many things can go wrong in the app and cause it to crash. **Firebase Crashlytics** collects, analyzes and organizes crash reports. It can also help you prioritize issues so that you can fix the most important ones first.

Your users will use your app in different circumstances — different devices, different networks and different locations. You need to provide the best user experience to all of them. To do that, you need metrics that tell you what's happening during critical moments of your app's use.

The only way to get that information is from the users themselves or by using **Firebase Performance Monitoring**. The Performance Monitoring SDK collects information about your app's performance, such as the app's startup time or details about HTTP transactions. You can also use the provided API to instrument your app to measure critical moments that you want to improve.

Growing a business

Firebase has several products that you can use to methodically grow your app, gain more users and help you earn more money.

In-App Messaging helps you engage users who are actively using your app by sending them targeted and contextual messages that nudge them to complete key in-app actions, like beating a game level or buying an item.

Google Analytics for Firebase gives you the power to build up groups of users, or audiences, out of just about anything you can measure in your app. It provides free, unlimited reporting on up to 500 distinct events.

Key points

- Firebase is Google's mobile platform that helps you quickly develop high-quality apps and grow your business.
- Firebase consists of three main pillars: Develop, Improve and Grow.
- Firebase Console is a single place where you need to go to set up and manage your app.

Where to go from here?

There's a lot more to explore in Firebase. You can find out more about different Firebase products and their key features in the official Firebase documentation: https://firebase.google.com/docs.

Chapter 13: Introduction to Firebase Realtime Database

By Fuad Kamal

Having a central place for storing application data is a common requirement for mobile applications. Let's say you're building a mobile game and you need to save user progress. You can save it locally on the phone. But what if the user logs in with the same account on a different device? That device doesn't know that the user has already made some progress and the user will need to start the game all over again. That can lead to unhappy users and bad app reviews.

In this case, you would need to save user progress to a remote database so that users can have access to the data from any number of devices they own. That database is usually hosted somewhere, on the Internet, making it accessible through a simple network connection. This concept is known as the **cloud**. You can think of the cloud as someone else's computer, or an entire infrastructure, which you've rented for various services.

Firebase Realtime Database is a solution that stores data in the cloud and provides an easy way to sync your data among various devices. It's powered by the Google Firebase platform, and is just a single piece in an otherwise large puzzle.

In this chapter, you'll learn how the Realtime Database works and its key capabilities. Furthermore, you'll add the Realtime Database to an Android project. Along the way, you'll learn how the Realtime Database takes care of security with database rules, how data is saved to the database and the best practices for the data structure.

Overview

Firebase Realtime Database is a cloud-hosted database that supports iOS, Android, Web, C++ and Unity platforms.

Realtime means that any changes in data are reflected immediately across all platforms and devices within milliseconds. Most traditional databases make you work with a request/response model, but the Realtime Database uses **data synchronization** and **subscriber mechanisms** instead of typical HTTP requests, which allows you to build more flexible real-time apps, easily, with less effort and without the need to worry about networking code.

Many apps become unresponsive when you lose the network connection. Realtime Database provides great **offline** support because it keeps an internal cache of all the data you've queried. When there's no Internet connection, the app uses the data from the cache, allowing apps to remain responsive. When the device connects to the Internet, the Realtime Database synchronizes the local data changes with the remote updates that occurred while the client was offline, resolving any conflicts automatically.

Client devices access the Realtime Database **directly**, without the need for an application server. **Security rules** take care of who has access to what data, and how they can access it. You'll learn more about security rules later in this chapter.

Firebase Realtime Database is not completely free. There are certain pricing plans. If you want your app to scale you'll need to pay for the number of connections, disk usage and network usage. You can check out pricing plans on the firebase pricing plans page here: https://firebase.google.com/pricing/.

Realtime Database is a **NoSQL** database. NoSQL stands for "Not only SQL". The easiest way to think of NoSQL is that it's a database that does not adhere to the traditional relational database management system (RDMS) structure. As such, the Realtime Database has different optimizations and functionality compared to a relational database. It stores the data in **JSON** format. The entire database is a big JSON tree with multiple nodes. When planning your database you need to keep this in mind to make your database as optimized as possible. You'll also learn more about data structure and best practices later in this chapter.

Setting up Realtime Database

In Chapter 12, "Firebase Overview," you added your app to a Firebase project. Now, you need to connect your app to Firebase, to enable its services.

Prerequisites

There are few requirements that you need to fulfill in order to setup Firebase with Android.

- To run your app on a physical device or an emulator you need to have at least **API level 9**, which is Android 2.3 *Gingerbread*.
- The device must have **Google Play Services** installed.
- Your app needs to use **Gradle 4.1** or higher.
- Your app needs to target **API level 16** or later.
- Uses Jetpack (AndroidX) (https://developer.android.com/jetpack/androidx/migrate) which includes `com.android.tools.build:gradle` v3.2.1 or later, and `combileSdkVersion` 28 or later

Connecting the app to the project

Go to the Firebase console and open the **WhatsUp** project that you created.

Firebase Getting Started Screen.

Click the **Android** icon to connect your Android app with Firebase.

Registering app

The first step is to register your app. For that, you need two pieces of information. The first one is your app's package name which you can find in the app-level **build.gradle** file as **applicationId**

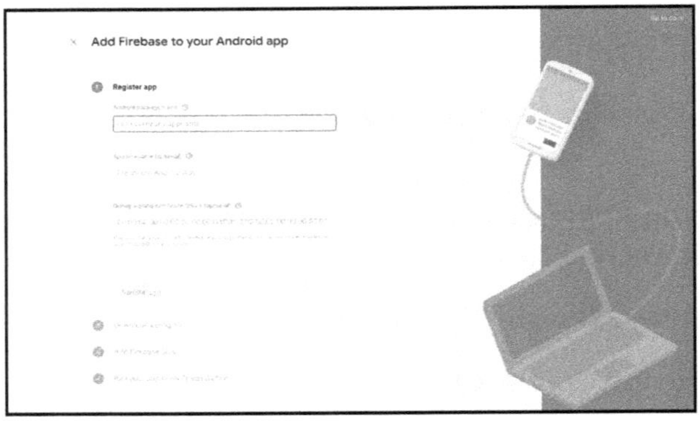

Add Firebase to your app Screen.

Enter **com.raywenderlich.android.whatsup** as the package name. App nickname is optional so you won't add it.

The second thing that you need to provide is the **SHA1** hash of your debug key. This is only required if you'll use specific Firebase features. In this project, it's needed for the **Authentication** feature. You can get your SHA1 hash in two ways, by using Android Studio, and Gradle, or by typing in a terminal command.

For the first option, open the **Gradle** tab from the right-hand side toolbar, and locate **signingReport**:

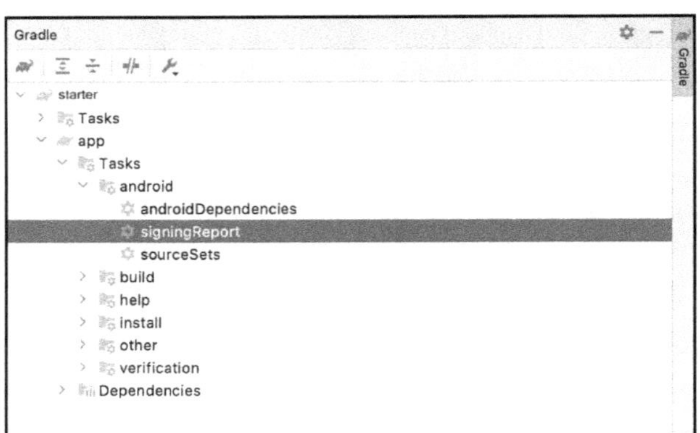

Gradle Signing Report Action.

Run it, and you should see the output in the terminal. The alternative is running the following command:

```
keytool -list -v -keystore ~/.android/debug.keystore -alias
androiddebugkey -storepass android -keypass android
```

Both commands give information about your debug **keystore**. In the Android Studio, open the **Terminal** panel. If one of the commands is executed, you'll see a line that starts with **SHA1**.

```
> Task :app:signingReport
Variant: debug
Config: debug
Store: /Users/gabrielaangebrandt/.android/debug.keystore
Alias: AndroidDebugKey
MD5: 62:F9:A3:52:05:87:E6:75:88:82:57:10:4F:17:CF:56
SHA1: 20:2F:8C:A2:0E:6C:59:B2:B8:1E:65:40:37:02:C6:51:02:AC:EF:46
SHA-256: 35:21:93:8B:F8:5A:00:1F:7B:C4:B2:43:41:35:26:BD:F2:FA:4A:CB:23:D1:1E:F1:0F:37:04:F8:04:2D:D9:F7
Valid until: Friday, 12 February 2049
```

Signing Report with SHA1 key.

Copy the value after that. That value is just a series of hex values, which represent your application's debug keystore signature. Paste that value into the **Debug signing certificate SHA-1** text box in the console. Click **Register app**.

Downloading config file

Next, you need to download the **google-services.json** config file by clicking the blue button, and add it to your Android project. Follow the instructions in the console to do that, so that you paste it to the correct location. This file contains your app configuration. If your Firebase configuration changes later you'll need to download an updated config file and replace the existing one.

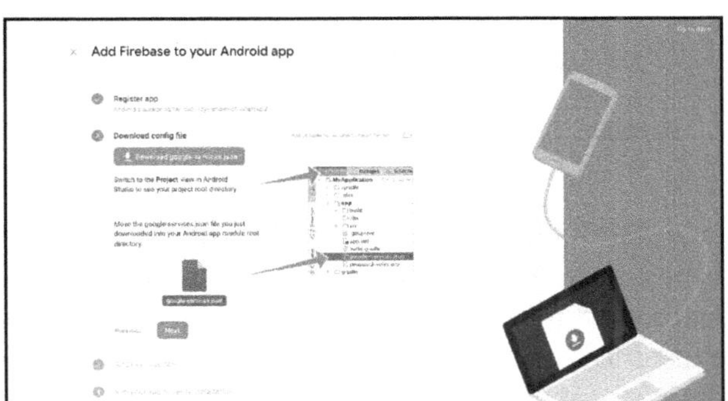

Download Google-Service JSON file.

Adding Firebase SDK

Next, you need to add the Firebase client libraries to your app. Follow the instructions in the console for this, as well.

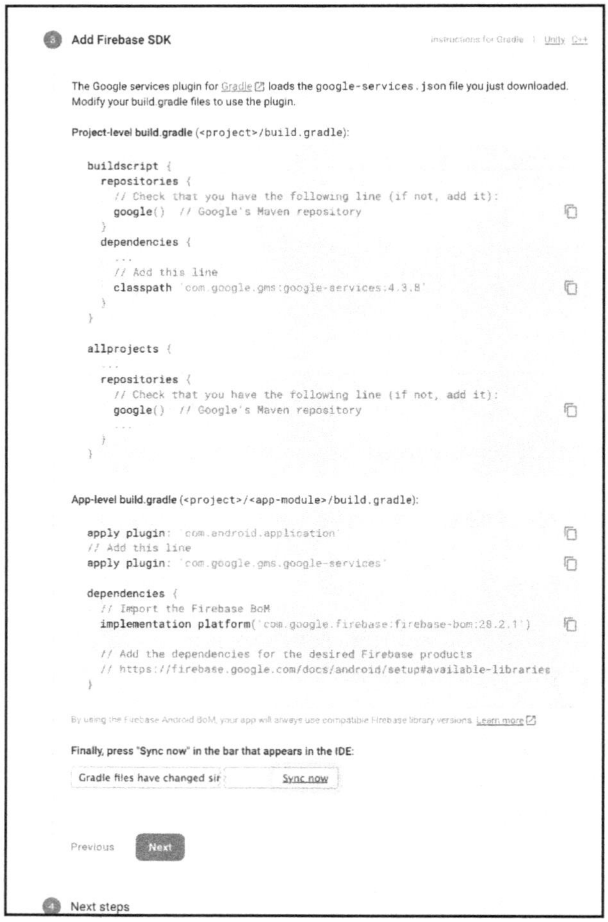

Adding Firebase SDK.

First, you need to add the **Google Services Gradle** plugin to your build script configuration. This plugin reads the **google-services.json** config file and injects some of its values into your build. Here, you'll also add a dependency to **Firebase core**. Make sure to use the latest version. You can check the documentation to find the latest version (https://firebase.google.com/docs/android/setup#available-libraries). Once you do that click **Next**.

Verifying installation

The last step is to verify if everything is set up correctly. For this, you only need to run your app on a device or an emulator. Before you do that, go to the `LoginActivity` class and uncomment the code. Repeat the process for the `HomeActivity` and `AuthenticationManager` classes. Run your app. If everything is set up correctly you'll get a verification message in the console.

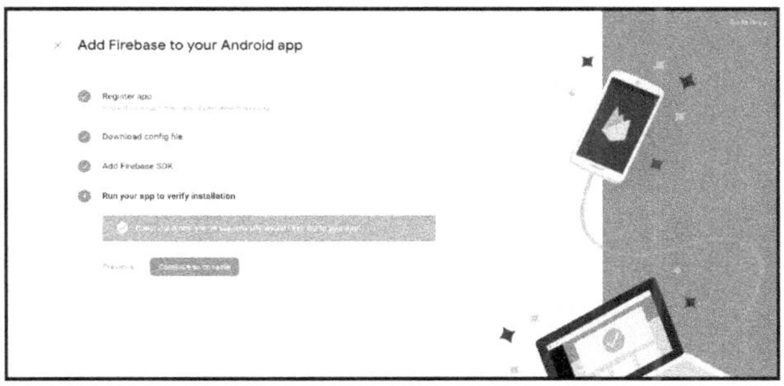

Installation verification.

You can click **Continue to console** now.

Adding Realtime Database

First, you need to create your database in the console. From the menu on the left select **Database**. Scroll to the **Realtime Database** section and click **Create database**. The security rules dialog will open.

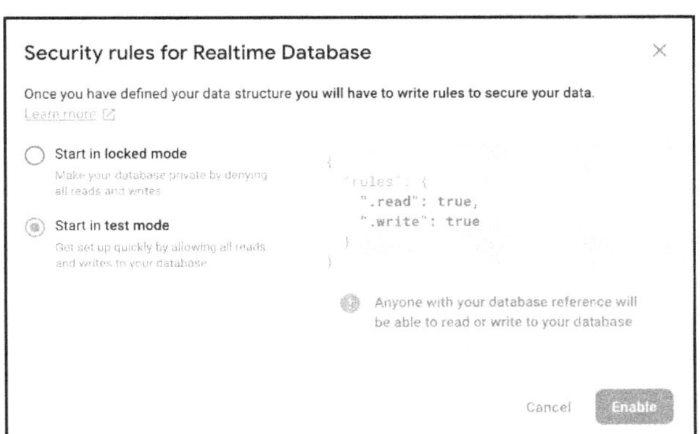

Security rules.

Select the second option, **Start in test mode**, and click **Enable**. You'll learn more about security rules in a bit.

Once your database is created you'll see its preview.

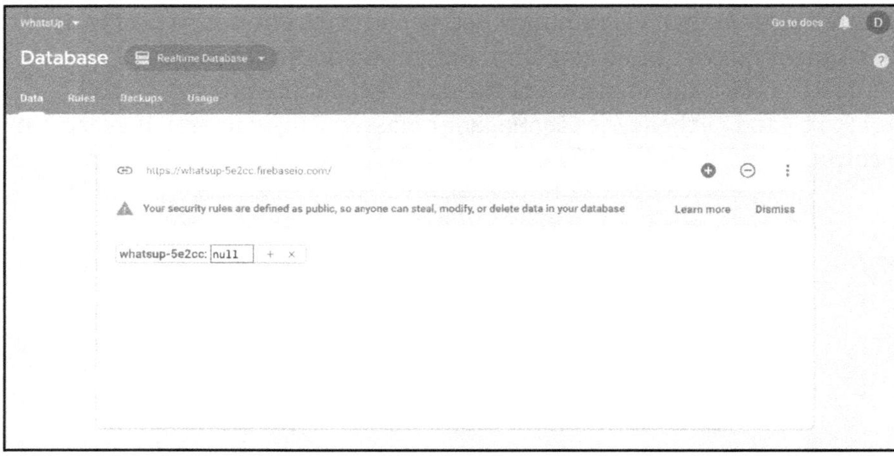

Database Preview.

To add the Realtime Database service to your app, you only need to add one more dependency. Open **build.gradle** and add the following dependency, making sure you're using the latest version:

```
implementation "com.google.firebase:firebase-database:20.0.0"
```

Database rules

In this section, you'll be working on the **WhatsUp** app which has an authentication feature so the app can know who your users are. **Authentication** is the process of verifying users are who they say they are, and giving them certain security access to your service.

User identity is an important security concept. Different users have different data and different capabilities. In this app, the user will be able to delete posts it created but not the other people's posts. Because of this, you need a way to control who has access to what data in your database. The process of determining who has access to what is called **authorization**.

To implement the various aspects of security, authentication and authorization would require a lot of work. Firebase has the Authentication service which can use for all those sides of security, and the Realtime Database service uses internal **Realtime Database Rules** for authorization.

Database rules allow you to control access for each user. They determine who has read and write access to your database, how your data is structured, and what indexes exist. Every time reading or writing is attempted, a request will only be completed if your rules allow it.

Firebase Database rules are also a **JSON object** which must have a top-level `rules` node. By default, the rules node contains two primitives, `.read` and `.write` and they determine who has read and write access. If `.read` and `.write` are set to **true**, everyone would have complete access to your data, so they can both read and write as they want. To protect your database from abuse, you need to customize those rules.

The Firebase Database Rules include built-in variables and functions that allow you to refer to other paths, server-side timestamps, authentication information, and much more. For this app, you'll write a rule that grants read and write access only for authenticated users.

This is what this rule looks like:

```
{
  "rules": {
    ".read": "auth != null",
    ".write": "auth != null"
  }
}
```

Navigate to the **Rules** tab, replace the rules with the above snippet and click **Publish**.

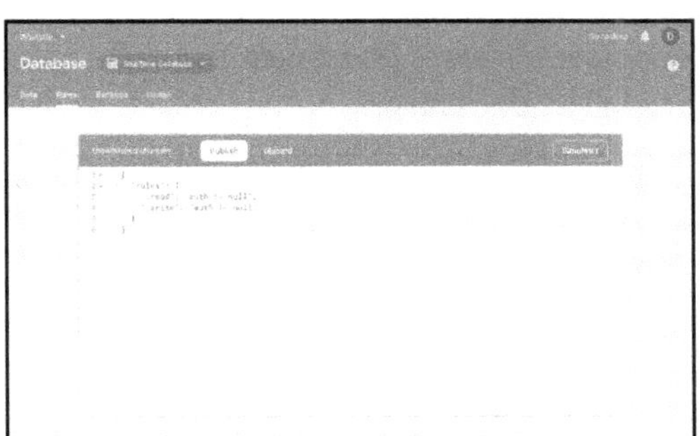

Adding specific Rules.

Now, only authenticated users are allowed to read from and write to your database.

You can learn more about database rules in the documentation here: https://firebase.google.com/docs/database/security/.

Communication with the Realtime Database

You need a way to talk to the Realtime Database. The first thing you need is a connection. To get a connection you need to create a database reference first. Open **RealtimeDatabaseManager.kt** and add the `databaseReference` property:

```
private val databaseReference =
FirebaseDatabase.getInstance().reference
```

This gets you a reference to the root of the Firebase JSON tree. You'll learn more about data structure later in this chapter.

For connectivity testing purposes, add a method to the `RealtimeDatabaseManager` that will write some dummy data to the database.

```
fun addDummyData() {
    databaseReference.setValue("Saving data on Android")
}
```

Next, open **HomeActivity.kt** and add the following property:

```
private val realtimeDatabaseManager by lazy
{ RealtimeDatabaseManager() }
```

Now, call `addDummyData()` from the bottom of `initialize()`:

```
realtimeDatabaseManager.addDummyData()
```

Run the app and sign in with your Google account by clicking **Sign in with Google**. Next, go to Firebase Console and select **Database** from the menu on the left side. You should see your data in the database.

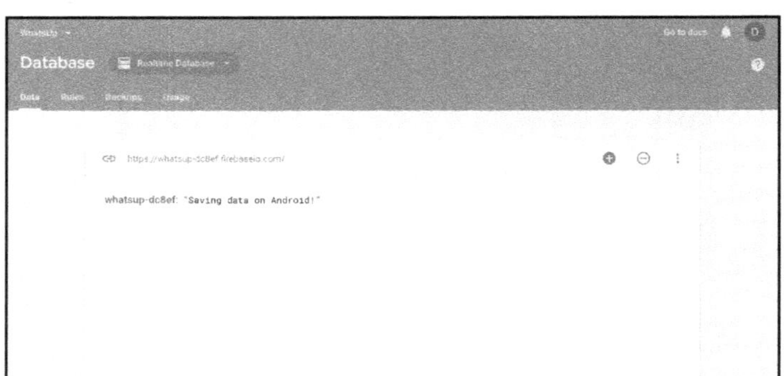

Database populated.

Congratulations! You have successfully communicated with the Realtime Database. Before you continue, delete the data from the database directly from the console by clicking the **X** button from the right side of the value. You'll learn a lot more about reading and writing to the Realtime Database in the next chapter.

Data structure

JSON format

As mentioned before, the Firebase Realtime Database stores data in **JSON format**. JSON stands for JavaScript Object Notation and it's a language-independent data format with a minimal number of value types: strings, numbers, booleans, lists, objects, and null. It consists of key/value pairs. The key/value pairs are separated by a colon and each pair is separated by a comma. It is easy for humans to read and write and for machines to parse and generate. This is a sample JSON object:

```
{
  "name": "Dean",
  "lastname": "Djermanovic",
  "age": 23,
  "gender": "male"
}
```

Best practices for data structure

The entire database is a big JSON tree with multiple nodes. When pushing new data to the database you either create a new node with an associated key or update an existing one. Therefore there is the danger of creating a deeply nested structure. Firebase Realtime Database allows nesting data up to 32 levels deep but that doesn't mean that this should be the default structure. When thinking about data structure you need to think about how your data is going to be consumed, you need to make the process of saving and retrieving as easy as possible.

If you have very complex structures with a lot of nesting you fetch all the data every time you read from the database, which is not needed in most cases. If you want to get the data from a specific node you get all the data below that node as well. Take a look at this restaurants structure for example:

```
{
  "restaurants": {
    "first_restaurant": {},
```

```
    "second_restaurant": {},
    "third_restaurant": {}
  }
}
```

Fetching the restaurant's data would get you all of its child nodes data as well. In addition, when you grant someone access to a node in your database you also grant them access to all of its children's data. You can limit this by specifying how many restaurants you want to fetch or to fetch only restaurants that satisfy some condition but in general, when you're loading data you're loading all of it. Because of this, it's good practice to keep your data structure as flat as possible.

Another good practice would be that you organize your data in a way that you don't fetch the data that you're not rendering on the UI. If you split your data into separate paths you can be more specific about what data you want to fetch. Traditionally, you would have a set of data and you'd build your UI on top of that, but with Firebase, since it's easy to write data, people build their UI and then they start building a data structure from the app. This flat data structure affects the performance in a good way since you don't need to fetch extra data that you won't use, which allows the UI to stay responsive and fast.

Generally, there's no right or wrong approach to structuring your data. Storage is cheap. You can have a million copies of the exact same string field in the Realtime Database and it will cost you almost nothing but the problem appears when fetching this data. With a little bit of practice, you'll be able to judge better what makes sense to nest and what doesn't.

Key points

- To use Firebase Realtime Database in your Android project you need to go through the **configuration** process first.
- The Realtime Database provides **database rules** to control access for each user.
- Firebase Authentication is very much connected to database solutions Firebase offers, since it controls the **access to data**, on a **per-user basis**.
- Firebase Realtime Database stores data in **JSON format**.
- Because the structure is a JSON, it operates with simple data like numbers, `Strings`, `Objects`, `Booleans` and `Lists`.
- Firebase Realtime Database data structure should be as **flat** as possible and designed with **scaling** in mind.

Where to go from here?

In this chapter, you saw how to configure Realtime Database and what are best practices when it comes to structuring your data. If you want to learn more you can check out official Firebase documentation (https://firebase.google.com/docs).

You also wrote your first data to the database. In **Chapter 14: Reading to & Writing from Realtime Database** you'll learn a lot more about reading from and writing to Realtime Database and you'll integrate it to the WhatsUp app. You'll be able to write posts from the app and upload them to the Realtime Database and other users will be able to read them as well.

Chapter 14: Reading to & Writing from Realtime Database

By Fuad Kamal

In the last chapter, you integrated Realtime Database into your app. You added Firebase SDK to your app and connected the app with the Firebase project. You also learned about database rules and you set them up to allow only authenticated users access to the database. You even wrote your first data to the database which was just a sneak peek of what you'll do in this chapter.

This chapter will teach you how to work with Realtime Database data. You'll learn how to read and write data as well as how to do basic manipulation with that data. First, you'll learn about performing **CRUD** operations on to the Realtime Database. CRUD is just an acronym for the four basic types of SQL commands: *Create*, *Read*, *Update* and *Delete*. You'll combine all these concepts together in order to build a fully functional app with Realtime Database as the backend.

Setting up Firebase

You need to set up Firebase in order to follow along. Do the following steps:

1. Create a project in the Firebase console.
2. Enable Google sign-in.
3. Set security rules to the test mode to allow everyone **read** and **write** access.
4. Add **google-service.json** to both **starter** and **final** projects.

To see how to do this, go back to Chapter 12: "Firebase Overview" and Chapter 13: "Introduction to Firebase Realtime Database."

Reading and writing data

Open the starter project, and build and run your app. If this is the first time you're running this app you'll need to sign in first in order to use it. To sign in, tap **Sign in with Google** and follow the steps on the screen. Next, click on the **floating action button**. A new screen opens where you can write your post. Write something and click **POST**.

Adding a Post.

As you can see nothing happens yet. Next, you'll add the logic for saving the post to the database.

Saving data to the database

Open **RealtimeDatabaseManager.kt**. Add the following line to the class:

```
private val database = FirebaseDatabase.getInstance()
```

The `database` object is the main entry point to the database. `getInstance()` gets you the default `FirebaseDatabase` instance. There are overloads of `getInstance()` if you want to get the database for the specific URL or specific app.

Next, you need to create an actual object which will contain data. Inside the class, add the code for creation of the `Post` object:

```
private fun createPost(key: String, content: String): Post {
    val user = authenticationManager.getCurrentUser()
    val timestamp = getCurrentTime()
    return Post(key, content, user, timestamp)
}
```

This function uses `AuthenticationManager` to get the current logged in user name, gets the current time and then returns the newly created `Post` instance.

Now that you have a post object, you need to store it. But first, add a constant above the class declaration:

```
private const val POSTS_REFERENCE = "posts"
```

You'll use this constant in retrieving reference from the database. Now, add the function for saving the post to the database:

```
 fun addPost(content: String, onSuccessAction: () -> Unit,
onFailureAction: () -> Unit) {
    //1
    val postsReference = database.getReference(POSTS_REFERENCE)
    //2
    val key = postsReference.push().key ?: ""
    val post = createPost(key, content)

    //3
    postsReference.child(key)
      .setValue(post)
      .addOnSuccessListener { onSuccessAction() }
      .addOnFailureListener { onFailureAction() }
  }
```

Here's what happens here:

1. The `DatabaseReference` class represents a particular location in the database and it's used to refer to the location in the database to which you want to write to or read from. `getReference()` returns a reference to the database root node. You won't save posts to the root node. Instead, you'll create a new node for the posts, which is why you added the `POSTS_REFERENCE` constant earlier. You pass that constant to `getReference()` and this returns a reference for the provided path. Now you can use `postsReference` to read or write data to this location.

2. Posts will be added as a child of the `posts` node. To add a post as a child it needs to have a **unique key** that will be used as a path to the specific post. The key needs to be unique because setting a value to the existing path would overwrite the previous value on that path. You don't want that. You can use `push()` to create an **empty node** with an auto-generated key. This method returns a database reference to the newly created node. You can call `getKey()` on the database reference to get the key to that reference. Next, you create a `Post` instance that you'll save to the database and you store the key of that post so you can refer to it later.

3. To access the newly created location you can use `child()` that returns a reference to the location relative to the calling reference. Finally, you use `setValue()` to save the post to this location. The Realtime Database accepts multiple data types to store the data: `String`, `Long`, `Double`, `Boolean`, `Map<String, Object>`, and `List<Object>`. You can also use custom Kotlin or Java objects to store the data model class directly to the database as you're doing here. Finally, you attach `OnSuccessListener` that gets called if the post is saved to the database successfully, and `OnFailureListener` that gets called if the post-saving failed.

Now, open **AddPostActivity.kt** and replace the `TODO` in `addPostIfNotEmpty()` with the following:

```
val postMessage = postText.text.toString().trim()
    if (postMessage.isNotEmpty()) {
      realtimeDatabaseManager.addPost(postMessage,
        { showToast(getString(R.string.posted_successfully)) },
        { showToast(getString(R.string.posting_failed)) } )
      finish()
    } else {
      showToast(getString(R.string.empty_post_message))
    }
```

Here you get the text from `EditText` and if it's not empty you save the text to the database and you close the current activity. Otherwise, you show an error message.

Build and run your app. Click on the **floating action button** on the home screen, add some text and tap **Post**. Current activity gets closed and the home screen is shown. You'll fix that in a bit. After you reopen the app, the added post will be displayed on the home screen.

To make sure your post is saved to the database, open the database in the Firebase console and you'll see your post here along with additional data that you added:

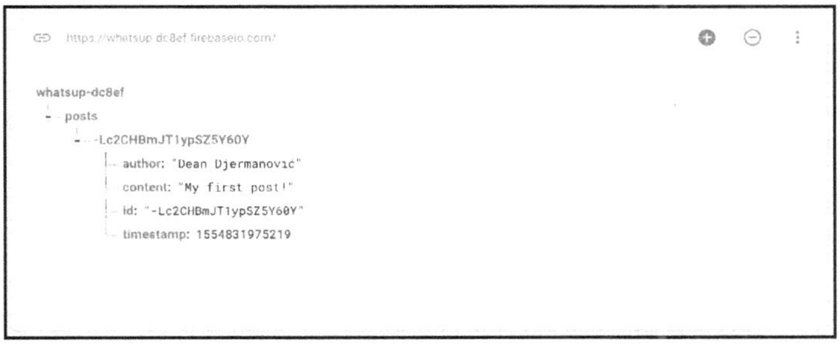

Firebase Console preview - Post is saved in the database.

Good job! You'll add the logic for displaying posts on the home screen next.

Fetching data from the database

When it comes to reading the data from the database you have two options. You can read the data once or you can be notified whenever data changes. Since you want to see every new post from other users instantly, you'll implement the second option.

To get all posts from the database and listen for value changes you need to use `ValueEventListener`. You need to attach this listener to the specific location in the database that you want to listen for changes from.

Open **RealtimeDatabaseManager.kt** and at the top of the class add:

```
private val postsValues = MutableLiveData<List<Post>>()
```

You'll use `LiveData` to notify the observers about post changes.

Next, below the previous line add:

```
private lateinit var postsValueEventListener: ValueEventListener
```

This is where you'll store your event listener.

Next, add the following function:

```
private fun listenForPostsValueChanges() {
    //1
    postsValueEventListener = object : ValueEventListener {
      //2
      override fun onCancelled(databaseError: DatabaseError) {
        /* No op */
      }

      //3
      override fun onDataChange(dataSnapshot: DataSnapshot) {
        //4
        if (dataSnapshot.exists()) {
          val posts = dataSnapshot.children.mapNotNull
{ it.getValue(Post::class.java) }.toList()
          postsValues.postValue(posts)
        } else {
          //5
          postsValues.postValue(emptyList())
        }
      }
    }

    //6
    database.getReference(POSTS_REFERENCE)
        .addValueEventListener(postsValueEventListener)
}
```

1. You add `ValueEventListener` as an anonymous inner class and you assign it to `postsValueEventListener` field. There are two methods that you need to implement.

2. `onCancelled(databaseError: DatabaseError)` gets triggered if reading from the database is cancelled. Reading can be canceled in case if there are server issues or if you don't have access to the location you're trying to read from due to database rules. `databaseError` contains more information about an error that occurred. In this case, you won't do anything if reading gets canceled.

3. `onDataChange(dataSnapshot: DataSnapshot)` gets triggered whenever data under the reference you attached the listener to gets changed; either new data is added or existing data is updated or deleted. This is the method where you perform desired operations on the new data. You get the data back as `DataSnapshot`. `DataSnapshot` contains all the data from a specific location in the database. `DataSnapshot` is just an immutable copy of your database data so can't use it to modify the data in the database.

4. By calling `exists()` on the `DataSnapshot` object you check if the snapshot contains a non-null value. If there is data in the snapshot you get all of the direct children of the snapshot and you map each one to the `Post` object by calling `getValue(Post::class.java)` on a child. `getValue(Post::class.java)` wraps the data to the specified `Post` class and returns an instance of the passed in class or `null` if there is no data in this location. Then you add `Post` instances to the list and you set this list to the `LiveData` field created earlier which will notify all active observers about new data.
5. If data doesn't exist you set an empty list as the new value of `LiveData`. This is needed in the case where all posts get deleted and the database is empty. In that case, `dataSnapshot.exists()` will return `false` and by setting empty list as the new value you'll reflect that.
6. You attach the listener to `POSTS_REFERENCE` because that is the location from where you want to listen for changes.

Now inside the class, add `onPostsValuesChange()`:

```
fun onPostsValuesChange(): LiveData<List<Post>> {
    listenForPostsValueChanges()
    return postsValues
}
```

This method just calls the function that attaches the listener and returns `LiveData`.

You only want to listen for posts updates when you're on the home screen. Once you navigate away from the home screen you don't care about posts updates anymore. To achieve that you need to remove event listener when you're no longer interested in the events.

Add this code inside the slass:

```
fun removePostsValuesChangesListener() {

database.getReference(POSTS_REFERENCE).removeEventListener(posts
ValueEventListener)
}
```

This method removes the passed in event listener, by calling `removeEventListener()`, from the specified location.

Open **HomeActivity.kt** and add the following method:

```
private fun onPostsUpdate(posts: List<Post>) {
    feedAdapter.onFeedUpdate(posts)
}
```

This method will get called every time posts update and it will set new data to the `RecyclerView` adapter.

Now, find `listenForPostsUpdates()` and replace the `TODO` with the following:

```
realtimeDatabaseManager.onPostsValuesChange()
  .observe(this, Observer(::onPostsUpdate))
```

This code enables listening for the changes in the posts. On every update, the system will call `onPostsUpdate()`.

Finally, override `onStop()`:

```
override fun onStop() {
    super.onStop()
    realtimeDatabaseManager.removePostsValuesChangesListener()
}
```

Once the activity stops, it also stops listening for the posts updates.

Build and run. You'll see the post that you previously added on the home screen.

The user can preview the post added to the database.

Build and run your app on a different device and log in with a different account. Add a new post and observe on your first device how the data is updated in the realtime.

Updating and deleting data

Tap on a post to open another screen that shows post details.

The Post Details Screen.

On this screen, you can edit your post by taping on its text. When you're done you can tap **UPDATE** the post content. By tapping **Delete** you can delete the post if you're the author of the post. There's also a **Comments** section here. The app also has the feature of adding a comment to the post which will be displayed here. If you try to tap any of these buttons you'll see that nothing happens. You'll implement those functionalities next.

Updating

Updating data in Realtime Database is almost the same as writing. You use the same method for updating - `setValue()`. Above the `RealtimeDatabaseManager` class declaration, add next constant:

```
private const val POST_CONTENT_PATH = "content"
```

You'll use this constant to indicate which field in the database you want to update.

Now add the following to the class:

```
fun updatePostContent(key: String, content: String) {
    //1
    database.getReference(POSTS_REFERENCE)
        //2
        .child(key)
        //3
        .child(POST_CONTENT_PATH)
        //4
        .setValue(content)
}
```

1. First, you get a reference to the location of the posts in the database.
2. Here you use the key to access the location of the post you want to update.
3. You can create a new object and write the entire object to this location but that isn't needed. You can update a specific field in the post by specifying the path to that field. Here you update only the content of the post.
4. Finally, you call `setValue()` with new content to update the content of the post.

Now, use this method in **PostDetailsActivity.kt**. Replace the `TODO` in `updatePostButton.setOnClickListener()` in the `initializeClickListener()` with this:

```
realtimeDatabaseManager.updatePostContent(post.id,
postText.text.toString().trim())
finish()
```

When the user taps **UPDATE** the post content will change and the current activity will close.

Build and run. Open any post in the list that was written by you, update the post content, tap **UPDATE** and verify both on the home screen and Firebase console that post content is updated.

Deleting

Deleting data in Realtime Database is very simple. You have two options. You can delete data by using `setValue()` and specify `null` as an argument or you can use `removeValue()` which will set the value at the specified location to `null`. You'll use the latter approach.

Open **RealtimeDatabaseManager.kt** and add the deleting post function:

```
fun deletePost(key: String) {
    database.getReference(POSTS_REFERENCE)
        .child(key)
        .removeValue()
}
```

Here you get a reference to the location of the posts, then you get the reference to the desired post and call `removeValue()` to delete it.

Open **PostDetailsActivity.kt**, navigate to `initializeClickListener()` and replace the `TODO` in `deletePostButton.setOnClickListener()` with this:

```
realtimeDatabaseManager.deletePost(post.id)
finish()
```

Build and run your app. Open any post in the list that was written by you and click the delete button. Verify on the home screen and Firebase console that the post is deleted.

Querying and filtering data

To show how to query data you'll add another feature to the app. You'll enable users to add comments to the post.

Open **RealtimeDatabaseManager.kt** and add two more constants above the class declaration:

```
private const val COMMENTS_REFERENCE = "comments"
private const val COMMENT_POST_ID_PATH = "postId"
```

`COMMENTS_REFERENCE` is used to refer to the location of comments and `COMMENT_POST_ID_PATH` is used when building a query. You'll do that in a bit.

Next, add `commentsValues` and `commentsValueEventListener` fields to the class:

```
private val commentsValues = MutableLiveData<List<Comment>>()
private lateinit var commentsValueEventListener:
ValueEventListener
```

Now, add a helper function for building a `Comment` instance:

```
private fun createComment(postId: String, content: String):
Comment {
    val user = authenticationManager.getCurrentUser()
    val timestamp = getCurrentTime()
    return Comment(postId, user, timestamp, content)
}
```

When adding `Comment`import, use `com.raywenderlich.android.whatsup.model.Comment. With this method you create a`Comment object in the same way as you created your first`Post` object.

Now, add the following function:

```
fun addComment(postId: String, content: String) {
    val commentsReference =
database.getReference(COMMENTS_REFERENCE)
    val key = commentsReference.push().key ?: ""
    val comment = createComment(postId, content)

    commentsReference.child(key).setValue(comment)
}
```

This function saves the comment to the database. It uses the same logic as the post saving function so you should be familiar with this by now.

Next, in **PostDetailsActivity.kt**, navigate to `initializeClickListener()` and replace the `TODO` inside `addCommentButton.setOnClickListener()` with the following:

```
val comment = commentEditText.text.toString().trim()
  if (comment.isNotEmpty()) {
    realtimeDatabaseManager.addComment(post.id, comment)
    commentEditText.text.clear()
  } else {
    showToast(getString(R.string.empty_comment_message))
}
```

Here you get the text from `EditText` and, if it's not empty, you save the comment to the database.

Build and run. Open details of any post from the list, add a comment and click **ADD COMMENT**.

A comment added successfully.

`EditText` gets cleared but nothing happens on the UI. Go to the Firebase console. You'll see there that comment is saved to the database.

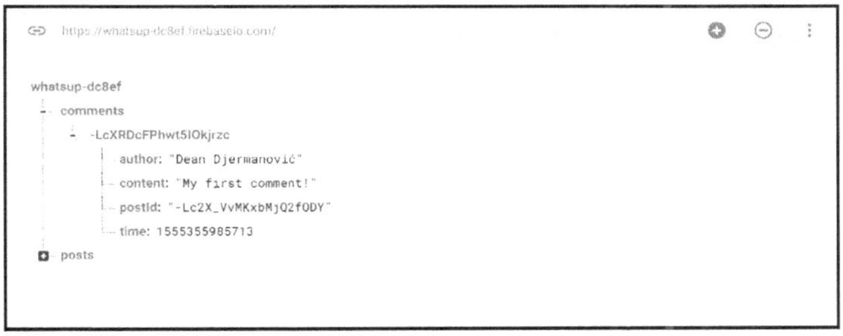

The Comment is visible in the Firebase console.

You can see there that comment has a `postId` child. This is how you'll know to which post comment belongs.

Finally, you can add logic for reading the comments from the database.

Open **RealtimeDatabaseManager.kt** again and add this code:

```
private fun listenForPostCommentsValueChanges(postId: String) {
    commentsValueEventListener = object : ValueEventListener {
      override fun onCancelled(databaseError: DatabaseError) {
        /* No op */
      }

      override fun onDataChange(dataSnapshot: DataSnapshot) {
        if (dataSnapshot.exists()) {
          val comments = dataSnapshot.children.mapNotNull
{ it.getValue(Comment::class.java) }.toList()
          commentsValues.postValue(comments)
        } else {
          commentsValues.postValue(emptyList())
        }
      }
    }

    database.getReference(COMMENTS_REFERENCE)
          //1
        .orderByChild(COMMENT_POST_ID_PATH)
        //2
        .equalTo(postId)
        .addValueEventListener(commentsValueEventListener)
}
```

This function listens for comments value updates and it's very similar to `listenForPostsValueChanges()`, but there are two differences:

1. `orderByChild()` returns a `Query` instance where children are ordered by the `postId` value. A query is a request for data or information from a database. The `Query` class is used for reading data and it has many useful methods that allow you to fetch the data in a way you want. You can filter data by some criteria, sort data, limit, etc. Check the official documentation (https://firebase.google.com/docs/reference/android/com/google/firebase/database/Query) to see what it offers.

2. `equalTo()` returns a `Query` instance that contains child nodes only where the node value is equal to the specified function argument. In this case, it will return a query with the comments for the specific post.

The rest of the code is the same as the code for listening for post updates.

Next, add a function, which will delete all of the comments for the specific post:

```
private fun deletePostComments(postId: String) {
    database.getReference(COMMENTS_REFERENCE)
        .orderByChild(COMMENT_POST_ID_PATH)
```

```
        .equalTo(postId)
        .addListenerForSingleValueEvent(object :
ValueEventListener {
          override fun onCancelled(databaseError: DatabaseError)
{
            /* No op */
          }

          override fun onDataChange(dataSnapshot: DataSnapshot)
{
            dataSnapshot.children.forEach { it.ref.removeValue()
}
          }
        })
}
```

It uses exactly the same logic for fetching the comments for the specific post as `listenForPostCommentsValueChanges()` and you're already familiar with how to delete data from the database.

Call this function from the bottom of `deletePost()` passing in the key of the post:

```
deletePostComments(key)
```

This makes sure that when a post gets deleted, its comments get deleted as well.

Next, add `onCommentsValuesChange()` which starts listening for comments updates and returns a `LiveData` object:

```
fun onCommentsValuesChange(postId: String):
LiveData<List<Comment>> {
    listenForPostCommentsValueChanges(postId)
    return commentsValues
}
```

Now, open **PostDetailsActivity.kt** again, navigate to `listenForComments()` and replace the `TODO` with the following:

```
realtimeDatabaseManager.onCommentsValuesChange(post.id)
  .observe(this, Observer(::onCommentsUpdate))
```

`Observer` in this case requires you to import `androidx.lifecycle.Observer`. This just starts listening for the comments update.

Next, back in **RealtimeDatabaseManager.kt**, add a function for removing the comments listener:

```
fun removeCommentsValuesChangesListener() {

database.getReference(COMMENTS_REFERENCE).removeEventListener(co
mmentsValueEventListener)
}
```

Finally, in **PostDetailsActivity.kt**, override `onStop()` and call `realtimeDatabaseManager.removeCommentsValuesChangesListener()` to remove the comments listener when you no longer want to listen for comment updates.

```
override fun onStop() {
    super.onStop()

realtimeDatabaseManager.removeCommentsValuesChangesListener()
}
```

Build and run. Navigate to the same post you added a comment to earlier.

The comment is visible on the Post Details Screen.

Now you can see your comment on the UI as well. Add more comments from the same and from the different account to see how comments are updated in real time.

Other features

Transactions

Realtime Database also allows you to write data to the database using a transaction. A database transaction is a unit of work that is independently executed and it must be atomic, consistent, isolated and durable. If the **WhatsUp** app had a feature to allow you to "like" a post you could use transactions to keep track of how many *likes* a given post had. Since there is a use case where multiple users could "like" the post at the same time, the transaction would allow you to always have fresh and correct data about *likes*.

Check the official documentation https://firebase.google.com/docs/database/android/read-and-write#save_data_as_transactions to see how to work with transactions.

Listening for child events

Previously you saw how to use value event listener. Often you'll also need to know about changes in children of a specific node. In that case, you'll need to use a child event listener. Child event listeners notify the app when child nodes are added, deleted or moved within a parent node. To add a child event listener you'll need to call `addChildEventListener()` on a database reference instance, and there are four methods that you'll need to implement. Check the official documentation https://firebase.google.com/docs/database/android/lists-of-data#child-events to learn more about child events.

Indexing

There can be a performance issue if your app frequently queries the database. To improve query performance you should consider defining indexing rules. A database index is a data structure that is used to quickly locate and access the data in a database.

You can learn more about indexing data in the official documentation https://firebase.google.com/docs/database/security/indexing-data.

Key points

- The `FirebaseDatabase` object is the main entry point to the database
- `DatabaseReference` represents a particular location in the database and it is used to refer to the location in the database to which you want to write to or read from.
- `push()` is used to create an empty node with an auto-generated key.
- Firebase Realtime Database has several types of listeners, and each listener type has a different kind of callback.
- `ValueEventListener` listens for data changes to a specific database reference.
- `ChildEventListener` listens for changes to the children of a specific database reference.
- You need to decide how to handle listeners when the user is not actively interacting with the app. In most cases, you want to stop listening for updates. To do that you need to remove the listener.
- For updating data in Realtime Database, use `setValue()`.
- You can delete data by using `setValue()` and specify `null` as an argument or you can use `removeValue()` which will set the value at the specified location to `null`.
- A query is a request for data or information from a database. The `Query` class is used for reading data and it has many useful methods that allow you to fetch the data in a way you want.
- A database transaction is a unit of work that is independently executed and it must be atomic, consistent, isolated and durable.
- To improve query performance you should consider defining indexing rules.

Where to go from here?

You covered a lot in this chapter. You have seen how to write data to the Realtime Database, how to listen for changes in the database and how to update and delete data. It takes a little bit of practice to get used to working with Realtime Database so feel free to play a bit with the current app. To see specifics about each method, what it does and how it does it, you can visit the official Firebase documentation to find out.

WhatsUp app works great for now, but what if you were using it in a place where the Internet connection is bad? What if you started uploading data and you lost Internet connection in the process? Can you write data to the database if you're offline? The good news is that Realtime Database provides great offline support. In Chapter 15, "Realtime Database Offline Capabilities", you'll learn how Firebase handles all of the mentioned cases. You'll make your WhatsUp app work seamlessly offline and you'll learn what happens under the hood that makes that possible.

Chapter 15: Realtime Database Offline Capabilities

By Harun Wangereka

So far, you've created an app that enables you to save posts to the database and read the posts from the database. The next step is to implement offline support. If you turn off your internet connection now and run your app, you'd see an empty screen because your app can't fetch the data from the database.

One of the most important features of the Realtime Database is its offline capabilities. If you were creating your backend system, you would need to persist the data by yourself. Firebase handles that for you, and it enables your app to work properly even when the user loses network connection. In this chapter, you'll learn how exactly it does that, and you'll add offline support to your app so that you could see posts on the screen and even add posts while you are offline.

Setting up Firebase

If you skipped previous chapters, you need to set up Firebase to follow along. Do the following steps:

1. Create a project in the Firebase console.
2. Enable Google sign-in.
3. Create a new Realtime Database. Set security rules to the test mode to allow everyone **read** and **write** access. You should *never* use these settings for your production apps.
4. Add **google-service.json** to both **starter** and **final** project's root directory.

If you need a reminder of how to do this, go back to Chapter 12: "Firebase Overview" and Chapter 13: "Introduction to Firebase Realtime Database."

Be sure to use the starter project from **this chapter**, by opening the **realtime-database-offline-capabilities/projects/starter** rather than continuing with the final project you previously worked on. It has a few things added to it, including placeholders for the code that you'll add in this chapter.

Enabling disk persistence

Before you start with coding, build and run the starter project. Make sure your device is connected to the Internet.

The sign in screen.

If you aren't logged in, do so. After successful login, you'll see your posts on the home screen. Open any post, disconnect your mobile device from the network and navigate back to the home screen.

> **Note**: The post and comments on screenshots can differ a bit than yours. You can use any post content you like!

The screen with all saved posts.

Notice that your posts are still there. By default, Firebase stores your data **in-memory**. Now, close the app and kill the app process from the **Recent apps** menu. Run your app again. Now, you'll see an empty screen.

Empty posts screen.

Caching data locally

To enable disk persistence, you only need one line of code. Open **WhatsUpApplication.kt** and add the following at the end of `onCreate()`:

```
FirebaseDatabase.getInstance().setPersistenceEnabled(true)
```

Setting the argument of `setPersistenceEnabled()` to `true` enables the app to store the data to the device's local storage — the **disk**. That is what makes the data available even after you kill the app.

The reason you had to enable disk persistence in the `Application` class, instead of the `RealtimeDatabaseManager`, is that `setPersistenceEnabled()` needs to be called once per app and *before* creating the first database reference.

Turn on the network connection on your device. Build and run. Your posts will appear on the home screen.

The screen with all saved posts.

Now, disconnect your mobile phone from the network, close the app and kill the app process from the **Recent apps** menu. Run your app again. You'll see the posts appearing on the home screen again. Nice job!

Writing data when offline

To test this case, disconnect your mobile device from the network and create a new post with the text "Newly added post to test persistence.". You'll see that the post appears on the home screen.

The post is added offline.

Then, open **the Firebase console** and check if your post is saved to the database. You'll notice that the post isn't there since you are offline and there is no connection to the database. But where is the post stored then?

The post isn't added to the database.

Now, connect your mobile phone to the network and observe the database data in the console. You'll see that a few moments after you connect your app back to the Internet your post appears in the database.

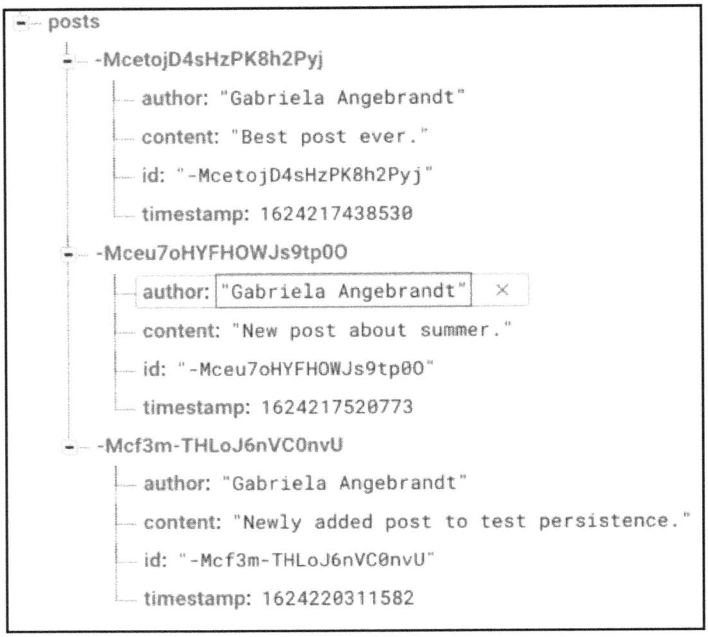

The post is visible in the database.

Setting the argument of `setPersistenceEnabled()` to `true` also keeps track of all the writes you initiated while you were offline and then when the network connection comes back, it resends all the write operations. This makes the user experience optimal even if the user loses the network connection for a moment because your app works as if it's connected to the Internet. After all, it uses local data from the disk for synchronization.

Enabling persistence also ensures any data or changes made while offline are kept even across phone restarts. All operations are queued and sent to the Firebase Realtime Database server once the app has a connection.

Keeping data in sync

Realtime Database stores a copy of the data, locally, only for active listeners. To understand this, delete your app's data by going to your device's **Settings ▶ Apps & notifications ▶ WhatsUp ▶ Storage** and press **Clear Storage**.

Make sure you're connected to the Internet and the posts are visible on the home screen. Then, disconnect the device from the Internet and open any post that you know has comments. You'll notice that there are no comments displayed even if you instructed the app to store data locally. Since Realtime Database stores data locally only for active listeners, your comments weren't saved because you haven't accessed them yet.

Don't worry, you'll fix this issue in a few moments.

Open **RealtimeDatabaseManager.kt** and remove `private` modifier from `COMMENTS_REFERENCE`. Your constant now looks like this:

```
const val COMMENTS_REFERENCE = "comments"
```

To save data locally for the location that has no active listeners attached, open **WhatsUpApplication.kt** , find `onCreate()` and change calls on the database instance to include `keepSynced()`:

```
FirebaseDatabase.getInstance().apply {
    setPersistenceEnabled(true)
    getReference(COMMENTS_REFERENCE).keepSynced(true)
}
```

Now, Realtime Database will download the comments and keep them in sync, even if there are no active listeners at that location. Whatever happens at this location — either data gets deleted or updated, you'll receive an update locally, as well.

Build and run. Connect your mobile device to the network, and after posts are loaded, disconnect your app from the network. Now open any post that you know has comments. You'll see your comments this time.

The post presenting comments when offline.

Default cache size is **10MB**, which allows you to store a substantial amount of data locally, and, in most cases, this should be enough. If you exceed that limit, any data that hasn't been used for a long time will be deleted. So it's an LRU cache kind of mechanism.

However, in a multi-user app, there is a huge chance of reaching race conditions. For example, if two users aren't connected to the Internet, and both create a post, one later than the other, and if they finally connect to the Internet at the same time, whichever user has a better and faster connection will write to the database first. After that, the other user can overwrite existing data in the database. This is important to know because, usually, this isn't the desired behavior.

Querying Offline Data

With persistence enabled, Firebase Realtime Database stores result from queries done when the app doesn't have an active network connection. The queries are done on data that has been previously loaded. It firsts loads data from the cache. Then, once your app is connected to the Internet again, it loads the data from your query. A query can return some items while offline. Then when online, more items will be added to your query results.

Other offline scenarios and network connectivity features

Firebase has many features that can help you when in offline mode and connectivity are an important part of your app. The features you're about to learn apply to your app regardless if the local offline persistence is enabled or not.

Real-time presence system

The **real-time presence** system allows your app to know the status of your users — are they **online**, **offline**, **away**, or some other status. This feature is inevitable for chat applications for example, because you want to know if the person you're texting is online. This feature may seem simple, but to build an entire app infrastructure or a mechanism, which handles this for you, can be quite troublesome.

Firebase has this infrastructure implemented and it allows you to use it out of the box. Firebase saves the user presence status info to the **/.info/connected** location that you can observe just like any other location in the database. The **.info/connected** reference just contains a `boolean` which indicates if the client is connected or not. The problem appears if you want to write something to the database when the user status changes to the offline status. For this case, you can use `onDisconnect()` from Firebase. This method tells the Firebase server to do something when it notices that the client isn't online anymore. It works properly, even in cases when the app crashes or the connection is lost, or any other nasty edge case.

On Android, Firebase automatically manages the connection state to **optimize battery usage** and **reduce bandwidth**. If the client app doesn't have any connection to the database, no active listeners, no pending requests, or similar, Firebase will automatically close the connection after **60 seconds** of inactivity. Alternatively, you can explicitly close the connection by using `goOffline()`.

To learn more about the presence feature, check the official documentation (https://firebase.google.com/docs/database/android/offline-capabilities#section-presence).

Latency

Generally speaking, **latency** is the time delay between the cause and the effect of some change. In Realtime Database that would be, for example, when the user triggers disconnecting from the server until the disconnecting action is done, or the delay between requesting a login entry, to an actual authorization response.

Firebase handles latency in a way that it stores a timestamp that is generated on the server as data in a value called `TIMESTAMP`. The timestamp is a static field in the `ServerValue` class and you access it by calling `ServerValue.TIMESTAMP`. You can use it to reliably know the exact time when the action actually finishes.

Key points

- Realtime Database allows you to enable **disk persistence** to make your data available when you're **offline**.
- Enabling disk persistence also tracks **all the writes you initiated** while you were offline and then when the network connection comes back it **synchronizes** all the write operations.
- Realtime Database stores a copy of the data, locally, only for active listeners. You can use `keepSynced()` on a database reference to save data locally for the location that has no active listeners attached.
- You can be able to **query** data that is available offline. Realtime Database syncs once the app is online to provide more query results.
- Firebase provides you with a **real-time presence** system, which allows your app to know the status of your users, are they **online** or **offline**.
- Firebase handles **latency** in a way that stores a **timestamp**, that is generated on the server, as data when the client disconnects and lets you use that data to reliably know the exact time when the user disconnected.

Where to go from here?

In this chapter, you learned how Firebase works offline and what features it provides to help you handle offline mode and connectivity issues. You also improved your app's **user experience** in a way that you enabled your app to work as expected even if the user is not connected to the Internet.

For more info and examples on enabling offline capabilities, visit the official documentation (https://firebase.google.com/docs/database/android/offline-capabilities).

Chapter 16: "Usage & Performance" is the last chapter about Realtime Database and it will teach you more about its performance and limits.

Chapter 16: Usage & Performance

By Harun Wangereka

In the previous chapters, you learned how to work with the Firebase Realtime Database. Realtime Database is built to handle high-traffic apps. To work effectively with Realtime Database, you have to be aware of its usage and performance limits. This chapter covers just that.

In this chapter, you'll cover the Realtime Database pricing model, general Realtime Database limits, reading and writing limitations and performance. You'll learn how to measure and optimize performance and how to profile your database.

Pricing model

Realtime Database is **free** — but that's only true up to a certain point. Visit the Firebase pricing page (https://firebase.google.com/pricing), and notice the text - "Start for free, then pay as you go.". Firebase is designed to work for free for smaller startups or experimental projects, like the one you'll build in this section. However, Firebase offers additional pricing plans too.

The Spark Plan is free and exists so that everyone can experiment and get their hands on Firebase, integrate it into their apps and see how it performs. The majority of the money that Firebase makes comes from big apps with lots of users. All of the products that Firebase has are included in all the plans that they offer. This means that you can try out any product you want for free.

When it comes to Realtime Database, the metrics that Firebase uses to decide how much to bill you for their services are:

1. Simultaneous connections: You can have up to 100 simultaneous connections for free. This limit can't be raised.
2. Data storage: You can store 1GB of data for free. Data in this context is text data and 1GB of text data is an enormous amount.
3. Downloaded data: You can download 10GB of data per month for free from Realtime Database.
4. Databases per project: You're not allowed to have multiple databases per project for free.

For more information about Firebase billing and how to optimize Realtime Database usage, check out the official Firebase billing guidelines (https://firebase.google.com/docs/database/usage/billing).

Limitations

As mentioned earlier in this chapter, Realtime Database is built to handle high-traffic apps, but it still has some limits. You'll examine some of those limits next. In general, all of them apply to Realtime Database, not for the free plans alone.

Realtime Database allows you to have 100 simultaneous connections for free, but 100,000 simultaneous connections in a paid plan. This doesn't mean that your app can't have 100,000 maximum users because not all of your users are connected at once. Simultaneous connections are devices or other clients *currently* connected to the database.

A single database can approximately send 100,000 responses per second. Responses are anything that comes from the database, like reading operations, or broadcast.

When writing to Realtime Database, the maximum size of a single write event is 1MB. That write event includes already existing data at the location that you're writing to plus the new data.

When it comes to the data in Realtime Database, the data is stored as a JSON tree, as you learned previously. The maximum number of child nodes must be less than 32 levels deep, the maximum length of the UTF-8 encoded key is 768 Bytes and the maximum size of the UTF-8 encoded string is 10MB.

Reading and writing operations are also limited. The size of the data stored in the database at a single location should be less than 256MB for a single-read operation. If you want to perform a read operation at a larger location, consider using data pagination with a query, shallow queries or backing up the data. The maximum time to run a single query is 15 minutes. The total number of cumulative **nodes** in a path that you want to listen to or query needs to be less than 75 million.

Realtime Database can handle 64MB per minute through simultaneous write operations on the database. The maximum size of a single write request is 16MB if you're writing through the SDK and 256MB if you're writing from the REST API.

To avoid those limits and scale your Realtime Database data, you can have your data divided across multiple Realtime Database instances. Since the limits mentioned above only apply to a single Realtime Database instance, this is a way to avoid them. Having multiple database instances also allows you to balance server load and improve performance. This concept is known as **database sharding**.

To learn more about Realtime Database limitations, visit the official Firebase documentation (https://firebase.google.com/docs/database/usage/limits). Learn more about scaling on the sharding page (https://firebase.google.com/docs/database/usage/sharding).

Performance

Monitoring

Realtime Database offers several ways to monitor database performance and find the source of eventual problems in your app. It offers the following tools that provide insight into performance data:

1. Realtime Database Profiler tool.
2. Firebase Console.
3. Cloud Monitoring.

You'll look into these tools next.

Realtime Database Profiler

One of the tools that Firebase provides is the **Realtime Database profiler tool**. This tool gives you an overview of reading and writing operations on the database in real-time, which includes information about the speed and operation payload size. The information doesn't have any historical data, so don't use it to estimate billing.

Firebase Console

Firebase console can also be a helpful debugging tool. The **usage** tab in the console gives you data about storage, bandwidth and simultaneous connections.

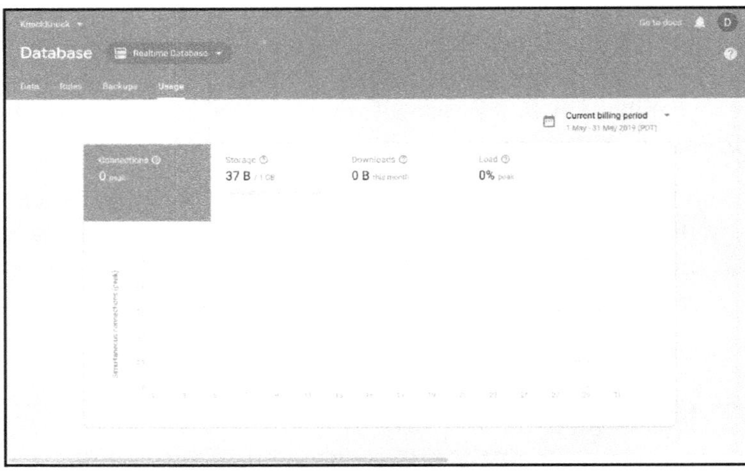

Console usages section

Cloud Monitoring

Firebase also offers Cloud monitoring. This has a granular approach to performance monitoring. It allows you to use the Metrics Explorer to see the individual performance, create diverse chart dashboards that display several combinations of performance metrics. It gives you ability to monitor your billed usage if you're on the paid plan, and also contains useful metrics to monitor performance.

With cloud monitoring, you can create alerts when your Database metrics meet a certain threshold. This is very helpful as you'll receive the alerts on your email as per your metric threshold settings.

To learn more about performance monitoring tools, check out the official page (https://firebase.google.com/docs/database/usage/monitor-performance).

Profiling

Database profiling is critical for finding bottlenecks or other issues that might be degrading the user experience. The Firebase command-line interface offers a variety of tools. One of these, the **Database Profiling** tool, analyzes the activity in the database over a specific period and generates a detailed report that you can use to troubleshoot the database performance.

The profiling results are split into three main categories: **speed**, **bandwidth** and **unindexed queries**. The speed category contains data about reading, writing and broadcast speed. The bandwidth category profiles database data consumption across incoming and outgoing operations. Finally, the unindexed queries category contains data about unindexed queries since those queries can be expensive.

Optimizing

The best way to optimize performance is to gather all of the data from the tools mentioned above. After you have gathered the data find out about best practices in the area that you want to improve and make changes accordingly.

Other ways of optimizing performance are, already mentioned, sharing data across multiple database instances and the following:

- Build efficient data structures.
- Index your queries.
- Reuse SSL sessions.
- Prevent unauthorized access.
- Limit download by use of query-based rules.
- Optimize connections.
- Remove unused or duplicate data.
- Ship scalable and easy to update code.
- Improve listener efficiency.

The method you choose to optimize performance is entirely dependent on the results you get from the data gathered. With the data, you can check on the best practices for each metric.

To learn more about optimizing database performance, check out the official documentation on optimization (https://firebase.google.com/docs/database/usage/optimize).

Key points

- Realtime Database is free up to a certain point.
- Realtime Database is built to handle high-traffic apps but it has some limits.
- Firebase provides you with tools that allow you to monitor, profile and optimize Realtime Database usage and performance.

Where to go from here?

In this chapter, you covered the usage and performance aspects of Realtime Database, which are critical to know for large-scale apps.

This chapter wraps up the Realtime Database part of this section. This is a good place to pause and revisit what you learned so far. Also, try to play with Realtime Database and check the official documentation to continue learning about what it can offer you as you build your apps.

In the coming chapters, you'll learn about **Cloud Firestore**, which is another Firebase product that's similar to Realtime Database.

Chapter 17: Introduction to Cloud Firestore

By Harun Wangereka

In the previous chapters, you learned how to use Realtime Database for storing data in the cloud. Firebase offers another product that you can use for storing data in the cloud: **Cloud Firestore**.

Cloud Firestore has a similar feature set as Realtime Database. It allows you to store data in the cloud and sync data across devices. It is designed to overcome all the drawbacks of Realtime Database — and it also stores data within a single JSON document.

In this chapter, you'll learn how to use Cloud Firestore and get familiar with the differences between Realtime Database and Cloud Firestore. More importantly, you'll learn how to determine when it's appropriate to use one over the other.

What is Cloud Firestore?

Cloud Firestore is a NoSQL database similar to Realtime Database. It stores data in a structure that looks like a tree, but where data is stored as documents.

Documents and **collections** are the primary building blocks of Cloud Firestore. It's helpful to think of documents as files. These files consist of key-value pairs known as **fields** — this is similar to how models work. The values can be anything - strings, numbers, binary data, or even nested objects in a map format that resembles a JSON object. Collections, on the other hand, are simply groups of documents.

When working with Cloud Firestore, there are a few rules to keep in mind:

- Collections can only contain documents. For example, you can't add a `String` object to the collection.
- Documents can't contain other documents; however, they can point to subcollections. For example, your collections can contain many documents, and those documents can point to other collections. This is how things are formatted in a tree-like structure.
- The root of the Cloud Firestore database can only contain collections.

For example, in the **WhatsUp** app you created earlier, you could have a *Posts* collection that contains a document for each post. Each document would point to a *Comments* collection that contains comments for that post, and the document that contains the comments would point to another collection, and so on.

When you worked with Realtime Database, you learned that you should avoid these deeply nested hierarchy structures. In Cloud Firestore, however, these deeply nested structures are typical because the queries are shallow, meaning that querying data from a document will get you *only* that document; you don't have to query the entire collection or the subcollections within the document. This also means that queries are more efficient and flexible than in a Realtime Database, especially when it comes to filtering and sorting the data.

With the **WhatsUp** app running with Cloud Firestore, you could have a collection of posts and any other collections you need to represent the data.

Cloud Firestore vs. Realtime database

Due to the similarity between Realtime Database and Firestore, you may be wondering how they're different. Both of these products offer a cloud-based database solution with real-time data syncing for mobile clients, so what gives?

You can think of Cloud Firestore as an **improved** version of Realtime Database because it's designed to overcome the drawbacks of the Realtime Database with things like **scaling**, **data structuring** and **querying**. Since Realtime Database stores data as one big JSON tree, it's challenging to organize and scale complex data.

Firestore has a new and intuitive data model. It handles complex data using subcollections within documents. Because of how it stores documents and data, Firestore has faster queries than Realtime Database, and it supports indexed queries with **compound sorting and filtering**. Additionally, in Realtime Database, you can't sort and filter the data in the same query. When you query the data, the result is the whole subtree. Firestore allows all kinds of query chaining that NoSQL databases allow. Instead of querying entire collections or a document, you can query subcollections within a document. Furthermore, in Realtime Database, you need to perform write operations in a single query; in Firestore, you can collect all of your data and write it as a batch operation. This means that it executes one large job in small parts to improve efficiency.

Firestore has a lot of advanced features too. Both Realtime Database and Firestore offer offline support; however, Realtime Database offers it only for mobile clients, while Firestore offers it for web apps as well.

With Realtime Database, you need callbacks for transactions. With Firestore, you don't. Transactions complete automatically when all of them are finished.

Scalability in Realtime Database isn't that big of a problem, but when the data exceeds the limits you learned about in Chapter 16, "Usage & Performance", you needed to shred your data across multiple database instances. In Firestore, you won't need to do that regardless of how big your database will be — it handles **database scaling** for you. This is a considerable improvement for large-scale projects.

Firestore also has support for complex queries when the user is offline. Realtime Database only offers support for simple queries of local data.

Like Realtime Database, Firestore is free, up to a certain point; you need to pay for your database to scale. Firestore charges based on the reading and write operations that you're performing on the database.

Because of the improvements that the Firestore offers compared to the Realtime Database, Firebase recommends using the Firestore for all new projects.

Cloud Firestore Data Structure

In this chapter, you learned that Firestore is a **NoSQL database**, meaning there is no SQL. But if there's no SQL, you can't build queries that will take one piece of data from one part of the database, and another piece of data from another part of the database, and merge them. In Firestore, to get data from two different parts of the database, you must make two different requests. If you run into that scenario, you likely need to re-structure your data in a way that you'll always be able to get what you need in **one request**.

You also learned that Firestore Database consists of collections and documents. Take the **WhatsUp** app, for example. While it's possible to have a *Posts* collection that contains individual posts as documents, **WhatsUp** has the feature where every post can contain comments. Maybe you can make it so that every post document contains a *Comments* subcollection, and that that collection contains comments for that post. With that setup, you could easily fetch the post and the comments in a single call. However, that's not how you want to do that.

When you think about it, you don't need to know about the post comments until the user opens the post by tapping on it. It's only when the post details screen appears that you need the comments. In this case, a better approach is to have a *Comments* collection stored as a separate collection rather than as a subcollection. You can then put the **post id** to the individual comment, so you'll know to which post the comment belongs. Finally, when fetching comments, you can filter them by the post id and get all of the comments that belong to a specific post.

There is one drawback to this approach, however, and that is data duplication. Every comment has an author so you'll likely want to know who wrote the comment. In **WhatsUp** this isn't the case, but in other apps, you could have another collection of users, and then the comment would need to contain the user data.

By doing that, not only do you fill the database with duplicate user data objects in each of the comments but also if the user chooses to change the data, you'll need to update all of the comments, as well. So, perhaps a better approach is to store the author id in the comment; then, when you need to get the user data, you can filter out the independent *Users* collection using the available id.

One significant advantage of the NoSQL database is that it can distribute data across **multiple machines** easily. In relational databases, when you have an app that's becoming more popular and needs more storage space, you'd need a more powerful and bigger machine. This is known as **vertical scaling**.

In many NoSQL databases, including Firestore, when you need more storage, Firestore spreads your data across many servers. This is known as **horizontal scaling**, and it's much easier to scale horizontally than vertically. Why? Because it's much easier to get many moderately powerful machines than to continually upgrade a single machine to handle everything. Machines have their limits too, you know!

Collections and Documents

You learned that Realtime Database stores data as one large JSON tree that contains keys and values. You also learned that these values can be objects containing other key-value pairs. Firestore is a collection of objects that are stored in a hierarchical structure that resemble a tree. Every object in a collection is represented as a document. The document consists of key-value pairs known as **fields** in Firestore. These values can be strings, numbers, binary data, or nested objects in a map format. The limitation, however, is that the document size must be less than 1MB.

In simple terms, collections are nothing more than a group of documents. A document can't contain other documents, but it can contain another collection known as **subcollection**. Collections are containers for documents. A collection can only contain documents. It can't directly contain raw fields with values, and it can't contain other collections. The document names within a collection are unique.

The general hierarchy in Firestore is usually collections first, then documents. A document can have a subcollection. Inside a subcollection you have documents and you can have subcollections too. This allows you to nest more data. The nesting limit is **100 levels** deep. Subcollections enable you to structure data hierarchically, making data easier to access. Your collections and documents should follow this hierarchy.

Cloud Firestore supports many data types. To learn more about them, visit the official documentation: https://firebase.google.com/docs/firestore/manage-data/data-types.

References

Firestore identifies each document by its location in the database. A **reference** is a lightweight object pointing to a location in your database. A reference doesn't perform any network operation. You can create a reference to a location even if it doesn't have any data. You can create references for your collections and documents. Collection reference and document reference are different types of references. This means the operations on each reference also differ.

Key points

- Cloud Firestore is a NoSQL database similar to Realtime Database.
- Firestore stores data as a **collection** of **objects** which are stored in a **hierarchical structure** that resemble a tree.
- Documents and collections are the main building blocks of Cloud Firestore.
- Documents consist of **key-value pairs** known as fields.
- Collections are a group of documents.
- Collections can only contain documents.
- The root of the Cloud Firestore database can only consist of collections.
- A document can't contain other documents, but it can contain another collection; these are known as subcollections.
- It's easier to query, filter and sort data using Firestore since it can all be done within a single request.
- It's best to use foreign-key-like fields in objects, as you don't want to duplicate data and clutter the database.
- Firestore scales horizontally; this is easier than Realtime Database which scales vertically.
- A reference is a lightweight object that points to the location of a collection or document.

Where to go from here?

In this chapter, you learned the basics of Cloud Firestore. You learned what Firestore is, the differences between Firestore and Realtime Database, and how Firestore structures the data. You still have a lot to cover, so be sure to visit the official documentation (https://firebase.google.com/docs/firestore) to understand the specifics of Cloud Firestore better.

In the next chapter, you'll learn how to manage Firestore data using Firebase Console and how to add and delete data from the database.

Chapter 18: Managing Data with Cloud Firestore

By Harun Wangereka

In the previous chapter, you learned the basics of Cloud Firestore. You learned what Firestore is, how it differs from Realtime Database and how it structures its data. In this chapter, you'll integrate Firestore into the app. You'll refactor the current **WhatsUp** app to use Firestore as the backend. The functionality of **WhatsUp** will remain the same.

In the process, you'll learn how to add data to Firestore, how to update and delete data, and how to use Firebase Console to manage Firestore data.

Getting started

You need to set up Firestore before you can start using it. If you followed along with Realtime Database chapters, you have already created the project in the Firebase console. If you didn't, go back to Chapter 12: "Firebase Overview" and Chapter 13: "Introduction to Firebase Realtime Database" to see how to create the project in the console and how to connect your app with Firebase.

Creating the Database

Open your **WhatsUp** project in the Firebase console. Select **Firestore Database** from the menu on the left.

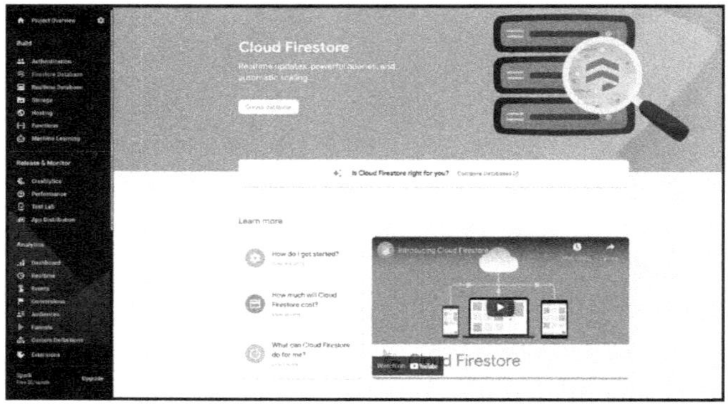

Firestore Landing Page

Tap **Create database** in the Cloud Firestore section at the top of the page. Next, you'll see the dialog with security rules. Firestore offers two security modes for you:

- **Test mode** will allow anyone to have read and write access to the database for a period of 30 days. You can adjust the date to the one you'd want.
- **Production mode** will deny all reads and writes to the database.

Choose the test mode for now. You'll learn more about the security of Cloud Firestore in "Chapter 20: Securing Data in Cloud Firestore".

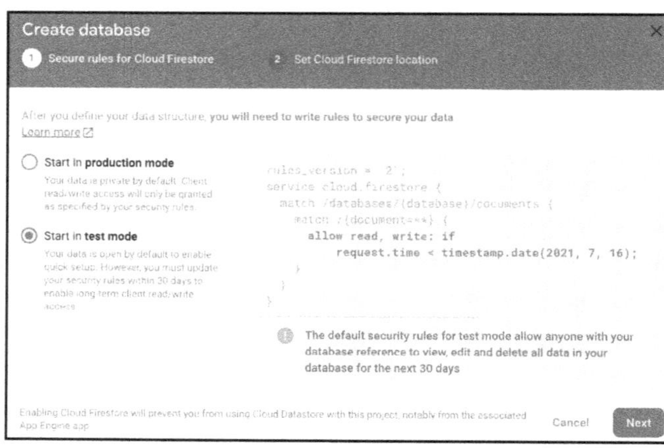

Firestore Security Rules

Tap **Next** to go to the next step of creating your database. You'll see the screen for setting your Cloud Firestore location.

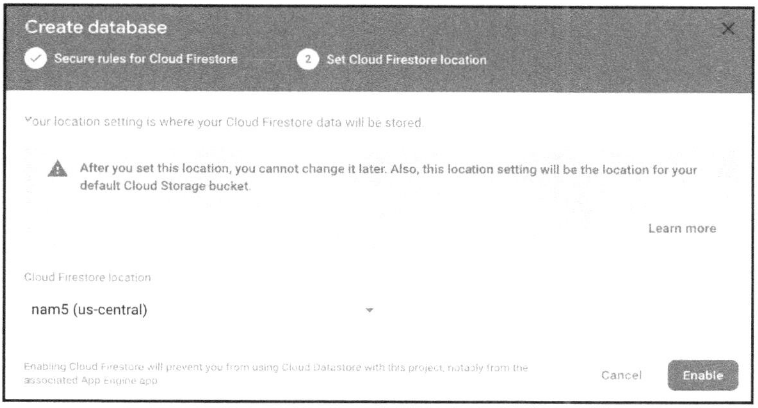

Firestore Location

Firestore allows you to set the location where it stores data. In the drop-down widget, choose either a multi-region or a single region from the available list of regions.

Tap **Enable**. You'll see your database on the screen after Firebase finishes creating it.

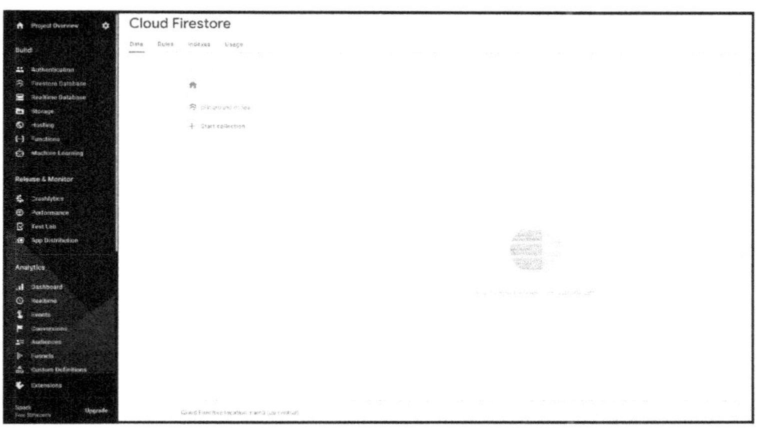

Firestore Database

Configuring your Application

You've created the database in the console. Now you need to configure your app so it can communicate with the database.

> **Note**: This chapter provides **starter** and **final** projects that you can use to follow along. To use these projects, you need to configure them first by creating a project in the Firebase and by adding the **google-services.json** configuration file to the project. Take a look at Chapter 12: "Firebase Overview" and Chapter 13: "Introduction to Firebase Realtime Database." to see how to do that.

Open the **starter** project for this chapter.

First, you need to add a Firestore client library for Android to the project. Open **build.gradle** and add the following dependency at the end of the `dependencies` block:

```
implementation 'com.google.firebase:firebase-firestore:23.0.2'
```

After adding this dependency, sync a Gradle. Click **Sync Now** in the notification shown after changing the file.

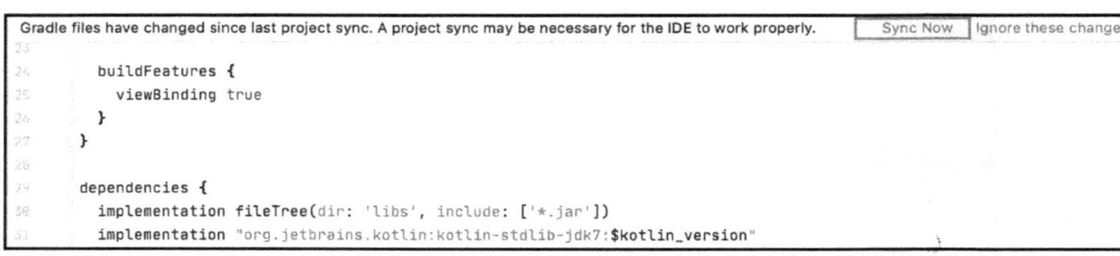

Build gradle notification.

The second thing you need to do is to initialize the Firestore instance. Navigate to **CloudFirestoreManager.kt** inside **firebase/firestore** package. Add a `database` field as a top-level variable below the `commentsValues` variable:

```
private val database = FirebaseFirestore.getInstance()
```

Resolve the import errors when the IDE prompts you. Here, you're getting a Firestore instance from`FirebaseFirestore`. You'll use it for all the communication with Firestore Database from the application.

With this setup, you're now ready to start writing and reading data from Firestore.

Writing Data

To learn how to use Firestore, you'll refactor the existing Whatsup app. The first part ready for refactoring is writing. Instead of writing data to Realtime Database, you'll write the data to Cloud Firestore.

In **CloudFirestoreManager.kt**, replace `TODO` inside `addPost()` with the following:

```
// 1
val documentReference =
database.collection(POSTS_COLLECTION).document()
// 2
val post = HashMap<String, Any>()
// 3
post[AUTHOR_KEY] = authenticationManager.getCurrentUser()
post[CONTENT_KEY] = content
post[TIMESTAMP_KEY] = getCurrentTime()
post[ID_KEY] = documentReference.id
// 4
documentReference
  .set(post)
  .addOnSuccessListener { onSuccessAction() }
  .addOnFailureListener { onFailureAction() }
```

In the code above:

1. First, you call `collection()` passing in the posts collection path stored in the `POSTS_COLLECTION` constant. As a result, the method returns a reference to the collection at the specified path in the database. Then, you use that collection reference to get the document reference by calling `document()`. This method points to the new document within that collection with an auto-generated ID. You'll use that document reference to get the document ID that you'll store in the database with the post object.

2. Here, you create data that you want to save to the document. You represent this data as a map where `String` is the type of the key and `Any` is the type of the value.

3. You need to populate the map with the values that you want to write to the database - you add author, post content, timestamp and the ID of the document.

4. The last part is saving the data. First, you call `set()` on the document reference. It will replace the data in the document if it already exists or it will create it if it doesn't. You pass in the map that contains the data that you want to write to that document. `set()` is an asynchronous operation and, once ready, it returns a `Task` object. Since the operation is asynchronous, you attach two listeners. One is `OnSuccessListener()` is called if the `Task` completes successfully, and `OnFailureListener()` is called if the operation fails. You pass in the actions that the system invokes depending on the result of the operation.

Open **AddPostActivity.kt**, find `addPostIfNotEmpty()` and replace `TODO` inside the `if` block with:

```
cloudFirestoreManager.addPost(postMessage, ::onPostAddSuccess, :
:onPostAddFailed)
```

Here, you're calling previously added code in `addPost()` on the `cloudFirestoreManager` instance. You also pass the message you want to add, and success and failure methods.

Build and run. Sign in if necessary. Tap the floating action button at the bottom right corner. Add some text and tap **Post**.

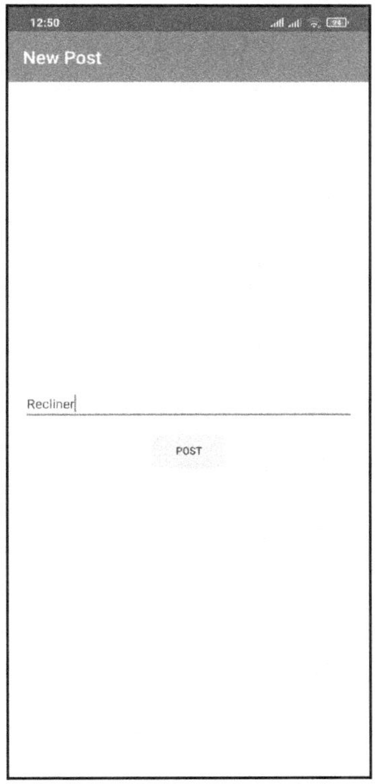

First Firestore Post.

You'll get a `Toast` message that says that the post is saved successfully. The home screen displays nothing.

That is because you haven't implemented the logic for reading yet.

Open the database in the console. You'll see your post there. If you don't see it try to refresh the page.

Posts on Firestore Collections.

Congratulations, you saved your first post to the Firestore database! From the screenshot, you have a **posts** collection that has a single document. The document has **author**, **content**, **id** and **timestamp** fields. Most likely, yours will have different content.

For cases where you only need to write small chunks of data, this is the approach you'll be using. In the next section, you'll be looking at using **transactions** to write a bunch of data at the same time.

Transactions

Firestore supports another way of writing data, **transactions**. Firestore has transactions for cases when you want to write a bunch of data to the database at once. While the transaction is executing, the user won't be able to read that partially changed state. If one of the operations that are in execution in a transaction fails, none of them will be applied because that could potentially leave the database in an inconsistent and undesired state. Firestore applies either all or none. One transaction operation can write to 500 documents maximally.

There is another type of transaction called **batched write**. Batched write allows you to perform a bunch of writes all at once, in other words, in a batch. It works in a way that you specify what you want to change and tell the SDK to change it. You don't have to worry about what happens if the operation fails halfway through. None of the changes will be applied in that case. Also, another user won't be able to change that same data that you are currently changing because those write operations are **atomic** which means that the operation is guaranteed to be isolated from other operations that may be happening at the same time. Batch operation is also much more efficient than doing many individual write operations. A good use case for batch write is when you want to change many related documents and your new value does not depend on the old value.

To learn more about transactions and batched writes check out the official documentation: https://firebase.google.com/docs/firestore/manage-data/transactions.

Updating Data

Next, you'll add an update feature to your app. You'll see that it's very similar to what you did when adding new data. Open **CloudFirestoreManager.kt** , look for `updatePostContent()` and replace `TODO` inside it with the following:

```
// 1
val updatedPost = HashMap<String, Any>()
// 2
updatedPost[CONTENT_KEY] = content
// 3
database.collection(POSTS_COLLECTION)
  .document(key)
  .update(updatedPost)
  .addOnSuccessListener { onSuccessAction() }
  .addOnFailureListener { onFailureAction() }
```

Here's what you're doing:

1. You create a map of data that you want to save to the database. This is similar to how you create new data.
2. You specify the data that you are updating. In this case, this is only the post content.
3. Finally, you get the reference to the posts collection. From there you get the reference to the document that you're updating by specifying a key. You then call `update()` on a document reference which updates fields in the document. The listener logic stays the same as in the case of writing new data.

Open **PostDetailsActivity.kt**, find `initializeClickListener()` and replace `TODO` in the `updatePostButton` on-click listener with:

```
cloudFirestoreManager.updatePostContent(
  post.id,
  postDetailsBinding.postText.text.toString().trim(),
  ::onPostSuccessfullyUpdated,
  ::onPostUpdateFailed
  )
```

In this code, you're calling your `updatePostContent()` and passing the `id` of the post you want to update. You're also passing the new message that you've added and finally, you pass your success and failure action methods. When you tap `UPDATE POST` it will update the database with the updated content.

Now you can update posts in the database as well. You'll be able to test this functionality when you put in place reading logic in "Chapter 19: Reading Data from Cloud Firestore".

Deleting Data

One last bit of functionality that you'll add in this chapter is post deleting. Open **CloudFirestoreManager.kt**, replace `TODO` inside `deletePost()` with the following:

```
database.collection(POSTS_COLLECTION)
  .document(key)
  .delete()
  .addOnSuccessListener { onSuccessAction() }
  .addOnFailureListener { onFailureAction() }
```

To delete a post, you first get a reference to the collection of the post by calling `collection()` on a database instance and passing in the path to the posts collection. Then you get a reference to the specific post document that you want to delete by passing in the key which is the ID of the post. Finally, you call `delete()` on a document reference which deletes the document referred to by the reference. This method deletes data asynchronously, so you also attach the listeners that get triggered when the deleting succeeds or fails.

Now, open **PostDetailsActivity.kt** and inside `initializeClickListener()` replace `TODO` of the `deletePostButton` on-click listener with the following:

```
cloudFirestoreManager.deletePost(post.id, ::onPostSuccessfullyDe
leted, ::onPostDeleteFailed)
```

Here, you make a call to your `deletePost()` which you've updated. You pass the `id` of the post you want to delete. Now, when you open post details you can delete a post by tapping `DELETE`. You'll also test this functionality when you implement reading logic in "Chapter 19: Reading Data from Cloud Firestore".

One important thing to mention here is when you delete a post document, if that document contained a subcollection, that subcollection wouldn't be deleted. When you delete a document only that document is deleted; Firestore doesn't delete the documents inside the subcollections.

Firebase Console

You can do all operations you implemented in this chapter, like adding data, updating and deleting, manually in the Firebase console.

Open **Firebase Console** in the browser and navigate to **Firestore Database**.

From here, you can view your database data. You can click on any collection to see the documents within that collection, and you can click on any document to see the details of that document.

You'll also notice a menu icon in every column title cell. Click on one of them. Then, you'll see the options to delete a document or a specific field of the document.

Documents Options Menu

You can also filter the documents inside the collection by clicking the filter button.

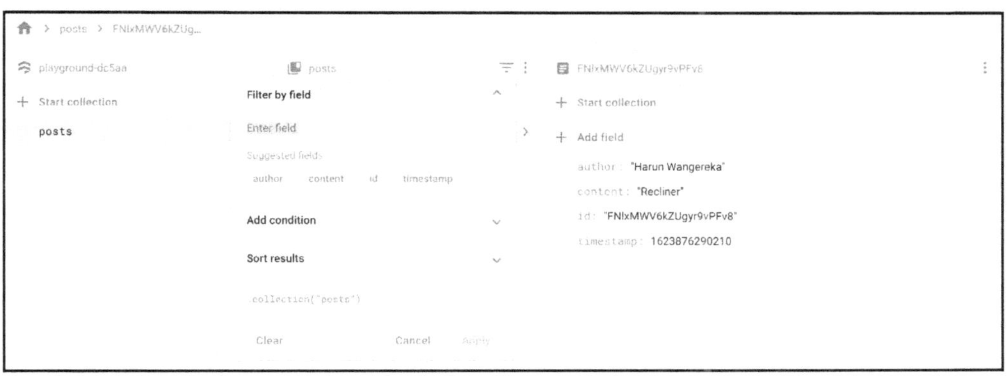

Filter Collections Data.

Visit the official documentation, https://firebase.google.com/docs/firestore/using-console, to explore more possibilities of the console.

Key points

- You can create a Firestore **database** in the Firebase console.
- You need to add a Firestore client **library** for Android to the project to use Firestore APIs.
- You need to initialize a Firestore instance to communicate with the database.
- You call `collection()` passing in the collection path to get a reference to the collection at the specified path in the database.
- You need to create and populate the map of data that you want to save to the database.
- You call `set()` on the document reference that will replace the data in the document if it already exists or it will create it if it doesn't to save the data to the database. You pass in the map that contains the data that you want to write to that document.
- Firebase supports **transactions** that you use in cases when you want to write a bunch of data to the database at once.
- You call `update()` on a document reference to update fields in the document.
- You call `delete()` on a document reference which deletes the document referred to by the reference.
- Adding, updating and deleting operations are **asynchronous**.
- You can use the console to manage data in the database.

Where to go from here?

You've implemented adding, updating, and deleting functionalities in this chapter and you saw how you can use the Firebase console to achieve that. You can visit the official documentation, https://firebase.google.com/docs/firestore/manage-data/add-data, to learn more about these operations.

You still don't have a way to test these functionalities. In "Chapter 19: Reading Data from Cloud Firestore" you'll add the ability to listen for data updates in real-time. You'll also learn how to read data from the database and do other data operations.

Chapter 19: Reading Data from Cloud Firestore

By Harun Wangereka

In the previous chapter, you learned how to write data to Firestore, and how to update or delete data from Firestore by implementing that functionality in the **WhatsUp** app. You also became familiar with the Firebase console and learned how to use it for managing data.

In this chapter, you'll continue working on your app. Since now you still don't have any data on the home screen when you run the app, you'll focus on implementing reading logic. In the process, you'll learn how to read data from Firestore, how to listen for updates in real-time, and how queries work.

Setting up Firebase

If you skipped previous chapters, you need to set up Firebase to follow along. Do the following steps:

1. Create a project in the Firebase console.
2. Enable Google sign-in.
3. Set security rules to the test mode to allow everyone **read** and **write** access.
4. Add **google-service.json** to both **starter** and **final** projects.

To see how to do this, go back to Chapter 12: "Firebase Overview" and Chapter 13: "Introduction to Firebase Realtime Database."

Be sure to use the starter project from **this chapter**, by opening the **reading-data-from-cloud-firestore** folder and its **starter** project from the **projects** folder, rather than continuing with the final project you previously worked on. It has a few things added to it, including placeholders for the code to add in this chapter.

Reading Data

Like the Realtime Database, Firestore allows to read data once or to listen for data changes in real-time.

To get the data once, you need to call `get()` on the collection reference from which you want to read the data or you can also use `get()` on the document reference, if you need to read data from a specific document. For example, this is how you'd read the data from the `posts` collection:

```
database.collection("posts")
    .get()
    .addOnSuccessListener { result ->
      ...
    }
    .addOnFailureListener { exception ->
      ...
    }
```

Since getting the data is asynchronous, you need to attach a listener that will notify you when the data fetching is complete. It returns the data as a `QuerySnapshot`. `QuerySnapshot` is a class that contains the results of a query and can contain `QueryDocumentSnapshot` objects if they are available. A `QueryDocumentSnapshot` contains data read from a document in your Firestore database. You'll see an example of this shortly.

Since you want your app to always have the latest data, you won't fetch the data only once. Instead, you'll put in place a listener, so you can receive events when the data changes.

Listening for Data Changes

If you don't have the project open by now, make sure to open it, and head over to **CloudFirestoreManager.kt**. Add a `postsRegistration` this field below `commentsValues` variable:

```
private lateinit var postsRegistration: ListenerRegistration
```

Add the IDE import when the IDE prompts you. `ListenerRegistration` represents a subscription of sorts, for a database reference, when you attach a listener to the reference. You'll use it to assign a `posts` listener to it and to remove it when needed, to clean up your code, and to stop receiving changes.

Still inside **CloudFirestoreManager.kt** , navigate to `listenForPostsValueChanges()`. Replace `TODO` inside the function with the following implementation:

```
// 1
postsRegistration = database.collection(POSTS_COLLECTION)
    // 2
    .addSnapshotListener(EventListener { value, error ->
        // 3
        if (error != null || value == null) {
            return@EventListener
        }
        // 4
        if (value.isEmpty) {
            // 5
            postsValues.postValue(emptyList())
        } else {
            // 6
            val posts = ArrayList<Post>()
            // 7
            for (doc in value) {
                // 8
                val post = doc.toObject(Post::class.java)
                posts.add(post)
            }
            // 9
            postsValues.postValue(posts)
        }
    })
```

Here's a breakdown of the code above:

1. You assign the listener to `postsRegistration` variable that you've declared, by attaching an `EventListener` to the database collection. You receive the database collection by calling `database.collection(POSTS_COLLECTION)`.
2. You call `addSnapshotListener()` on the collection reference which starts listening for the data changes at its location.
3. When `onEvent()` is called you first check if an error occurred by checking if the error argument *is not* `null`, or if the value *is* `null`. If it is you'll return from the function since you cannot consume the event.
4. You check if the received data actually contains documents - it isn't empty.
5. You update the `postsValues` with `emptyList()` when the value is empty. Which means no posts are available.

6. If there are values, instantiate an `ArrayList` to store them.
7. Iterate through each document in the value snapshot.
8. Parse each document as a `Post`, and add it to `posts`.
9. Update the `postsValues` with parsed posts.

To resolve the import error add this import for `EventListener` class in your imports

```
import com.google.firebase.firestore.EventListener
```

To read the data, you pass in the listener of type `EventListener` that Firestore calls whenever data changes or if an error occurs. `EventListener` is a generic interface for any type of event listening, and contains only `onEvent(T value, FirebaseFirestoreException error)` that you're required to implement. `onEvent()` will be called with the new value or the error if an error occurred. You get the result data as a `QuerySnapshot` object. This is the easiest way to communicate data changes or errors. Since it's **generic**, it can work for any collection.

Open **HomeActivity.kt** and navigate to `listenForPostsUpdates()`. Replace the `TODO` inside the function with the following:

```
cloudFirestoreManager.onPostsValuesChange()
  .observe(this, Observer(::onPostsUpdate))
```

Here, you register an observer for values on the posts collection. When you receive new data, you'll reflect that by displaying it on the screen.

You also need to remove the listener when you no longer want to receive data change events. To do that, open **CloudFirestoreManager.kt** and navigate to `stopListeningForPostChanges()`. Replace the function code with the following:

```
fun stopListeningForPostChanges() = postsRegistration.remove()
```

Here, you call `remove()` on a `ListenerRegistration` object. This removes the listener from the location that this listener is assigned to.

Now go back to **HomeActivity.kt** and add this code:

```
override fun onStop() {
    super.onStop()
    cloudFirestoreManager.stopListeningForPostChanges()
}
```

Here, you call your `stopListeningForPostChanges()` method. It stops the listener when the activity stops.

Build and run. You should see the posts now on the home screen:

Listening to Firetore Collection.

You can test the real-time updates by deleting the posts from the console. You"ll see the app will instantly reflect the changes.

Performing Queries

Sometimes, you don't want to read only the documents of certain collections. Sometimes you need to filter out, match by values, or simply skip a certain amount of documents. To do this, you use database **queries**. Currently, you don't have any nested documents in the `posts` collection. Up next, you'll add comments to it to make it a bit more complex.

Adding Comments

Open **CloudFirestoreManager.kt**, and navigate to `addComment()`. Replace `TODO` with the following code:

```
// 1
val commentReference =
database.collection(COMMENTS_COLLECTION).document()
// 2
val comment = HashMap<String, Any>()
// 3
comment[AUTHOR_KEY] = authenticationManager.getCurrentUser()
comment[CONTENT_KEY] = content
comment[POST_ID] = postId
comment[TIMESTAMP_KEY] = getCurrentTime()
// 4
commentReference
    .set(comment) // 5
    .addOnSuccessListener { onSuccessAction() } // 6
    .addOnFailureListener { onFailureAction() } // 7
```

To sum it up, here's what happens:

1. Create a new document in Firestore, and store its reference.
2. Create `HashMap<String, Any>`, to store the comment data.
3. Store the data in `comment`.
4. Use `commentReference` to communicate the save operation.
5. Set the reference value to the new comment.
6. In the case of a Success, call `onSuccessAction()`.
7. In case something goes wrong - a Failure occurred, call `onFailureAction()`.

Open **PostDetailsActivity.kt** and find `initializeClickListener()`. Replace `TODO` inside the `addCommentButton` click listener with:

```
cloudFirestoreManager.addComment(
            post.id,
            comment,
            ::onCommentSuccessfullyAdded,
            ::onCommentAddFailed
          )
```

In this code, you call `addComment()` with the comment from `EditText`. You're also passing the `id` of the post and methods to handle success and failure. This will save the comment to the database when you tap **ADD COMMENT**.

Build and run. Tap on any post in the list. Enter some text into the comments `EditText` and tap **ADD COMMENT**:

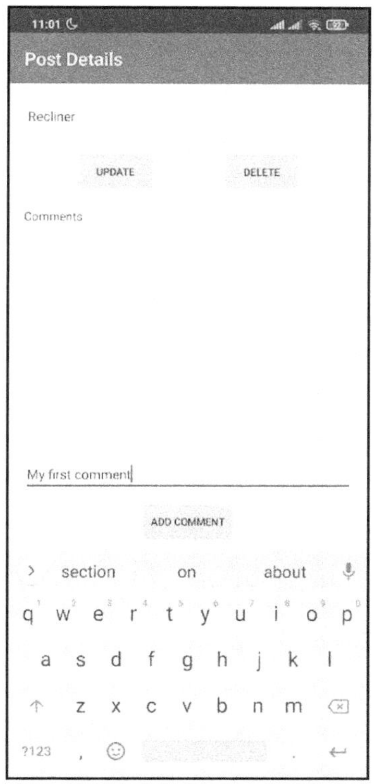

The screen for creating a comment.

Your comment is now saved to the database. Open the database in the console to confirm that. You should see your comment there.

Comments Collection in Firestore Database.

Listening for comments

You can add comments to the database now, but you still can't read them. Since you store comments in a separate collection from posts, to read them you'll need to write a query that returns comments for the specific post. Every comment document has a `post_id` property that indicates to which post the comment belongs.

Open **CloudFirestoreManager.kt**. Add a `commentsRegistration` field below the `postsRegistration` variable:

```
private lateinit var commentsRegistration: ListenerRegistration
```

You'll use this field to assign the comments listener to it and to remove the listener when needed like before.

Next, navigate to `listenForPostCommentsValueChanges()`. Replace `TODO` inside the function with the following:

```
// 1
commentsRegistration = database.collection(COMMENTS_COLLECTION)
    // 2
    .whereEqualTo(POST_ID, postId) // 3
    // 4
    .addSnapshotListener(EventListener { value, error ->
        if (error != null || value == null) {
            return@EventListener
        }
        if (value.isEmpty) {
            postsValues.postValue(emptyList())
        } else {
            val comments = ArrayList<Comment>()
            for (doc in value) {
                val comment = doc.toObject(Comment::class.java)
                comments.add(comment)
            }
            commentsValues.postValue(comments)
        }
    })
```

Here's what you're doing:

1. As before, you assign a listener to the `commentsRegistration` reference.
2. `whereEqualTo()` creates a query that filters the documents in the collection that contain the specified field and value in that field.

3. You pass in two parameters. One is POST_ID, which represents the post_id property in your collection. The second parameter, postId represents the value for comparison. This query will only return the documents that belong to the specified post. whereEqualTo() returns Query that you can read or listen to.

4. Once again, you attach EventListener and parse the comments list, if there are any, updating the UI when you're done.

Next, open **PostDetailsActivity.kt** and navigate to listenForComments(). Replace TODO inside the function with the following:

```
post?.id?.let {postId ->
    cloudFirestoreManager.onCommentsValuesChange(postId)
      .observe(this, Observer(::onCommentsUpdate))
}
```

Add necessary import from the lifecycle package. With these lines, you are listening for the comments changes for that particular post and when the data changes you update the UI.

Go back to **CloudFirestoreManager.kt** and look for stopListeningForCommentsChanges(). Replace the function with the following:

```
fun stopListeningForCommentsChanges() =
commentsRegistration.remove()
```

Here, you remove the comments listener from the location that you assigned to commentsRegistration.

Open **PostDetailsActivity.kt** and add the following code below onStart():

```
override fun onStop() {
    super.onStop()
    cloudFirestoreManager.stopListeningForCommentsChanges()
}
```

In the code above, you call stopListeningForCommentsChanges() which stops the listener when the activity stops.

Build and run. Open a post that has at least one comment. You'll see all comments appear in the post details section of the app.

Adding Comments in Realtime.

Adding more comments to the post will appear instantly since you've attached a listener. Firestore notifies the listener of any changes in the `comments` collection.

Deleting comments

One last thing that you need to add is the ability to delete the comments. You'll delete the comments for the particular posts when you delete that post.

Open **CloudFirestoreManager.kt** and navigate to `deletePostComments()`. Replace `TODO` inside the function with the following:

```
// 1
database.collection(COMMENTS_COLLECTION)
    .whereEqualTo(POST_ID, postId)
    //2
    .get()
    //3
    .continueWith { task -> task.result?.documents?.forEach
{ it.reference.delete() } }
```

In the code above, you:

1. Create a reference to the comments collection and filter the comments that belong to the specific post.
2. Call `get()` to retrieve the filtered-by-post comments, **asynchronously**.
3. After you load the comments, you delete them from the database, one by one.

Using `continueWith()` on a `Task` instance returns a new `Task`. The `Task` completes with the `result` of applying the specified `Continuation` to this `Task`. A `Continuation` function once called, continues execution after completion of a `Task`. You fetch the comments for the specific posts and delete them by traversing the result documents and calling `delete()` on each document reference.

Finally, in **CloudFirestoreManager.kt**, at the end of `deletePost()` add:

```
deletePostComments(key)
```

This will delete the comments tied to that post, when you delete a post.

Build and run. Open the post that you added a comment to before. You'll now see the app displays your comment. Add another comment and you'll see that it's displayed on the screen immediately.

Listening to Comments Updates.

Now, delete the posts that you added comments to and observe the database in the console. Notice that comments for that post are deleted, as well.

Working offline

Like Realtime Database, Firestore can also work **offline**. Cloud Firestore stores a copy of data that your app is using, locally, so that you can have access to the data if the device goes offline. You can perform operations like reading, writing and querying on the local copy. When your device goes back online, Firestore automatically syncs the data with the data that is stored remotely!

Firestore offline persistence is enabled by default for mobile clients. You can test this in your **WhatsUp** app.

Here are the steps:

- Add some posts if you don't have them already. You can add some comments to that post as well if you like.
- Disconnect the device from the network and kill the process of your app. Start your app again and you'll notice that your data is still displayed on the screen.
- Add another post. Tap the floating action button on the home screen and enter some content for the post and tap **Post**. Nothing happens because you only consider post saved when it is saved to the remote database.
- Go back to the home screen by tapping the system back button. The app displays the post that you added while offline on the home screen. This is because the app saved it to the local cache. If you open the console and look into the database you won't see that post in the database.
- Connect your device back to the network. You'll get a `Toast` message on the device that the post is saved and now you can see your post in the remote database.

If you don't want to have the offline feature enabled, you can disable it when initializing Cloud Firestore.

Check the official documentation (https://firebase.google.com/docs/firestore/manage-data/enable-offline) to learn more about offline support.

Other features

Cloud Firestore has many other features. You'll go through some of them next.

Ordering and limiting

You've already seen how you can specify which documents you want to fetch from the collection by using `whereEqualTo()`. But there's much more you can do, on top of `whereEqualTo()`:

- You can use `orderBy()` on the collection reference to sort the data by the specified field. By default, Firestore sorts the documents in ascending order by document ID.

- You can use `limit()` on the collection reference to only return up to the specified number of documents.
- You can also combine all of `where()` for filtering with `limit()` and `orderBy()`.

Pagination

You can have a lot of data stored in your database, but at times you don't need all the data. Pagination allows you to split your database data into chunks so that you don't need to fetch it all at once.

Firestore provides you with the **pagination** feature, which works in a way where you don't need to execute one large query. Instead, you use multiple smaller queries **sequentially**. Firestore library has some useful methods that you can use to divide your query into smaller queries, like `startAt()`, `startAfter()`, `endAt()` or `endBefore()`.

Check the official documentation (https://firebase.google.com/docs/firestore/query-data/query-cursors) to learn more about pagination.

Indexing

To ensure good performance for every query, Firestore requires an index. Firestore automatically creates indices for the basic queries for you.

Check the official documentation (https://firebase.google.com/docs/firestore/query-data/indexing) to learn more about how to add indexing manually and how it works.

Key points

- Firestore allows to **read data once** or to **listen for data changes** in real-time.
- To get the data once, you would need to use `get()` on the collection reference.
- The `ListenerRegistration` interface represents a Firestore subscription listener.
- You can call `addSnapshotListener()` on a collection reference to start listening for data changes at a specific location.
- **Queries** are used to get only a **subset** of the documents within a collection.
- Cloud Firestore stores a copy of data that your app is using, locally, so that you can access the data if the device goes offline.
- You can also use `orderBy()` and `limit()`, on the collection reference, to get only specific documents from a collection.
- **Pagination** allows you to split your database data into **chunks** so that you don't need to fetch all your data at once.
- To ensure good performance for every query, Firestore requires an index, when creating them.

Where to go from here?

You covered a lot in this chapter. You learned how to read data from Firestore and listen for data changes in real-time. You also learned what queries are and how to use them only to fetch specific documents from a collection.

To learn more about those features, you can check out the official documentation (https://firebase.google.com/docs/firestore/query-data/get-data).

WhatsUp is now complete, but it has one big flaw. Anyone can read and write the data to the database. In "Chapter 20: Securing Data in Cloud Firestore", you'll learn how to secure the data in the database and restrict access to the data.

Chapter 20: Securing Data in Cloud Firestore

By Harun Wangereka

In the previous chapters, you implemented all the features to the **WhatsUp** app except the most important one. You haven't implemented any security rules, which means anyone has access to your data.

In this chapter, you'll learn what security rules in Cloud Firestore exist and how to add them to your database to make your data safe.

What are Security Rules?

To set up your own security system you'd need to set up your own server that acts as a proxy between your mobile clients and the remote database. That server would need to process all the requests that are sent to the database and make sure that the client is accessing only the data that it is allowed to see.

Security rules handle security for you. You don't need to set up your own security system.

How Security Rules Work

Security rules check the requests that are coming to the database and let through those that meet the criteria and reject the ones that don't. So for example, if your database only allows writing data to the authenticated client and an unauthenticated user tries to write something to the database, then the database will reject that request.

Any request that comes to the database involves the document. You're either trying to write the document to the database, read the document from the database, update an existing document, or something similar. Cloud Firestore will take a look at the security rules that apply to the document that your request contains. It will then run a set of tests that you wrote to determine if it will allow the request or not.

In a nutshell, security rules consist of two things:

1. Specifying which documents you are securing.
2. What logic you're using to secure them.

Getting started

To see how the security rules look like open your Firestore Database in the console. Open the **Rules** tab at the top.

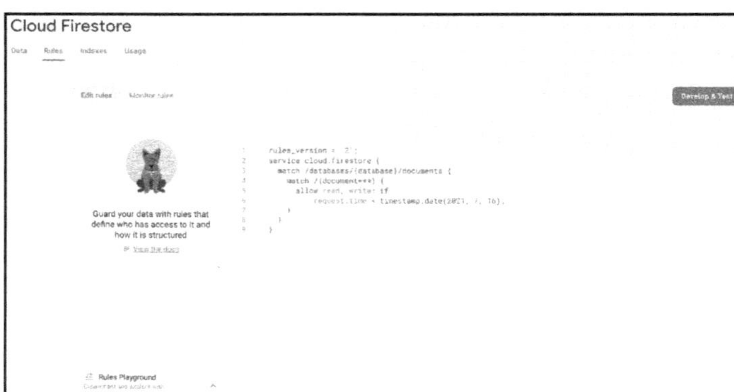

Cloud Firestore Security Rules.

This is where you can see your current logic for the security rules. These are the default security rules that you added while creating Firestore Database. To be able to create your own rules, you need to understand the security rules syntax as in the image above.

You start by specifying your Security Rules versions as:

```
rules_version = 2
```

By default, version one of the security rules is the one used. So here, you're specifying version two of the security rules. Using this version enables you to do more queries like collection group queries. This version also changes the following behavior of recursive wildcards:

- Recursive wildcards match zero or more path items. In version one, the wildcards can't match an empty path and must return one or more path items.
- In version one, recursive wildcards can only be at the end of a `match` statement. In version two, you can place your wildcard anywhere in the `match` statement. Check the official documentation (https://firebase.google.com/docs/firestore/security/get-started#security_rules_version_2) to see the differences in the behavior.

On the next line you have a `match` block:

```
match /databases/{database}/documents
```

This line indicates the path that all the documents belong to. By default, all the documents belong to the **/databases/{database}/documents** path. `{database}` in curly brackets is a wildcard that matches any database name. You'll learn more about wildcards later. Next, you have another `match` block:

```
match /{document=**} {
      ...
}
```

This is where you set the rules for the specific document by specifying the path to that document. `match` specifies the path to the document. `document=**` is a recursive wildcard that matches any document in the entire database.

In your current database, you have a *posts* collection that contains a specific post. The path to the specific post looks like this:

```
/databases/{database}/documents/posts/{postId}
```

If you only want to write a security rule that applies to that specific path you'd do it like this:

```
match /databases/{database}/documents {
    match posts/{postId} {
      ...
```

```
    }
}
```

From the above snippet, the first `match` block, As you can see, Firestore lets you nest the paths.

Now, your **posts** collection could have a subcollection. You could add a separate rule for that subcollection like this:

```
match /databases/{database}/documents {
    match posts/{postId} {
      match subcollection/{documentId} {
        ...
      }
    }
}
```

There is one important thing to notice when looking at these nested rules. The rules you add to the top-level `match posts/{postId}` **do not** apply to the inner match statements. Security rules in Cloud Firestore do not cascade.

Adding Security Rules

Your **WhatsUp** app is still not safe. You'll add security rules next to restrict the access to data. Open **Firestore Database** in the console and tap **Rules**. Replace the exisiting rule with:

```
rules_version = '2';
service cloud.firestore {
  match /databases/{database}/documents {
    match /{document=**} {
      allow read, write: if request.auth.uid != null;
    }
  }
}
```

This rule allows *read* and *write* access on all documents for any signed-in user. The *allow* expression specifies when to allow the writing or reading of data.

When you're done with writing the rules to the editor click **Publish**.

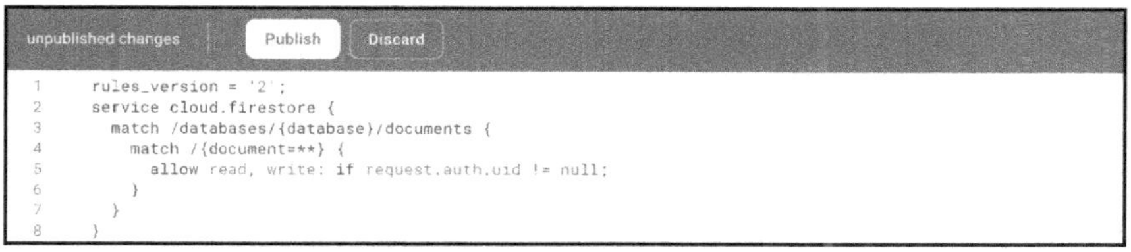

Firebase Security Rules Editor.

Usually, it takes a minute for the security rules to make an effect, but sometimes it can take up to 10 minutes. Before you start testing make sure you wait a couple of minutes.

Testing the Security Rules

Firestore has the **Rules Playground** which you can use to test your rules. You'll be using the Rules Playground to test the rule you've created.

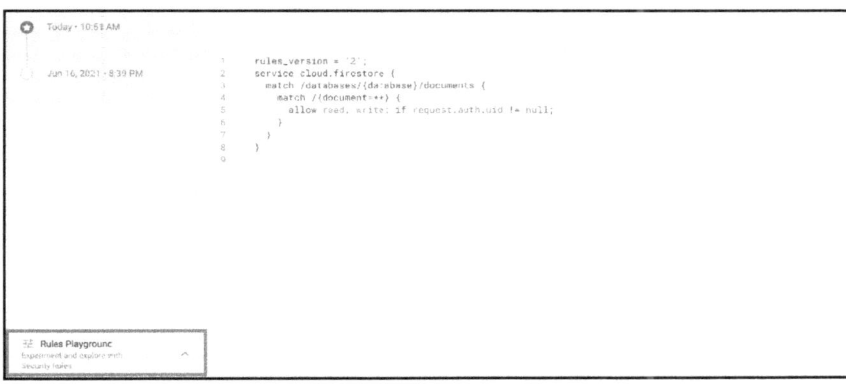

Security Rules Playground.

Click the **Data** tab, open *posts* collection and copy the ID of one post. Go back to **Rules** and tap the **Up arrow** in the Rules Playground section. This opens the Rules Playground window.

Next, do the following:

1. Under the *Simulation type* field leave it set to **get**.
2. Under the *Location* field enter the path to the specific post. In my case the path looks like this:

```
posts/posts/FNlxMWV6kZUgyr9vPFv8
```

The `posts/FNlxMWV6kZUgyr9vPFv8` is the ID of the post. Replace that value with the ID you copied earlier.

Leave the **Authenticated** switch in the inactive state.

Now, tap **Run**. You should see an error message:

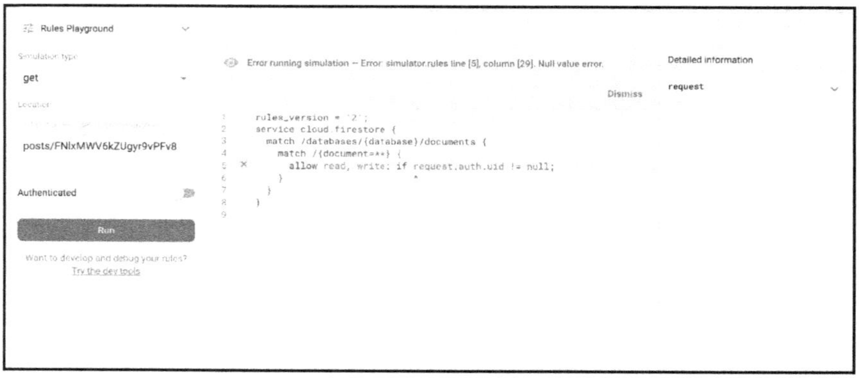

Security Rules Failure.

Your request didn't succeed because you simulated an unauthenticated request. The Rules Playground shows you the rule which your request doesn't meet and shows you the line.

Now change the **Authenticated** switch to an **active state**. Leave the authentication fields that appear with their default values, and tap **Run** again.

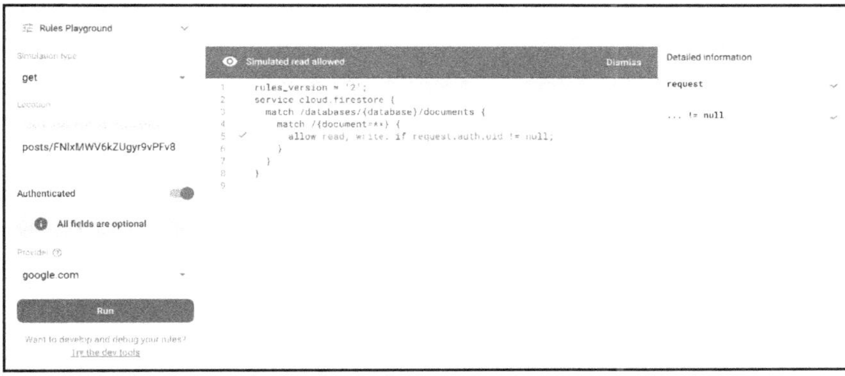

Security Rules test request is successful.

Your request is now successful since it meets all the conditions in your rules. Now all users that want to read and write to your database have to be authenticated. It prevents unauthorized reads and writes which at times can be from unwanted parties and can increase your usage and cost.

Monitoring Security Rules

Firebase also provides statistics for your set rules. You can access your rules data by tapping the **Monitor rules** tab which is next to the **Edit rules** tab.

The rules graph.

From this, Firestore provides the following information:

- Total allows. This is the number of reads and writes for your apps and users who meet your set criteria.
- Total denies. Number of reads and write denials for your apps or users.
- Total errors. The number of errors encountered in your rules.

There's a graph for the statistics too.

Key points

- **Security rules** check the requests that are coming to the database. The rules let through those that meet the criteria and reject the ones that don't.
- Security rules consist of two things. One is specifying which documents you are securing. The second thing is what logic you're using to secure them.
- In the **Rules** tab in the Firebase Console, you can see your current security configuration.
- `match` statement specifies the path to the document.
- `allow` expression specifies when to allow the writing or reading of data.
- Security rules in Cloud Firestore **do not** cascade.
- Cloud Firestore provides the **Rule Playground** feature that you can use to test your rules.

Where to go from here?

In this chapter, you learned the basics of the Cloud Firestore's **Security rules**. Your **WhatsUp** app now only allows authenticated users to access the data.

To learn more about writing conditions, structuring and testing Security rules check out the official guidelines: https://firebase.google.com/docs/firestore/security/rules-structure.

Chapter 21: Cloud Storage

By Harun Wangereka

With Realtime Database and Cloud Firestore, you saved data to the database. But what about files like photos, for example? While small pieces of data like posts, comments or users tend to be a few kilobytes of text, photos are much larger. Storing and retrieving photos extends the startup and loading time when reading the database. You don't want to store photos in a database because it should be fast.

In this chapter, you'll learn how to store media files using another Firebase feature — **Cloud Storage**. You'll learn how to store an image in the cloud and how to get a URL to the image to display it in your app.

> **Note**: If you skipped previous chapters, you need to set up Firebase to follow along. Do the following steps:
>
> 1.Create a project in the Firebase console.
>
> 2.Enable Google sign-in.
>
> 3.Set security rules to test mode to allow everyone **read** and **write** access.
>
> 4.Add **google-service.json** to both **starter** and **final** projects.

> **Note**: To see how to do the steps above, go back to **"Chapter 12: Firebase Overview"** and **"Chapter 13: Introduction to Firebase Realtime Database"**.
>
> Be sure to use the starter project from **this chapter** by opening the **21-cloud-storage** folder and its **starter** project from the **projects** folder, rather than continuing with the final project you previously worked on. This chapter's starter project has a few things added to it, including placeholders for the code to add in this chapter.

Cloud Storage Overview

Cloud Storage is a Firebase product used for saving files associated with your app. You can use it to store large documents or media files like images or videos.

Since Cloud Storage operates with large files, it's fundamental to provide robust network connection mechanisms and fallbacks. Cloud Storage handles all the potential network problems for you. Depending on your connection, upload or download can take a while. If you lose the network connection in the middle of an upload or a download, the transfer will continue where it left off, after you reconnect to the network. This makes transferring your data very efficient.

Cloud Storage also has security features that will safely store your files away from the public. You can decide who can write data to and read data from the storage.

The foundations of Cloud Storage are the folders that you create to organize your data. You can then decide which users can access which folders.

There's more theory you could learn, but for now, you'll use the Firebase console to set up Cloud Storage. You'll use the **WhatsUp** app to store, download and display images to users on the app screen.

Getting started

Open your **WhatsUp** app in the Firebase console. Select **Storage** from the **Build** menu on the left.

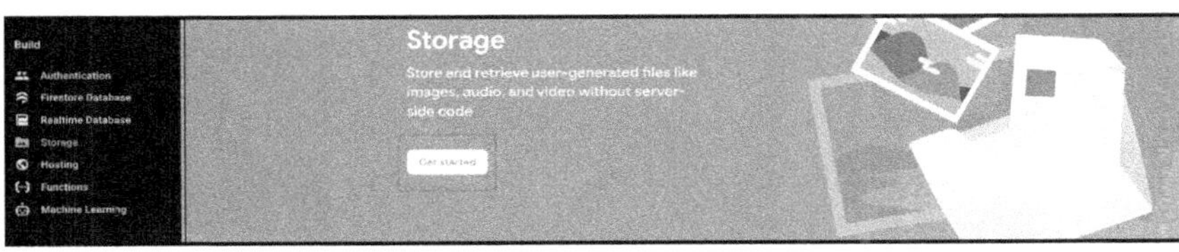

Cloud Storage Getting Started Menu.

Tap **Get started** to set up Cloud Storage.

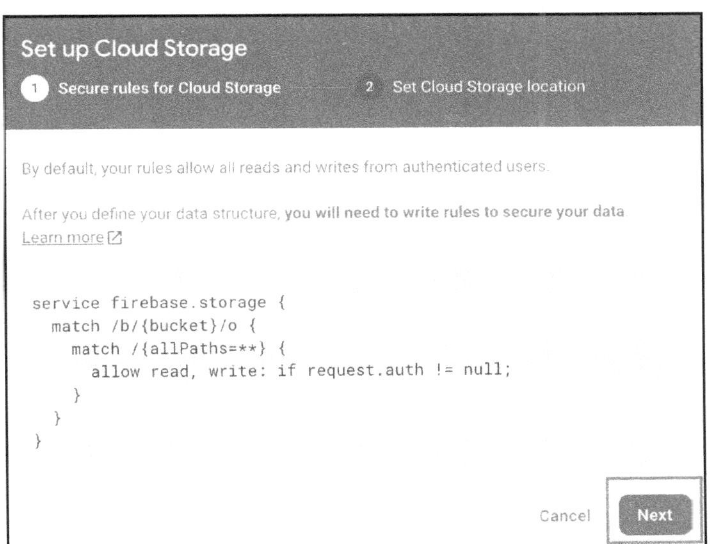

Adding Security Rules in Cloud Storage.

For your first step, you need to set up security rules for your storage. Leave the default rules that allow reads and writes from **authenticated users**. Tap **Next**.

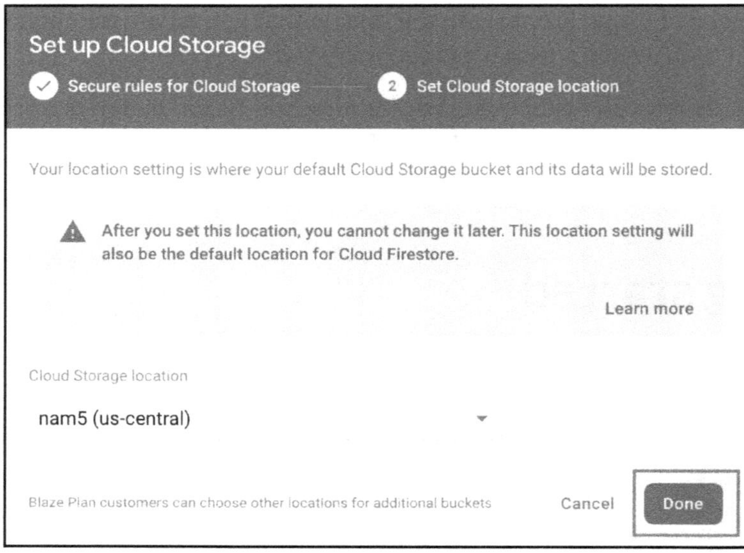

Location Settings.

In the second step, you need to choose the location for your Cloud Storage. You can choose the location of your preference from the drop-down list that appears. Tap **Done** once you finish. Your Cloud Storage is now ready for use.

Cloud Storage Home Page.

You can see that your storage is empty; you haven't added any files yet. Next, you're going to change this. Tap the **little folder icon** in the top-right corner to create a new folder.

Creating a New Folder.

Name your folder **photos** and tap **Add folder**. You'll use this folder to store the photos.

Add a New Folder.

Cloud Storage is now set up and ready for use. Next, you'll integrate it with your app.

Integrating Cloud Storage

Open the **starter** project for this chapter. Build and run. You'll see the main screen for adding posts.

Cloud Storage Starter App.

On this empty screen find a **floating action button** in the bottom-right corner. Very soon you'll implement action for that button. Then, once you tap it, it will open **File Explorer** on your device.

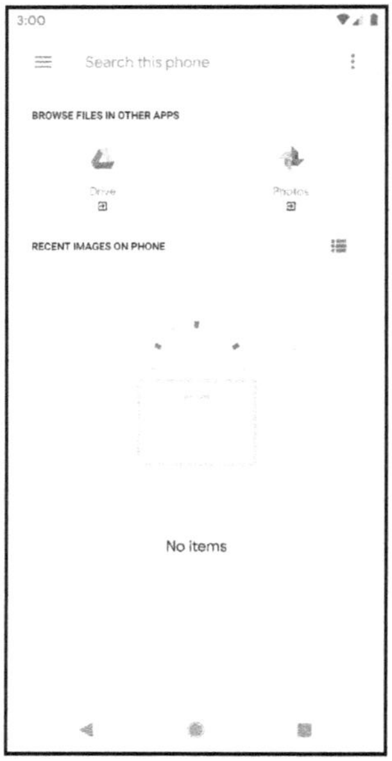

Phone File Explorer.

This is where you'll choose the image that you want to store to Cloud Storage.

> **Note**: File Explorers may vary in appearance depending on your Android version, phone manufacturer and whether you've installed third-party file manager applications.

Next, you'll implement the logic for uploading the image. When a user selects an image, you'll upload it to Cloud Storage. Then, you'll get a URL of that image which you'll use to display the image on the home screen.

Open **CloudStorageManager.kt** , replace the `TODO` inside `uploadPhoto()` with:

```
//1
val photosReference =
firebaseStorage.getReference(PHOTOS_REFERENCE)
//2
selectedImageUri.lastPathSegment?.let { segment ->
  //3
  val photoReference = photosReference.child(segment)
```

```
  //4
  photoReference.putFile(selectedImageUri)
      //5
      .continueWithTask(Continuation<UploadTask.TaskSnapshot,
Task<Uri>> { task ->
        val exception = task.exception
        if (!task.isSuccessful && exception != null) {
          throw exception
        }
        return@Continuation photoReference.downloadUrl
      })
      //6
      .addOnCompleteListener { task ->
        if (task.isSuccessful) {
          val downloadUri = task.result
          onSuccessAction(downloadUri.toString())
        }
      }
}
```

In the code above:

1. First, you get a reference to the **photos** folder that you created earlier, by calling `getReference()` on `firebaseStorage`. This is where you'll upload your photo.
2. You get `lastPathSegment` of the image URI. You'll use it as the name of the file that you're going to save.
3. Get a reference that points to the location to which you'll store the image.
4. Here you call `putFile()` to store the image to `photosReference`. You also pass in the content URI of the image. This method stores the image asynchronously. It returns an instance of `UploadTask` that you'll use to track the upload progress.
5. Next, you call `continueWithTask()` on the `UploadTask` object to get the download URL of the image you're uploading when the image upload finishes. When importing, use `com.google.android.gms.tasks.Continuation`.
6. If the `Task` request is successful, you return `photoReference.downloadUrl`. Otherwise, you throw an exception.
7. Finally, you attach `OnCompleteListener` so you'll receive a notification when the upload finishes.
8. If the task is successful, you get the download URI by calling `task.result`. You pass that result to `onSuccessAction()`.

Now, open **HomeActivity.kt**, below your `onPhotoUploadSuccess()` add:

```
private val pickImages =
registerForActivityResult(ActivityResultContracts.GetContent())
{ uri ->
    uri?.let { selectedImageUri ->
      binding.progressbar.visibility = View.VISIBLE

cloudStorageManager.uploadPhoto(selectedImageUri, ::onPhotoUploa
dSuccess)
    }
  }
```

Here, you using the new **Activity Result API** to register your `pickImages` callback. This callback uses an inbuilt contract, `ActivityResultContracts.GetContent()`, in the API. It makes it easy for you to launch the image picker option. When you select your image from the File Explorer, you'll get the URI of the selected image from the callback. You pass the URI using `uploadPhoto()` on the `cloudStorageManager` object.

Finally, in `initialize()`, replace the `TODO` inside `addPostFab` click-listener with:

```
pickImages.launch(IMAGE_TYPE)
```

With this line, you launch your `pickImages` contract. You pass `mimeType` for your content. In this case, it's `image/jpeg` since you only want to upload image files. With this, your app is ready to choose and upload images to Cloud Storage. :]

Build and run. Now, open the File Explorer by using the floating button. Select an image from the File Explorer. It will immediately upload to Cloud Storage.

When the upload finishes, you'll see the image on the home screen.

Selected Image Uploaded.

Go to the Firebase console and open your app's Cloud Storage. You'll see the photo you uploaded in the **photos** folder.

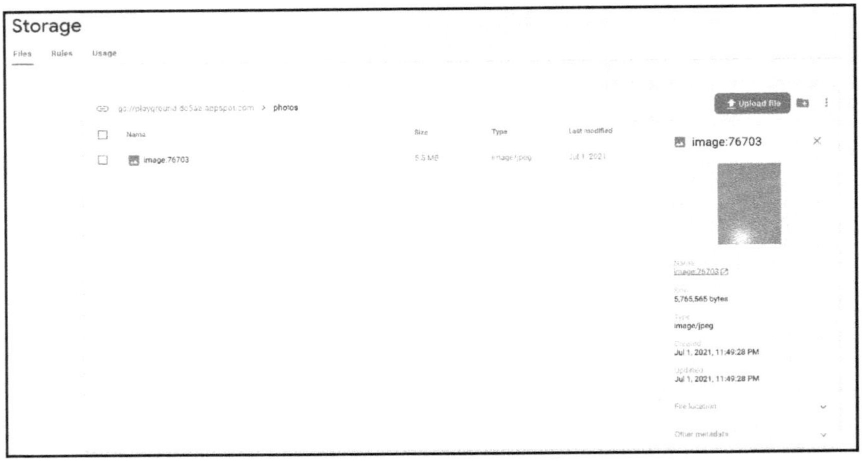

Cloud Storage Images List.

Awesome! You've successfully connected your app to Firebase Cloud Storage!

Key points

- **Cloud Storage** is a Firebase product used for saving files associated with your app.
- If you lose a network connection in the middle of the upload or a download, the transfer will continue where it left off after you reconnect to the network.
- Cloud Storage also has **security features** that will make your files secure.
- The foundations of Cloud Storage are **folders** that you can create to organize your data.

Where to go from here?

This chapter was only an introduction to Cloud Storage to show you how to store media files to the cloud. You learned how to set up Cloud Storage and how to upload and download files from it. Cloud Storage has many other features. To learn more about them visit the official guidelines https://firebase.google.com/docs/storage/android/start.

22 Conclusion

Congratulations! After a long journey, you've learned a lot about persistence in Android. You can use the API and tools provided by the Android SDK as well as the Room library, which Android Architecture Components provide. On the other hand, if you want to resolve persistence with the latest tools, you now know how to use Google's Jetpack DataStore. If your app needs to manage persistence, along with security and offline capability, you can now know the fundamentals of using the Firebase suite.

Remember, if you want to further your understanding of Kotlin and Android app development after working through *Saving Data on Android*, we suggest you read *Android Apprentice* and *Kotlin Apprentice*, which are available on our online store:

- https://www.raywenderlich.com/books/android-apprentice
- https://www.raywenderlich.com/books/kotlin-apprentice

If you have any questions or comments as you work through this book, please stop by our forums at http://forums.raywenderlich.com and look for the particular forum category for this book.

Thank you again for purchasing this book. Your continued support is what makes the tutorials, books, videos, conferences and other things we do at raywenderlich.com possible, and we truly appreciate it!

Wishing you all the best in your continued work with Kotlin and saving data on Android.

–The *Saving Data on Android* book team

www.ingramcontent.com/pod-product-compliance
Lightning Source LLC
Chambersburg PA
CBHW061158240926
51846CB00006B/1051
9781950325436